Tanya Shaffer

Somebody's Heart Is Burning

Tanya Shaffer has spent much of the past decade wandering the globe and writing about it. An actor as well as a writer, she has toured nationally and internationally with her award-winning solo performances *Let My Enemy Live Long!* (based on her African travels) and *Miss America's Daughters*, and her original play *Brigadista*. Her travel stories have appeared on *Salon.com*, in *Speakeasy* magazine, and in numerous anthologies. A native of Lawrence, Kansas, she now calls the San Francisco Bay Area home. Visit her on-line at www.TanyaShaffer.com.

Somebody's Heart
Is Burning

Somebody's Heart
Is Burning

❖

A Woman Wanderer in Africa

Tanya Shaffer

VINTAGE DEPARTURES ◆ Vintage Books
A Division of Random House, Inc. ◆ New York

A VINTAGE DEPARTURES ORIGINAL, MAY 2003

Copyright © 2003 by Tanya Shaffer

The photos on pages x, 14, 50, 59, 114, 123, 162, and 214 courtesy of Ali Caddick. The photo on page 298 courtesy of Ultimate Africa Safaris Inc. All other photos courtesy of the author.

Library of Congress Cataloging-in-Publication Data
Shaffer, Tanya.
Somebody's heart is burning : a tale of a woman wanderer in
Africa / Tanya Shaffer.—1st Vintage Departures ed.
p. cm.
"Vintage Departures original."
ISBN 1-4000-3259-8
1. Africa, West—Description and travel.   2. Shaffer, Tanya.
3. Women travelers—Africa, West—Biography.   4. Travelers—
Africa, West—Biography.   I. Title.
DT472 .S45 2003
966.03'29'092—dc21
[B]   2002193353

Book design by Mia Risberg

www.vintagebooks.com

Printed in the United States of America
10   9   8   7   6   5   4   3   2   1

To my father,
who is all heart,

my mother,
who loves a journey,

and to David,
who brought the weary traveler home.

I hear a robin singing, singing,
Up in the treetop high, high
To me and you, he's singing, singing
The clouds will soon roll by.

Somebody's heart is burning, burning
Somebody's heart is burning, burning
Somebody's heart is burning, burning
Because he sees me happy.

—ENGLISH LANGUAGE FOLK SONG TAUGHT
IN GHANAIAN COLONIAL SCHOOLS

❖

Let my enemy live long and
see what I will be in future!

—PROVERB SEEN PAINTED ON THE
SIDE OF A BUS IN GHANA

Contents

Somebody's Heart
Is Burning

Looking for Abdelati

Here's what I love about travel: Strangers get a chance to amaze you. Sometimes a single day can bring a blooming surprise, a simple kindness that opens a chink in the brittle shell of your heart and makes you a different person when you go to sleep—more tender, less jaded—than you were when you woke up.

When my relationship with Michael got too complicated, I did what I always do under such circumstances: fled the country. I know some people think this isn't the healthiest possible way to deal with personal crises, but I figure it's my life, and if I want to run from it, I can.

My wandering habit began in childhood, when I was obliged to trundle myself back and forth between my dad's house in Kansas, where I spent the school year, and my mom's California

3

apartment, where I passed the summer and winter breaks. To everyone's surprise, I loved the journey. Whenever my hand passed from my parents' protective grip into the cool, neutral grasp of a flight attendant, I felt a reckless, giddy thrill. As I grew older, my meanderings led me farther and farther afield. I'd stay put for a year or so, begin to build my career as an actor-slash-writer, and then off I'd go. As I traveled to increasingly poorer places, I began to volunteer. I didn't like feeling like a parasite, and the work connected me to a community and gave me a sense of purpose. It also allowed me to stay a long time without spending much money. I picked coffee in Nicaragua, met with human rights groups in Guatemala, dug ditches in the former Czechoslovakia, and tilled the land in rural Maine.

This time, I was headed for Africa. After a year of exhaustive research, I'd located a suitable volunteer project in Ghana, a small country on the west coast of the continent, which was renowned for the friendliness of its inhabitants. The organization I was going to work for was extremely flexible. It operated year-round, offering two- to three-week construction projects in villages across the country. On each project, a team of foreign and Ghanaian volunteers worked in conjunction with the villagers to build something: a school, hospital, women's center, or other public edifice. I had little knowledge of construction, but I'd worked on similar projects in the past, and I knew they'd take anyone. Somebody's got to shovel and carry, and what I lacked in strength, I made up for in endurance. I'd considered projects that might've made more use of my skills—teaching English, for example—but those required a commitment of at least a year, sometimes two or three.

I decided to travel to Ghana the long way, taking in as much of the world as I could en route. I flew to Paris and wended my way by train through the sun-soaked fields of France and Italy, then caught a boat to Morocco, where I'd signed up to spend two and a half weeks planting a public park in an ugly industrial city called Kenitra. Seventeen grubby days later, our group of fourteen Moroccans and five foreigners had transformed an uneven plot of dust-dry land into a relatively level one. We'd accomplished this with our shovels and, ultimately, a tractor, which appeared on the last day to finish off the remaining third of the ground. Why it hadn't appeared earlier remains a mystery. The next group, our project leader informed us, would plant the grass and the trees.

When the project ended, I hooked up with a young Spaniard named Miguel for a week of exploring before hopping a plane to sub-Saharan Africa and my next volunteer adventure.

Miguel was one of the five foreigners on our project, a twenty-one-year-old vision of flowing brown curls and buffed golden physique. The fact that his name was Spanish for Michael felt like one of the universe's cruel little jokes. Although having him as a traveling companion took care of any problems I might have encountered with Moroccan men, he was inordinately devoted to his girlfriend, Eva, a wonderfully brassy, wiry, chain-smoking Older Woman of thirty with a husky Scotch Drinker's voice, whom he couldn't go more than half an hour without mentioning. Unfortunately, Eva had to head back to Barcelona immediately after the three-week work camp ended, and Miguel wanted to explore Morocco. Since I was the only other person on the project who spoke Spanish, and Miguel spoke no French or Arabic, his tight orbit shifted onto me, and we became traveling companions. This involved posing as a married couple at hotels, which made Miguel so uncomfortable that the frequency of his references to Eva went from half-hour to fifteen-minute intervals, then five as we got closer to bedtime. Finally one night, as we were getting set up in our room in Fès, I grabbed him by the shoulders and said, "Miguel, it's okay. You're a handsome man, but I'm over twenty-one. I can handle myself, I swear."

On my last day in Morocco before heading to West Africa, Miguel and I descended from a cramped, cold bus at 7 A.M. and walked the stinking gray streets of Casablanca with our back-packs, looking for food. Unlike the romantic image its name conjured, Casablanca was a thoroughly modern city, with rectangular high-rises sprouting everywhere and wide boulevards already jammed with cars. Horns blared, and the air was thick with heat and exhaust. My T-shirt, pinned to my skin by my backpack, was soaked with sweat. We were going to visit Abdelati, a sweet, gentle young man we'd worked with in Kenitra. He was expecting our visit, and since he had no telephone, he'd written down his address and told us to just show up—his mother and sisters were always at home. Since my plane was leaving the following morning, we wanted to get an early start so that we could spend the whole day with him.

Eventually we scored some croissants and overly sugared *panaches* (a mix of banana, apple, and orange juice) at a roadside café, where the friendly owner advised us to take a taxi rather than a bus out to Abdelati's neighborhood. A taxi would only cost fifteen to twenty dirham, he said—less than three dollars—and the buses would take all day.

It took us an hour to find a cab. When we did, the poker-faced driver informed us that the address which Abdelati had written down for us was somehow suspect. When we got to the neighborhood, he told us, he would have to ask directions.

"Here we go," Miguel whispered, rolling his eyes. "Eva would hate this."

The first person to whom the driver showed our scrap of paper was a policeman, who scratched his head and asked our nationalities, looking at our grimy faces and scraggly attire with bemused tolerance. After some small talk, he pointed vaguely toward a park a few blocks away, where a group of barefoot seven- or eight-year-old boys were kicking a soccer ball. Our driver walked over and asked where Abdelati's house was. One of the boys told him that Abdelati had moved, but he could take us to the new house. This struck me as odd, since Abdelati had just given me the address a week ago, but since a similar thing had happened to us in Fès, I chalked it up as another Moroccan mystery and didn't worry about it too much.

The little boy came with us in the cab, full of his own importance, squirming and twisting to wave at other children as we inched along. The roads were narrower now, sometimes barely wide enough for the car to pass through. Finally the little boy pointed to a house, and our driver went to the door and inquired. He came back to the cab saying Abdelati's sister was in this house visiting friends and would come along to show us where Abdelati lived.

Soon a lovely, delicate-featured girl of about fifteen emerged from the house. I was surprised to see her dressed in a Western skirt and blouse, since Abdelati's strong religious beliefs and upright demeanor had led me to think he came from a more traditional family. Her skin tone differed from his as well, reflecting Morocco's complex racial mosaic. Whereas Abdelati appeared quite African, his sister was an olive-skinned Arab. She too joined us in the cab and directed us to a white stone house a few winding blocks away.

We waited in the yard while the girl went inside the house and returned, accompanied by several cousins and a brother-in-law, all of whom greeted us with cautious warmth. Unlike the girl, the older female cousins wore traditional robes, though their faces were not veiled. There's a wide range of orthodoxy in Moroccan cities, caught as they are between Europe and the

Arab world. This family seemed to encompass a generous portion of the spectrum.

We paid our taxi driver, and I tipped and thanked him profusely, until he grew embarrassed and drove away.

We were ushered into a pristine middle-class Moroccan home with an intricately carved wooden doorway and swirling multicolored tiles lining the walls. The mother told us in broken French that Abdelati was out, but would soon be back. We sat on low cushioned seats in the tiled living room, drinking sweet, pungent mint tea, poured from a foot above out of a tiny silver teapot, and eating sugar cookies. (Tea in Morocco is like Guinness in Ireland—it has to be poured from the proper height in order to be aerated on the way down.) Different family members took turns sitting with us and making shy, polite conversation, which frequently lapsed into uncomfortable silence. Whenever anything was said, Miguel exclaimed, *"Que pasó?"*

with extreme eagerness, and I dutifully translated the mundane fragment into Spanish for him: "Nice weather today. Tomorrow perhaps rain." At this he'd sink back into fidgety frustration, undoubtedly wishing Eva were there.

An hour passed, and as the guard kept changing, more family members emerged from inner rooms. I was again struck by the fact that they were all light-skinned Arabs. How did Abdelati fit into this picture? Was he adopted? I was eager to find out.

After two hours had passed with no sign of Abdelati, the family insisted on serving us a meal of couscous and fish. The food was a delectable blend of sweet and savory, with plump raisins, cayenne pepper, slivered almonds, and loads of garlic.

"Soon," was the only response I got when I inquired as to what time Abdelati might arrive.

"You come to the *hammam*, the bath," the young sister said, after we'd finished lunch. "When we finish, he is back."

"The bath?" I asked, looking around the apartment.

The sister laughed. "The women's bath!" she said. "Haven't you been yet?" I shook my head. We'd had our own facilities on the volunteer project. The bathroom in our low cement dormitory had spigots from which we filled our buckets and dragged them into the toilet stalls to bathe.

She pointed at Miguel. "He can go to the men's; it is right next door."

"*Que pasó?*" said Miguel anxiously, sitting up.

"She wants to take us to the baths," I said.

A look of abject horror crossed his face.

"The-the baths?" he stammered. "You and me?"

"Yes," I said, smiling widely. "Is there a problem?"

"Well . . . well . . ."

I watched his agitation build for a moment, then sighed and put my hand over his.

"Separate baths, Miguel. You with the men, me with the women."

"Oh." He almost giggled with relief. "Of course."

✥

The women's bath consisted of three large connecting rooms, each one hotter and steamier than the last. In the innermost room, you could barely see two feet in front of you. The floor was filled with naked women of all ages and body types, sitting directly on the slippery tiles, washing each other with mitts made of rough washcloths. Tiny girls and babies stood in plastic buckets filled with soapy water—their own pint-sized tubs. The women carried their buckets to and from the innermost room, swinging the pails like elephants' trunks. There they filled the buckets at a stone basin from a spigot of boiling water, mixing in a little cold from a neighboring faucet to temper it.

In a culture where the body is usually covered, I was surprised by the women's absolute lack of inhibition. They sat, mostly in pairs, pouring the water over their heads with small plastic pitchers, then scrubbing each other's backs—and I mean *scrubbing*. Over and over they attacked the same spot as though trying to get out a stubborn stain, leaving reddened flesh in their wake. They sprawled across each other's laps. They washed each other's fronts, backs, arms, legs. Some women washed themselves as if they were masturbating, hypnotically circling the same spot. Two tiny girls, about four years old, scoured their grandmother, who lay spread-eagled on the floor, face down. A prepubescent girl lay in her mother's lap, belly up, eyes closed, relaxed as a cat, while the mother applied a forceful up and down stroke to the length of her daughter's torso. At the steamy heart of the baths, where the air was almost suffocating, a lone young woman reclined, back arched and head thrown back, soaping her breasts in sensual circles. With her stomach held in and her chestnut hair rippling down her back, she appeared serene and majestic—a goddess in her domain.

Abdelati's sister, whose name was Samara, was amazed at my spiky, close-cropped hair. She called to a couple of other girls, who scooted over on their bottoms and ran their fingers through it, giggling.

"Skinny!" she exclaimed, poking at my belly. *"Il faut manger!"* She made eating gestures with her hands.

Turning me around, she went at my back with her washcloth mitt, which felt like steel wool.

"Ow!" I cried out, "Careful!"

This sent her into gales of piercing laughter, which drew the attention of the surrounding women. They joined her in appreciative giggles as she continued to sandblast my skin.

"You must wash more often," she said, pointing to the refuse of her work—little gray scrolls of dead skin that clung to my arms like lint on a sweater.

When it came time to switch roles, I tried to return the favor, but after a few moments Samara became impatient with my wimpiness and grabbed the washcloth herself, still laughing. After polishing the front of her body, she called over a friend to wash her back. The girl scrubbed valiantly, while Samara giggled and sang.

"What was it like in there?" asked Miguel, when we met again outside. He looked pink and damp as a newborn after his visit to the men's baths. I wondered whether his experience had been anything like mine.

"I'd like to tell you all about it," I said eagerly, "but . . ." I paused for emphasis, then leaned in and whispered, "I don't think Eva would approve."

When we got back to the house, Abdelati's mother, older sister, and uncle greeted us at the door.

"Please," said the mother, "Abdelati is here."

"Oh, good," I said, and for a moment his face danced in my mind—the warm brown eyes, the smile so shy and gentle and filled with radiant life.

We entered the lovely tiled room we'd sat in before, and a handsome young Arab man in crisp Western pants and bright white button-down shirt stepped forward to shake our hands.

"Bonjour, mes amis," he said cautiously, his eyes darting uncertainly from my face to Miguel's.

"Bonjour." I smiled, slightly confused. *"Abdelati—est-ce qu'il est ici?"* Is Abdelati here?

"Je suis Abdelati."

"But . . . but . . ." I looked from him to the family and then began to giggle tremulously. "I-I'm sorry. I'm afraid we've made a bit of a mistake. I-I'm so embarrassed."

"Qué? Qué pasó?" Miguel asked, urgently. "I don't understand. Where is he?"

"We got the wrong Abdelati," I told him, then looked around at the assembled family who'd spent the better part of a day entertaining us. "I'm afraid we don't actually know your son."

For a split second no one said anything, and I wondered whether I might implode right then and there and blow away like a pile of ash.

Then the uncle exclaimed heartily, *"Ce n'est pas grave!"*

"That's right," the mother chimed in. "It doesn't matter at all. Won't you stay for dinner, please?"

I was so overwhelmed by their kindness that tears sprang to my eyes. For all they knew we were con artists, thieves, anything. Would such a thing ever happen back home?

Still, with my plane leaving the next morning, I felt the

moments I could share with the first Abdelati and his family slipping farther and farther away.

"Thank you so much," I said fervently, "It's been a beautiful, beautiful day, but please . . . Could you help me find this address?"

I took out the piece of paper Abdelati had given me back in Kenitra, and the new Abdelati, his uncle, and his brother-in-law came forward to decipher it.

"This is Baâlal Abdelati!" said the second Abdelati with surprise. "We went to school together! He lives less than a kilometer from here. I will bring you to his house."

And that is how it happened, that after taking photos and exchanging addresses and hugs and promises to write, Miguel and I left our newfound family and walked briskly through the narrow streets with this new Abdelati as our guide, until we arrived at the home of our old friend Abdelati just as the last orange streak of the sunset was fading into the indigo night. There, I threw myself into the arms of that dear and lovely young man, exclaiming, "I thought we'd never find you!"

After greetings had been offered all around, and the two Abdelatis had shared stories and laughter, we waved goodbye to our new friend Abdelati and entered a low, narrow hallway, lit by kerosene lamps.

"This is my mother," said Abdelati.

And suddenly I found myself caught up in a crush of fabric and spice, gripped in the tight embrace of a completely veiled woman, who held me and cried over me and wouldn't let me go, just as if I were her own daughter, and not a stranger she'd never before laid eyes on in her life.

2

Dirty Laundry

Sometimes I think I'll never go back to the U.S. The words are seductive, and once in a while I play them in my head, a tantalizing refrain: never go back, never go back. Of course it's all drama, because what do you fill that "never" with? You still have to spend the rest of your life somewhere.

I couldn't escape Michael. My time in Morocco, consuming as it was, had not erased the memory of our parting. He'd held me so tightly at the airport that I could feel his heart knocking against the wall of his slender chest. He wouldn't let go until they'd called final boarding three times. When I finally managed to pull away, he ducked his head in embarrassment, his eyes leaking tears.

I blamed myself for leaving, but I blamed him, too. In recent months, he'd started talking marriage, and talk of marriage made me extremely uncomfortable. He knew this, but he wouldn't stop.

After countless hours of negotiations, accusations, recriminations, and apologies, we'd agreed to leave things open while I was away. We'd stay in touch, of course, but we were free to see other people, and there were no guarantees on either side about what would happen when I returned. The length of my trip was indefinite; I didn't want to feel constrained by the idea that he was waiting for me.

I hadn't counted on the wiliness of memory. I'd go almost an entire day without thinking of him, and then I'd turn a corner and there he'd be, his sudden, cheeky grin reflected in the face of a policeman or trinket hawker, his loose-limbed walk adorning a museum guard. His letters arrived at the Moroccan work camp every few days. Each one was quintessentially Michael: quirky, humorous, tender, filled with misspellings and the whimsical poetry of daily life. Although reading them made me homesick and confused, I felt anxious and impatient on days when they didn't arrive. I tried to keep a tone of neutrality in the ones I sent back—to let him know that I missed him without raising false expectations. It was a difficult line to walk.

❖

I arrived in West Africa tired and cranky. I hadn't slept well the night before, and Abdelati's six-year-old sister had burst into my room at five-thirty in the morning with a pot of tea. The flight itself had been an exercise in nausea control.

A con artist accosted me in front of the airport in Abidjan, the capital of Ivory Coast. He'd emerged from a small army of men who hovered outside the sliding glass doors of the baggage claim, jockeying for the attention of travelers. He was a slim

African man in his early twenties, dressed in what a cynical volunteer once called "third world chic"—dark blue jeans with bright orange stitching up the sides and a carefully pressed St. Louis Cardinals T-shirt. I made the mistake of meeting his eyes. After that, there was no shaking him.

"*Bonjour, Madame.* My name is Jean-Pierre. Let me take you to your hotel. They know me; I will help you to get a better price," he said to me in French.

"I've got no money for you, okay, *pas d'argent.*"

"I don't want your money. I help you choose the hotel. If I bring you there myself, they give me commission."

"I already know which hotel I'm going to."

A boozy expat on the plane had looked through my guidebook and steered me away from the hotel I'd circled in Treicheville, the "African" quarter.

"Too dangerous," he'd said. "Stay in the Central Section, or at least here, this one's right next to the Central Section." He poked a stubby finger at the page. "Anywhere else, they'll sniff you out and rob you in a New York minute." He laughed.

Although I pegged him as a racist, I decided to go with his suggestion for my first few nights. Later I would stay in the African parts of town. I hadn't come to Africa to avoid Africans.

I got into a taxi. Jean-Pierre was next to my open window, still talking.

"Please," he said. "This is how I live. I show tourists to the hotel, I get commission."

"I'm not a tourist. I'm on my way to do some volunteer work in Ghana."

"You pay nothing! The hotel, they pay."

I sighed, and taking that as a yes, he got in. The taxi took off without setting the meter or agreeing on a price.

"Wait," I said, "*attend*," and Jean-Pierre, sitting beside me, repeated the phrase in a local language. How could an airport taxi driver not speak French?

"Tell him he has to set the meter," I told Jean-Pierre. I'd read this in my guidebook: *"In Abidjan, make sure they set the meter."*

He spoke to the driver, who just kept driving. Then he turned to me.

"There is no need," he said. "He knows the price."

"There is a need," my voice grew shrill, "because if he doesn't set it, I'm getting out."

"Small, small." He laughed, making a calming gesture with his hand. He spoke to the driver some more. The driver barked with laughter, then slapped the meter. It came on, its electronic digits bright and reassuring. I settled back in my seat.

I was too tired to take in the rows of dilapidated wood and cardboard shacks and the women wrapped in bright, dissonant cloth with bundles on their heads. Too weary to crane my neck at the colorful markets with their expanse of tables piled high with everything from vegetables to virility potions to auto parts. I'd traveled enough in the "developing world" that these things seemed strangely familiar. Even the thick tropical vegetation reminded me of someplace else. *Jesus,* I thought, *what's happened to me? It's my first day in sub-Saharan Africa and already I'm bored.*

I did notice the peeing, though. It seemed every man in the city had sought out the most conspicuous corner he could find on which to urinate. Again and again I saw them, poised like statues in that telltale wide-legged stance, facing the wall. I leaned back in my seat.

❖

There's a river around central Abidjan, like a moat. As we approached the bridge to enter the downtown area, the driver suddenly swerved into a gravel parking lot.

"*Ici,*" said the driver.

A hand-painted wooden sign reading "*Hôtel*" was propped against the door of an enormous stone rectangle of a building. The windows on the ground floor were boarded up.

"Are you sure this place is open?" I asked Jean-Pierre.

"*Bien sûr!*" He jumped out and opened my door.

I paid the driver and he peeled off, covering me in dust.

Jean-Pierre grabbed my backpack and headed through the door.

"Improvements," he said, gesturing at the boarded-up windows.

The stairway was narrow and dark after the bright gray outdoors. We climbed two flights and entered a deserted lobby with dirty green carpeting, a sagging sofa, and a counter that looked like a bar. At least there were windows—that stairwell made me feel claustrophobic.

A man popped up behind the counter as though he'd been crouched there, waiting. He did not seem to know Jean-Pierre. I told him I'd like a room and asked the price. Before he could answer, Jean-Pierre jumped in, speaking to him in the local language. The man answered him curtly. He turned his attention to me.

"Please, the cost is 4,000 CFA," he said. The price, roughly thirteen dollars, was slightly more than the guidebook said. Expensive for this part of the world, but I was prepared to splurge on my first night. He reached under the bar and got a key and a form to fill out. I was ready to drop from exhaustion.

"Can I put my things in my room?" I asked. "I'll be back in a minute."

"Please," the man at the desk said. Jean-Pierre accompanied me down a short, unlit hallway.

"See," he said proudly. "I got you a good price."

I said nothing. I dumped my things, locked the room, and headed back to the desk. I had two things on my mind: shower and laundry. I hadn't done laundry since the volunteer project ended, and all my clothes were stuffed in my backpack in fetid lumps.

I paid the man at the desk, who introduced himself as Adjin. I thanked Jean-Pierre, and turned toward my room.

"Pardon," said Jean-Pierre, "you have forgotten my commission."

"Jean-Pierre," I said, "you told me the hotel pays the commission."

"No! You pay the special, low price. Then you pay me commission. I got you a good price."

I turned to Adjin.

"Did you give me a special price?" I asked.

Adjin frowned, and Jean-Pierre burst into a string of words. Adjin ignored him.

"You paid the regular price," he told me.

"You see," I said to Jean-Pierre, "I don't owe you anything."

"But I have helped you to get here!"

I handed him 300 CFA. "Goodbye," I said.

"Uh!" He made a high-pitched sound of disbelief.

"Jean-Pierre, I'm tired. You said you didn't want anything from me. That is enough."

I refused to feel guilty about the pained, vexed look in his eyes. Michael would've given him more money, even if he knew he was being ripped off. He was like that, generous as rain, giving of himself until there was nothing left. It was healthy to move the money through, he said, otherwise you got constipated. Consequently, I sometimes had to loan him the rent.

I went to my room, shut the door, and locked it. It was a basic room: a single bed with a mosquito net hanging above it,

suspended from the ceiling by a rope and a wooden ring. A ceiling fan, a wooden chair, a tiny barred window facing a cement wall. But the bathroom held an overhead shower with running water, albeit cold. That was more than I'd had in a month. I showered, lay down on my bed, and slept.

When I emerged in the late afternoon, I asked Adjin if he knew of a place where I could do my laundry. I'd spent much of the last month on my knees in the dirt, and my light-colored cotton clothes were covered with ground-in grit. I'd scrubbed and scraped at them, but it had done nothing to lighten the dingy gray. I figured that in Abidjan, which the guidebook called the "gleaming high-rise capital" of Ivory Coast, I'd treat myself to a spin with a washing machine.

Adjin told me there was a woman connected with the hotel who would do the laundry for me.

"How much will it cost?" I asked him.

"Let me see the items."

I plopped the bag on the counter.

"It's not so much," I said. "A skirt, a shirt, a pair of pants. . . ." I pulled the pieces out one by one. "And a bunch of little stuff." I waved my hand toward the underwear and socks at the bottom.

Adjin looked the items over, then said, "It will cost you 500 CFA. You can collect them this evening."

I headed downtown to change money. As I walked across the bridge, I looked down and saw a man standing on the stony riverbank, peeing into the river. I decided to leave for Ghana and my next volunteer project as soon as possible.

I walked among Abidjan's rectangular high-rises, none of which gleamed. The air was humid as the Moroccan bathhouse, the temperature pushing a hundred degrees. Raw sewage ran down the side of the street, its odor mingling with exhaust and the faint scent of rotting vegetables. Next to the gutters, women sat stirring large metal pots of pale mush over charcoal burners or roasting skewers of gristly meat. They grabbed at my arm as I went by, scolding me in French, *"Venez, venez."* Come.

I didn't want to come. I didn't want to touch their food, let alone eat it. I wanted to go home. But that was a place—and a person—to which I might never go back.

✛

Getting service in the bank required assertiveness. Crowds of Africans and foreigners roiled around the windows with no semblance of a line. After spending half an hour in their midst with no visible progress, I began to push. As I braced my body against the human mass, a voice next to my ear croaked in melodic English, "Now you get the idea."

I looked up at a towering Italian with curly silver hair, a Jimmy Durante nose, and a vocal cadence that made every statement a punch line. His name was Luigi, and he was vacationing in West Africa with two friends, all of them members of the Italian left, formerly the Communist party. He offered me a ride to Accra, the capital of Ghana.

"Don't take the bus," he said. "The buses are horrible. Filthy and crowded. Always breaking down."

"Not very proletarian of you," I said.

He looked startled for a moment, then bellowed with hilarity.

"When I make holiday, I become bourgeois!"

I'd thought to take public transportation and meet locals, but there'd be plenty of time for that in Ghana. I agreed to meet Luigi and his friends at their hotel the next morning.

That night the laundry wasn't back.

"She will bring it tomorrow morning," said Adjin.

"What time?" I asked, "because I'm meeting some friends at ten."

"Fine, fine."

The next morning, Adjin said, "She will bring it soon. Sit and wait. Small, small." He laughed, making the same calming gesture with his hand that Jean-Pierre had made in the taxi. "Give me your address, and when you are back in your country, we will write to each other."

I looked at him in surprise. We hadn't exchanged ten words, and now he wanted to write to me?

"I'll give it to you when I get the laundry," I told him. I decided to meet the Italians and come back later.

"Where do you go now?" Adjin asked.

"I told you I was meeting friends at ten." I looked at my watch. "It's ten."

Adjin really laughed at that one.

"You people," he said at last, wiping his eyes, "you live by the clock."

❖

An hour later, I pulled up to the hotel in the back of a rented Peugeot. Luigi and his friends got a tremendous kick out of the boarded-up windows and the hand-painted *"Hôtel"* sign. I felt oddly slighted by their derision.

"They're doing some repairs," I explained huffily as I climbed out.

At the top of the stairs, Adjin greeted me with a beaming smile.

"The laundry is here," he announced triumphantly.

"Do I get a discount for lateness? Just kidding."

He handed me the bill. The total was 1,700 CFA.

"Hey," I said. "This isn't what we agreed on! You said 500."

Adjin shrugged. "I didn't see everything. All the slips."

Every pair of underwear was itemized by the word "slip."

"Well, I showed you what was here. This is more than three times what you said it would be."

He shrugged again.

"This is what the woman charges."

This wasn't right. I had to resist this stuff. Not give in to guilt. Otherwise I'd be taken for a ride every step of the way. I'd seen it happen often enough.

"I'm going to pay what we agreed on," I said. "Five hundred CFA."

"But the price, it is not up to me," said Adjin. "It is the woman who does the laundry. If you don't give it to me, I must pay her from my own pocket."

"You should have thought of that when you quoted me a price. I can't afford this." I slapped the bill. "If I'd known it would be this much I would have washed it myself."

"Oh!" he said, with some surprise.

"I'm not rich, you know. I'm not a tourist. I'm a volunteer."

"Why don't you stay and speak to her yourself. She will come soon."

"I can't stay," I said, exasperated. "My friends are waiting for me in the car." I paid him the 500 CFA and turned to go. The laundry, folded and wrapped in brown paper, was heavy in my hands.

"It's a little damp," he said. Then he called after me, "You forget."

I turned around. He had a big smile on his face.

"You have forgotten to leave me your address."

I didn't understand this guy at all. Sighing, I went to the bar and wrote out my address.

"Are you sure you will not speak to her?" he asked as I left.

I set the laundry beside me on the back seat as we drove away from the hotel. I refused to feel guilty. 1,700 CFA was over five dollars—not a lot at home, but a small fortune here. I didn't want to be a dumb tourist, conned and conned again. If I was going to draw this trip out as long as I hoped to, every dollar counted.

"What is the matter, comrade?" Luigi asked jovially. "The cat has captured your tongue?"

As we pulled out of town we passed a broad hillside, completely covered in laundry. Shirts, pants, dresses, and bedsheets were spread across the high grasses as far as the eye could see. In the river below, women knelt on flat rocks, wringing and scrubbing, their bodies swaying back and forth. Suds drifted lazily downstream in the brown water.

❖

Ivory Coast is one of the wealthier countries in West Africa, and the roads are very well kept. Our Peugeot wound its way over smooth black tarmac amid a spectacular tropical tangle: festooning vines, palms with wide, flat leaves, gangly saplings with frizzy heads. Men and women tromped along the sides of the road, carrying bundles of sticks and baskets of bananas on their heads. In the midafternoon we stopped at a restaurant, ducking beneath the thatched overhang just as the rain hit. For a moment I thought of Michael, how he loved that time of day, the way the greens and yellows popped out in the dying light. I drank orange Fanta from a rusty-necked bottle and munched popcorn as the boys played checkers. And for a moment, I touched something . . . happiness? *Why here? Why now?* Why did I run halfway across the globe if this was all it took—just to sit, in the company of others, with rain, laughter, mild air, fragrant earth?

❖

Late that night, deep in the rain forest between Abidjan and Accra, in a room furnished exactly like the one I'd slept in the night before, I unwrapped the brown paper packages. My light-colored clothes gleamed in the dark room. They were spotless. Every trace of Moroccan grime, dust that I'd thought permanently ground in, was gone. Someone must have spent hours, to succeed so thoroughly where I had repeatedly failed. Each item, every shirt and sock and pair of underwear, lay neatly pressed against the brown paper, brighter and more beautiful than when it was new.

3

The Girl
Who Drank Petrol

When I think of Hannah, I always see her in the same spot. She's near downtown Accra, striding along a red dirt path above the beach. Flecks of ash dance in the air. Beside the path a woman sits on a low stump, roasting plantains on an iron grill, while far below the raggedy silver ocean laps at the pale sand. Hannah walks fast, feet turned out, cheeks pink with exertion, curly golden hair bouncing, chest and chin up, bright green eyes fixed straight ahead. She is purposeful and oblivious, at home in her city, her Ghana, her world.

The first time I saw the Dutch volunteer called Hannah, she was sitting on the sun-bleached wooden steps of the volunteer hostel at high noon, surrounded by African men. I'd arrived in Ghana from Ivory Coast the night before and was making my first tentative sojourn into the achingly bright day. The assembled men shouted boisterously, cheerfully one-upping each other, vying for Hannah's attention. She reclined against the top step, all pink cheeks and yellow curls, flirting and sassing like some kind of postmodern Scarlett O'Hara. I was just about to scoot past her onto the footpath into town, when she turned to me abruptly and said, "Did you know I almost died?"

"Really?" I asked uncertainly.

"Yes!" she said brightly. "Only two weeks ago! I had malaria, but it was the kind where you are not aware that you have it, and you become more and more . . . how do you say . . . like a slow and creeping worm? You walk like this," she stuck out her arms like a zombie, "and laugh all the time like this," she demonstrated a vague, high-pitched giggle, "and you have no desire to eat anything. I ate no food for five days. Then when I went to the hospital, the doctor said if I had waited one day longer I would have died." Her accent was soft and rounded, difficult to place.

"Our sistah was looking sooooo skinny!" one of the African men chimed in. "We make her chop *fufu* six times a day now, so she will be plump and beautiful again." He poked her in the side.

"Chop *fufu*?" I said.

"Chop," said Hannah, gesturing toward her mouth and chomping her jaw up and down. "*Fufu* is Ghana food—you must try some very soon." The man poked her again and she giggled, "Stop it, Gorby!"

"Gorby?" Everything felt bewildering in the hard, flat light.

"My camp name," he said, extending a strong, slender hand. "Claude Mensah, a.k.a. Mensah Mensah Gorbachev, at your service." He grinned at me with such genuine warmth that I giggled in response.

"But we just call him Gorby," said Hannah. "Don't we?" She rubbed her hand across his close-cropped hair. "And he is my dear, dear friend. Gorbachev is his camp name. And this is

Ninja, Momentum, Ayatollah, and Castro." I shook hands all around, dizzied by the wattage of smiles. "At camp, the Africans take foreign names and the foreigners take African names. Have you been to camp yet?"

I shook my head. "I just got here last night."

The work projects, which took place in the rural areas, were called camps. Foreign volunteers paid $200 for a year's membership and then participated in as few or as many camps as they chose during that time. At camp, the volunteers were given room and board. When not at camp, they were welcome to stay here, in the Accra hostel, for as long as they liked. The hostel was a low-ceilinged wooden building, painted olive drab like a military barracks, which housed both a volunteer dormitory and the organization's offices. The dormitory was a long, low-ceilinged room, which fit about thirty bunk beds. Each upper bunk had a hook above it on which the volunteer could hang a mosquito net. Those on the lower bunks attached their nets to the metal lattice of the bed above. The overhead fan worked sporadically, and the rough wooden floor bestowed many splinters on tender pink soles. Sunlight filtered in through small, screened windows. In midsummer, when the hostel was packed with volunteers, the bunks were supplemented by mattresses on the floor.

The hostel was for foreigners only. Ghanaian volunteers were expected to live at home when not participating in camps, although they were welcome to visit during the day. Ghanaians who complied with certain criteria could participate in the camps free of charge. No one seemed to know exactly what those criteria were, but all the Ghanaian volunteers were literate, spoke good English, and had families that were financially able to spare them. With a few exceptions, they were city youth, getting a taste of the countryside. Some of them seemed as alien to the lives and customs of the villagers as we foreigners were.

A few local young men who were not volunteers hung around the hostel during the day, practicing their English and hoping to develop friendships with foreigners that would lead to marriage, employment, or at the very least sponsorship for a journey abroad. These men were clean-cut and solicitous, and many of the foreign women were all too eager to take advantage of the opportunity for roadside romance (and if that's all it turned out to be, the men didn't seem to mind too much either). As a brunette, I didn't get quite the attention the blondes did, but I got enough. Too much, even. I was still far too confused about the relationship I'd left behind to think about flirting. Michael's and my letters had slipped back into a tone of such intimacy it was as if we were still together. On my stronger days, this felt like a burden—I worried that my homesick heart was writing checks my itinerant body wouldn't keep. But on days when I felt most unrooted, it was a tremendous comfort to know that he was there.

Periodically throughout the day, Mr. Awitor, the head of the organization, emerged from an inner office to chase away nonvolunteers with harsh words in one of the local languages. He often added in English—presumably for our benefit— "If I see your face here again, I will surely telephone the police."

"We don't mind them," the foreign volunteers insisted, but he simply shook his head and walked back inside, murmuring under his breath that we would surely mind when our costly cameras and sunglasses went missing. The young men always reappeared an hour or two later anyway. Though Mr. Awitor's tone was menacing, they'd learned by now that the threatened phone call was never made.

Some foreigners participated in one camp and simply stayed on at the hostel for the rest of the year, bumming around Accra and smoking potent local marijuana, called "bingo" or "wee." Hannah, however, had been in Ghana for three months and already participated in four camps.

"We must choose your name!" Hannah clapped her hands with delight. "What shall we call her, Gorby?"

"We must call her Korkor," he said, "like my baby sistah."

"Korkor," I said. It sounded like kaw-KAW. "What does it mean?"

"It means second-born, in Ga," said Gorby.

"Are you second-born?" asked Hannah.

"To my mother I am." I was about to explain that my father had older children from a previous marriage, but Hannah interrupted.

"Perfect! Gorby is . . . how do you call it . . . Soo-kick?"

"Psychic," I said.

"Psychic! Gorby is psychic!"

"What's your camp name?" I asked Hannah.

"Mine is Abena," she said, "Tuesday-born in Fanti. Everyone here has a day name. But then there are also nicknames and family names and Christian names. Africans have so many names, it is very confusing."

"Not to us," said the man called Momentum.

"Only to girls from Holland," added Gorbachev. He flashed her an adoring grin.

Later Hannah confided in me that back home in Amstelveen, the suburb of Amsterdam where she grew up, she'd never considered herself attractive. She had not been popular in school, she told me. She was always isolated. Boys picked on her, girls whispered about her, and she had few friends.

"But you're so beautiful!" I stammered. "Not to mention smart, and sweet, and vivacious. You would've been very popular at my high school, I can promise you that."

She looked at me warily. "I don't think I should thank you for telling me lies. I may be smart, but I am not beautiful."

"You're—"

"Stop it," she said sharply, and something in her tone prevented further protest. "I know what I am. Anyway, it is all past. I am not in Holland now. I am in Ghana, and here I will be a new Hannah, a completely new girl."

I never found out what the old Hannah was like, but this new girl was a charmer. She insinuated herself into my brittle heart the way a child might, and in fact she was like a child, begging for attention, pouting when she didn't get it, pointing out her own best attributes at full volume, basking in the world's love. Among the volunteers, she was the favorite daughter of Africans and foreigners alike, doted on and pampered. She was a baby, really, not even twenty, and though there were others around that age (I was practically the grandmother of the group at twenty-six going on twenty-seven), there was something about her that made you want to protect her, to take care.

Hannah had a flair for drama. Once she leaned over in the night to take a swig from her water bottle and got a big swallow of gasoline instead. She ran to the bathroom and spent the rest of the night vomiting. The burning sensation lingered in her throat throughout the following day.

"I drank petrol!" she crowed to the group on the steps the next day. "You must tell your children and grandchildren this story, so that the girl who drank petrol will become a legend. You must tell them that after that day this girl had the power to light a fire with only her breath."

✤

In Accra I was initially put off, as I had been in Abidjan, by the gaping holes in the sidewalk, the open sewers running down the sides of the streets, and the curbside food stands swarming with flies. The fumes of gasoline, human waste, and charred meat nauseated me. I was beleaguered as well by boisterous strangers who accosted me on the street, shouting, "What is your name? Let me be your friend! Give me your address! Bring me to your country!" I wondered sourly whether these overtures constituted the legendary Ghanaian friendliness.

But within two weeks I no longer noticed the sewage or the flies, and I was gobbling up street food like it was going out of style. I relished it all—the dark green *kontumbre* with its texture of creamed spinach; the thick, savory groundnut stew (Ghanaian for peanut) with sticky rice balls; salty *Jollof* rice flavored with bits of egg and fish; tart, juicy pineapple; sweet oranges stripped of their peels but still clothed in their white felt underskins; starchy cocoyams; *kenke*; *banku*; *shitoh*; *akieke* . . . All the stews were heavy with palm oil, its drowsy flavor reminiscent of coconuts and cashews. But far and away my favorite street food was *keli-weli*, a spicy-sweet concoction made of small chunks of plantain fried to a crisp in palm oil, then sprinkled amply with ginger and chili pepper for a sharp, tangy bite.

Simply put, I loved Accra. While embracing the amenities of running water and electricity, it maintained a character all its own. No New York–style high-rises to be found here. Instead it unfolded, neighborhood by colorful neighborhood, a curious mixture of African and European influence, opening outward from the center like an elaborate tropical bloom. Accra was alive. Every city block pulsated with energy, from the solid cement buildings of the downtown area to the tin-roofed shacks of the poorer neighborhoods, from the sweltering maelstrom of the Makola Market to the crumbling castle that housed the government offices. In any one of these places, you were as likely to see a man dressed head to toe in full African regalia as you were to see a woman in jeans, tube top, and high-heeled shoes. And the colors! Brilliant shades of orange and red, turquoise and lilac, fuchsia and teal. The African fabrics would make a flamingo look drab. The prohibitions against combining reds and pinks or circles and stripes were absent here. Fabrics of every description lived side by side in delirious dissonance, a dizzying visual feast. The hairstyles too were astonishing. Some adorned the women's heads like helmets, with sharp spikes sticking out in every direction. Others were elaborate multi-tiered sculptures, their interlacing layers balanced against each other like houses of cards. Still others were interwoven with beads and ribbons, which complemented the colorful outfits with extra splashes of light.

On top of all this, I'd fallen completely in love with the people. Strangers still waylaid me daily, but what initially felt like aggression I now saw as vitality tinged with humor. I understood that the people on the street didn't actually expect to go home with me. They enjoyed engaging for its own sake, and while they were at it, they figured they might as well take their shot. This was the quality that struck me the most about the Ghanaians: for better or worse, they *engaged*. Riding across town in a *tro-tro* (Ghanaian for minivan), I often found myself in the midst of a rowdy argument, with people on all sides shouting at each other in the local language. These arguments were almost always good-natured, ending with laughter and backslapping when the participants disembarked. I recalled sadly that in the United States I had once taken a Greyhound halfway across the country without speaking to a single soul.

There were nights when Hannah, Gorbachev, and I, along with Ayatollah, Momentum, and a shifting group of European volunteers, would smoke bingo (purchased from a mysterious man called Bush Doctor who hovered around the path near the hostel) and tear ravenously through the streets of Accra at mid-

night, searching for food. Eventually we'd find one of the few stands that hadn't closed down for the night. The nodding attendant, usually an old woman, would wake with a start and make us egg sandwiches on thick chunks of white bread smeared with Laughing Cow cheese. We'd each down two or three sandwiches and a cup of Milo, a warm chocolaty beverage, before setting off for the hostel, our laughter echoing through the night streets, our running feet keeping pace with the rats that darted in and out of the sewers.

"A rat stepped on my foot!" Hannah shrieked one night. "I am marked by the King of Rats! Like, do you know, 'the Nutcracker'? Now you must tell people, I knew a girl who—every night at midnight exactly—she would get down on the ground and squeak like a rat, or no, a girl who had power to change a bad person to a rat."

Hannah's need to mythologize herself touched me. It was what we all yearned for, I thought, to be seen, recognized. We all wanted to be heroes or martyrs, to create lives worthy of legend. She just wore her desire a bit more nakedly than the rest.

❖

Our volunteer efforts were a mixed bag. While some of the projects ran smoothly, others were woefully ill-conceived. The idea was simple enough: We'd go into a village, start up a project, and leave behind materials so that the villagers could finish the project after we left. The problem was that in many cases no one seemed to have consulted the villagers in advance. Unless there was a committed individual in the village to galvanize the community into action, the hospital or school might easily remain unfinished, while the building materials were slowly spirited away to patch failing roofs or add adjoining rooms to people's homes. It was also unclear why certain villages were chosen for projects several years in a row, while others nearby remained unvisited. Since the presence of so many foreigners brought a lot of energy to the local economies, I suspected personal connections might be involved.

One of the more disheartening stories I heard involved a camp in which the volunteers dug a foundation for a schoolhouse right next to an identical foundation that another group had dug and abandoned. When the volunteers asked why they couldn't simply build on the existing foundation, they were told that it was forbidden to interfere with the work of another group. Another tale involved a village to which a group had returned several years in a row and done nothing but make bricks. As the story went, the village was so overrun with bricks that the local people were using them as tables, chairs, even bassinets.

Most of the foreign volunteers I worked with in Ghana fell into one of two groups: those who came with an already ingrained sense that the work we were doing here was futile (but doing it was marginally better than doing nothing at all), and those who arrived filled with hopeful romanticism about their own ability to "help." Members of the second category were often terribly disillusioned when their projects hit a snag, and tended to resemble the members of the first category by the time they left. Members of the first group, on the other hand, were occasionally jolted back to the second by the sheer exuberance of Ghanaian life.

Outwardly, I allied myself with the jaded camp—I'd done enough volunteering in the past to know that it often benefited the supposed help-*ers* more than the help-*ees,* but my cynical veneer was ridiculously thin. Beneath my world-weary affectation, I longed with my entire being to be knocked over the head by a driving sense of purpose. I approached each new project harboring a shameful secret: a vast, uncool reservoir of hope. In the guise of offering service, I came to the construction site seeking nothing less than redemption. Perhaps we all did.

◆

Whenever I returned to Accra, I looked for Hannah. She alone seemed peculiarly free of either grudge or expectation concerning our role here. She soaked up everything with unbiased delight. I envied her capacity for simple enjoyment and secretly hoped that if I spent enough time with her, some of it might rub off.

A few months after our initial meeting, I came back from a project on the northern coast to find that Hannah had gotten romantically involved with a Ghanaian volunteer who went by the camp name of Rambo. Rambo was devilishly handsome, with silky skin the color of polished walnut, pronounced cheekbones, and striking gray-green eyes. He dressed to fit his nickname, in Western tank tops that exposed his enormous biceps, camouflage pants, and heavy-soled boots. He was studying mathematics at Legon University and was rumored to be a brilliant student. He came from that minuscule portion of the Ghanaian population that could be called middle class, meaning he had been raised in a home with both a television and a phone. His father had some mysterious government post, which Rambo cryptically described as "near the top." He spoke flawless English in a deep, purring voice, and was famous for his ability to drink any European under the table when it came to *apeteshi*, the strong home-brewed liquor that was popular in the Ghanaian countryside.

Throughout the steamy afternoons and into the balmy evenings, Hannah sat beside Rambo on the steps of the hostel. She listened intently as he talked to the other African volunteers in Fanti, Ga, or Twi, his arm slung heavily across her shoulders or hooked around her neck like a boa constrictor. Often she leaned over to kiss his cheek or nibble at his ear. He allowed this briefly before pushing her away with a murmured reprimand.

She began to wash his laundry on a regular basis. As I sat in the dirt courtyard behind the hostel with my plastic bucket, wringing the dust from my own grungy socks and shirts, I'd see her laboring over the heavy camouflage pants or scrubbing away at a spot of dirt on a white tank top. When I suggested to her that Rambo could just as easily do his own laundry, she shrugged.

"How do you say, when you are with the Romans . . . ?" She giggled nervously.

Hannah had little time for her old friends.

"I have known this man," Gorbachev grumbled to me privately, "and I have not liked him. I am very sure that he seeks only to marry a white sistah so that he may leave this country. He wants to be a doctor in Europe or America, where he can make a lot of money and own many cars. Our Sistah Abena, she is so innocent. She trusts every person."

A week later I returned to the empty hostel from the Makola Market in the middle of the day. The Makola Market was the largest in Accra, and its endless rows of outdoor stalls provided the ideal place to revel in the beauty of African fabrics. I was laying out my purchases—three exquisite batiks dyed in richly saturated blues, purples, and greens—draping them across my bed to admire, when I heard a strange, stifled sound, like someone choking. Looking around, I saw, through the gauzy veil of a mosquito net, a huddled lump on Hannah's bed, covered by a sleeping bag. Alarmed, I rushed over.

"Hannah? Is that you? What's going on?"

In one violent motion the sleeping bag flopped flat on the bed and there she sat, shaking and red-faced.

"He will marry her!" she screamed. "He is all made of lies! He will marry *her!*"

"Who? Who will marry who?"

"Rambo," she sobbed, throwing herself at me through the mosquito net. I ducked beneath the netted shroud and wrapped my arms around her. She heaved and wailed against my shoulder.

"I'll kill him!" she cried. "I will give him petrol to drink. I will turn him into a rat. Then I will make him marry only me, after he is *dead.*"

"Hannah, Hannah, sweetheart . . ." I murmured. She sobbed in my arms for close to an hour, occasionally breaking away to hurl accusations at Rambo and his unnamed bride.

Eventually, the story came out. That morning, while Hannah was still in bed, a former volunteer named Isabella had arrived from Spain. Rambo had introduced her to the omnipresent crowd on the steps as his fiancée. He'd been anxiously awaiting her return, he said; they would be married at the end of the month. Hannah heard the commotion and wandered out in her oversized T-shirt to find Rambo lip-locked in the sort of public display of affection he was never willing to engage in with her. When he came up for air, Rambo met her eyes for a long, cool moment, then looked away. She ran and threw her arms around him, shouting that he was hers. He pushed her away, and told the astonished Isabella—whom Hannah alternately described as ugly as a rhinoceros and beautiful as Sophia Loren—that this crazy girl had been hanging around the hostel bothering the volunteers and would soon be shipped back to Sweden or Germany, wherever she came from.

"But that's ridiculous!" I sputtered. "She'll hear the truth before the day is out. She'll know he can't be trusted."

But Rambo and Isabella had taken Isabella's things and left the hostel. Hannah had run after them, trying to grab the luggage out of Rambo's hands. Several of the assembled men held her back, chuckling and clucking, trying to soothe her. Now she no longer wanted to live in the hostel, no longer wanted to see the faces of those men.

Hannah had long ago befriended Sistah Essi, the feisty, sparkly-eyed young proprietress of a tiny beachside restaurant called The Last Stop. Located about a quarter mile from the hostel, The Last Stop was a favorite volunteer hangout, a breezy open-air shack with sand underfoot, located a short sprint from the ocean. Essi lived with her two daughters, ages one and three, in a room adjoining the restaurant. She assured Hannah it would be no problem for her to pitch her tent on the beach, and offered Hannah meals in exchange for helping out in the café.

Hannah's good nature returned after a week or so, but her eager-to-please, puppy-dog energy had been replaced by something calmer and more distant. That was when she began her walking. At any time of the day or night you might see her, striding through the streets or along a red dirt path above the beach, chin and chest thrust forward like a woman on a mission. She walked that way for hours, unafraid and unapproachable, perfectly poised on the crust of Africa, perfectly alone.

"Where's she going?" one volunteer or another would wonder aloud as we sat on the balcony of the Wato Bar, another favorite hangout, watching daylight turn to dusk. As the cloth wicks on the kerosene cans took flame one by one in the streets below, we'd crane our necks just in time to see Hannah slip quickly between the food stands and disappear.

As time went on, she became fluent in Fanti, which she practiced with Gorbachev and the other African volunteers while serving us our food at The Last Stop. There were over sixty languages spoken among Ghana's eighteen million people. Fanti belonged to Akan, the dominant language group, which most

Ghanaians understood. Hannah's English, too, sounded increasingly Ghanaian, her accent, sentence structure, and turns of phrase growing more African with each passing day. Her relationship with the African men had changed, too. She no longer flirted the way she once had. She was friendly, even affectionate, but a distance remained.

"Why don't you go out with Gorbachev?" I asked her once. "He's such a sweet, gentle man, and you know he worships you."

"*Eh!*" she clucked. "Ghana men and me, we are finished. Ghana men are *weak!*" she shouted, echoing a common insult the African volunteers threw at each other on the camps. "Now I want only Ghana. Ghana here," she pounded the table. "Ghana is sooo sweet. Amsterdam was never my place. Ghana here, this is my place."

❖

When the rains came, Hannah began spending nights in the small room attached to The Last Stop, with Sistah Essi and her two girls. Hannah and Essi had become very close, and often when Gorbachev and I went down there for a midday meal I could hear them giggling behind the kitchen partition while they chopped vegetables and stirred the stews. Sometimes I had to call out three or four times before Hannah would come out and greet us with a friendly, "*Eh!* Sistah Korkor, Brothah Gorbachev, you are welcome!"

Essi's husband, Kweku, was in the army and came home every month or two for a few days. He was known around the hostel as an odd character and a heavy drinker; the Ghanaian volunteers were reluctant to visit The Last Stop when he was in town. Whenever he appeared, Hannah moved back to her tent and, as though by tacit agreement, her relations with Essi became stiff and formal. Kweku was suspicious of her motives for working at The Last Stop, and one night she heard him shouting through the walls, while the two little girls whimpered and wailed.

"They are so rich," he shouted in Fanti, "to come here, from so far away, and stay for many months, doing nothing, buying whatever goods they please. Why then should she work like this, eating our food?"

Hannah could not make out Essi's reply, but when she heard what sounded like a hand striking flesh, she put her head under her sleeping bag and counted to a thousand. She offered to leave the next day, but Essi begged her to stay.

"Sistah Korkor, Essi hates that man," Hannah said. "If I were her, I would surely find a way to kill him." We were sitting on one of The Last Stop's uneven wooden benches at dusk, wiggling our toes in the cooling sand. A gentle breeze rose off the ocean, and a pale sunset tinted the foam pink.

"I know," I said. "It's awful. And I have the feeling it's pretty widely tolerated, too." The previous day, I'd overheard a Ghanaian volunteer telling one of the foreign men that if he himself had a sister whose husband beat her, he would not accept her back into the family. Her husband wouldn't beat her for no reason, he explained; she'd had to have done something wrong.

"I wish Essi would throw him out," Hannah said. Tears stood in her eyes. "She and I, we can run the restaurant. For what does she need him? He takes her chop money and buys *apeteshi*."

I sighed. "She'd probably leave him if she could. Who knows what her options are? We can't really see the full picture."

"I see her! She is afraid, that is all. But I will help her. I will stay with her and help to run the café."

"How long do you plan to be here, Hannah, really? Aren't you going back to Holland, to school?"

"No, no, no!" She started to cry. "For what do I go back to that place? I am Ghana woman now. That place has nothing that I need."

◆

I left the next day to go to another camp, and didn't see Hannah for almost a month. When I returned she was still staying with Essi, and she seemed more entrenched in her "Ghana woman" image than ever. She generally refused to speak English now, though she'd relent and engage in fragmentary conversation with me when pressed.

"Our sistah from Holland is now more Ghana than we Ghanaians!" Gorbachev quipped.

One Saturday night, Hannah, Gorby, and I went with a few other Ghanaian volunteers to Labadi Beach, on the outskirts of Accra, for a dance party. While a tight-knit interracial group danced beneath bright white spotlights and the disheveled silhouettes of palm trees, the three of us walked down the beach to a quiet place where we could smoke our extremely potent wee. Buoyed up by a giddy high, Hannah and I stripped off our skirts and charged into the water, which was scarcely cooler than the air. We stood holding hands, with the waves licking our waists, and looked out toward the horizon. There was no moon, and I could see no line between ocean and sky: just blackness, with sporadic zigzags of white that vanished as soon as they appeared. A thrill of danger raised goose bumps all over my body. I couldn't see what was coming—I never knew the size of a wave until it broke around me. For all I knew, the next one would crash down on top of our heads and sweep us out to sea.

It was three in the morning when we crammed into a shared taxi back into town with three other Europeans. We were sopping and exhausted, hangovers already on the way. Gorbachev and I walked Hannah down to the beach by the Last Stop, but when we got there we experienced a jolt of disorientation: Hannah's tent was nowhere to be seen.

"Did you move it?" I asked Hannah.

"No." She shook her head in bewilderment, looking around her in a kind of daze.

"Thieves?" said Gorbachev.

We walked toward the spot where the tent had been. I stepped on something squishy, and when I reached down I felt fabric, slick and synthetic, with feathers leaking out of it. Exploring further, I found a zipper.

"Oh no," I said softly. Taking another step I tripped on a slender plastic pole.

"This . . . this is . . . someone has . . ." Gorbachev sputtered, as we discovered pieces of clothing, paper, and plastic, ripped and scattered around the beach. Down near the water I stumbled over a mass of nylon, sopping wet. It was Hannah's tent.

Hannah began to cry. Gorbachev was shouting, "Who . . . Who has . . ."

A burst of light exploded from The Last Stop. A male figure leaped out into the night with a flaming torch in his hand.

A torrent of abuse came from his mouth in Fanti, interspersed with sporadic words of English. Amid the torrent the words "spy," "thief," and "CIA" jumped out at me, and then, later, "white witch" and several times, "my wife."

"She's not your wife!" Hannah shouted suddenly. "She doesn't love you! She hates you! She loves me!"

After that, everything blurs together. Kweku lunged toward us with the torch, and then Gorbachev was holding my hand and the three of us were running blind along the beach. At some point we turned uphill, staggering toward the porch light of the hostel, which glimmered feebly on the horizon. Hannah, on

Gorbachev's other side, screamed a string of Fanti words into the wind as we ran, stumbling and gasping, toward the light.

◆

The next morning, Hannah was gone. At my panicked insistence, Mr. Awitor made inquiries and learned that she had called her parents in Amsterdam, who had arranged for a ticket home the same day. By the time I awoke, she was already at the airport. I don't know whether she got up at dawn and went to the beach to salvage her possessions. Some volunteers went down there to search, but they found nothing. She would at least have needed her money and passport, I pointed out, but Gorbachev said that Hannah always carried those things with her, in a money belt worn under her dress, "like a foreigner."

For me she left no note, nothing. And I never found out whether she'd said goodbye to her beloved Essi. I didn't go back to The Last Stop for many months. When I finally did, Essi chattered cheerfully, avoiding my eyes, and I couldn't bring myself to ask.

"She loved Ghana so much," said Gorbachev sorrowfully. "And this horrible man, he must drive everything to ruin."

"But why would she just leave like that?" I asked for the hundredth time. "She could have found another place to live. And she could have visited Essi when Kweku was away."

"Sistah Korkor," said Gorbachev, looking at me sadly. "Our Sistah Abena, you know, she was a very kind girl, but she was not strong like you. It is very good fortune that she was born in this world to parents who were able to send for her."

◆

Later, when I was back in the States, I got a letter from Hannah. The tone was exuberant, filled with exclamation points. It sounded more like the girl I'd first seen on the hostel steps than the woman run off the beach by a friend's irate husband. She was now in nursing school, she said. One day, she'd gone for a long walk in a part of Amsterdam that was unfamiliar to her and stumbled onto a Ghanaian restaurant. She went inside and was amazed to find all her favorite foods: *fufu* and pepper sauce, *kenke*, garden egg stew, groundnut soup, even *apeteshi* to drink. Imagine the waiters' surprise and delight when she began speaking to them in Fanti! Soon she was going there every day. They invited her to parties, and she discovered a whole community— a little Ghana in Amsterdam. For the first time in her life, she felt almost at home in her hometown. And that feeling reminded her of what she'd nearly forgotten: how right it all was before it all went wrong.

"Oh, Sistah Korkor!" she wrote, and I could hear her voice as clearly as if she were standing before me, flushed and tremulous and filled with hope.

"I remember now how very sweet Ghana was! How tender the air, the nighttime smell of ocean. Also Essi, her laughter too loud at my ear. Now I know what I must do, and school is no longer boring! I want to study and learn, so I can take my degree quickly and soon, so soon, I can leave this place forever and go home."

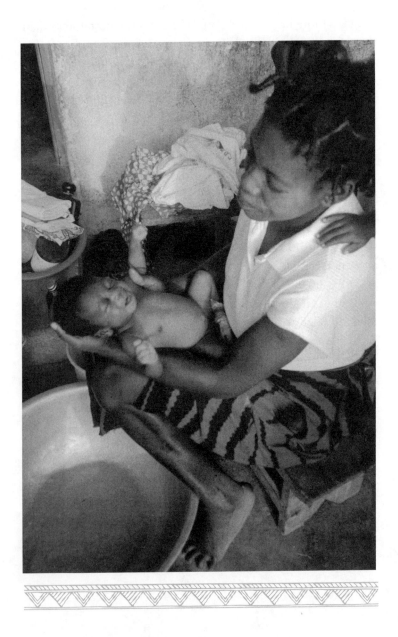

4

Yao

Love, baskets of love for the baby Yao. Gardens of it. Oceans. In a village swarming with children, each of them vital and mercurial enough to remind your heart that it can split wide open, Yao has made an impression on us all. Each day, men and women, African and foreign volunteers alike, set down our shovels for a moment, wipe the dust and sweat from our eyes, and watch Minessi as she strolls by, tall, dark, and regal, with Yao strapped to her back. Yao swivels his little head, working hard to take us all in with his enormous dark eyes. And what eyes! Compassionate enough to forgive a world's transgressions, alert enough to awaken a planet asleep.

Forgive my gushing. I'm in love.

My first camp found me building teachers' quarters in the village of Afranguah, in the Central Region. Unlike some of the projects I'd heard about, this one had the full support of the villagers and seemed destined to reach completion. The village women worked enthusiastically beside us, carrying buckets of water on their heads, pulling up weeds, hammering nails. Though the doors and window frames were made of wood, our primary building material was cement, which we mixed ourselves and molded into bricks, then left overnight to dry. At first it was unclear to me who was in charge—people just seemed to know what to do—but gradually a kind of hierarchy emerged. The camp leader could be seen from time to time consulting a piece of graph paper and instructing some of the experienced Ghanaian campers, who then passed on instructions to the more skilled Western volunteers. If I was assertive, some task or other would eventually trickle down to me. I soon discovered that I could just as easily sit in the shade doing nothing all morning without anyone caring or even noticing. I did my best to avoid this temptation.

On the second day, I approached a volunteer called Ballistic, who was planing some wooden boards.

"Can I try that?" I asked.

"You cannot do it," he said, without looking up.

"I'd like to try," said I, bristling.

At which he reiterated, "You surely cannot do it."

I got on his case then, asking him how he'd like it if he asked me to teach him an English song, as he had the previous day, and I responded that he couldn't learn it? After that he became my committed teacher and remained so for the next several hours, resulting in numerous uneven boards and two very sore arms.

It was the month of June, right in the middle of Ghana's long rainy season, ostensibly the coolest time of the year. Even so, the midday sun was so excruciating for us Westerners that our workday had to be arranged around it. On an average day, we rose around five-thirty, started work by six-thirty, and broke at eleven-thirty. If it was overcast, or breezy enough to be tolerable, we'd return to work around two for a couple more hours. The rain usually hit in the late afternoon, washing away the heat and leaving the evening fragrant and cool.

Every afternoon, as soon as we finished work, I'd tear back to the schoolhouse where we slept, grab a bucket of water and a calabash bowl, and duck behind the woven reed screens we'd set up for privacy. There, I'd shed my clothes and dump calabashes of water on myself while I soaped off the day's grit, leaving a few inches in the bottom of my bucket for a final whoosh of cool. Then, while the other foreign volunteers hung around the camp trading travel stories, I'd scoot down to Minessi's hut to spend some time with baby Yao before the evening meal.

Afranguah was a village of several hundred souls, with neither running water nor electricity. The inhabitants were poor, but not destitute. The children were bright and energetic, thin and scrappy, without the swollen bellies and patchy, red-tinged hair that signal malnutrition. The village had a deep borehole with a pump attached which yielded clear, sweet-tasting water, thanks to a far-reaching cooperative effort between the Ghanaian government and several international aid organizations.

An unpaved road ran through the center of town, surrounded by rectangular cinderblock houses smoothed over with stucco and topped off by corrugated tin roofs. Paths leading away from the center led to more cinderblock houses, interspersed with rectangular mud huts. My favorite of these huts had big yellow flowers growing out of its thatched roof. The surrounding countryside was lush and verdant, thick with vines and a jumble of deciduous trees. The jungle, a European volunteer told me, had been chopped down hundreds of years before and replaced by this secondary growth. The landscape was lovely, with its fecund red-brown earth, but it lacked the rain forest's primordial complexity.

Minessi lived in one of the small stuccoed houses gathered around the center of town. She could usually be found in the communal courtyard outside her hut, washing laundry or preparing *fufu*. The women of Afranguah made *fufu* by pounding boiled cassava or yam in a large bowl, made from a scooped-out tree stump, until it acquired a smooth elasticity. While the Ghanaians loved *fufu*, most foreigners found it an acquired taste, due to the peculiar consistency. The proper way to eat it was to take a fist-sized handful and swallow it down without chewing. Since doing this produced a gag reflex in the uninitiated, we novices took smaller bites, chewing it like gum until it broke apart.

The women threw their entire bodies into the pounding. Using heavy wooden pestles four to five feet long, they repeatedly flung their arms high above their heads and brought them down with tremendous force. Each time I watched Minessi do this, I was struck by the extraordinary grace and dignity of her movement. While most of the women in the village were short and stocky, Minessi's figure was tall and tapered, with wide hips and a long, elegant neck. Her arms were lean, sinewy ropes. Her pounding looked like a ritual expulsion—a fierce, elegant dance.

On a typical day, Minessi would look up from her pounding as I approached. She'd smile her languid, unhurried smile and unstrap Yao from her back. Her near-black skin was smooth and lustrous; her wide-set eyes tilted slightly upward. It was obvious where Yao got his looks. The schoolteacher Amoah, an effusive, genial man whose hut was next to Minessi's, would greet me each day with a warm cry of "Sistah Korkor, you are welcome!" Amoah's three children would run up to me, and we'd trade exuberant greetings in Fanti. Then I'd sit on the low stool in front of Minessi's hut, take Yao in my arms, and rock him, singing softly in his ear. He'd explain a few things to me in his own language, a kind of universal babyspeak, which resembled neither English nor Fanti so much as the call of a rapturous bird.

Minessi spoke a bit more English than the other women in Afranguah, which is to say that her vocabulary extended beyond basic greetings. Our conversations went something like this:

MINESSI: You like Yao!

ME: Yes, I do.

MINESSI: You like Yao too much!

Then she'd begin to laugh. Her laughter was like a thunderstorm, starting as a rumble, low and distant, occasionally building to a full-on roar. Soon I'd be laughing with her, and Yao too. The three of us spent a lot of time like that, laughing together for no reason at all.

"Minessi, listen," I said one day, holding Yao's mouth close to her ear. His breathing was raspy and labored. Minessi listened for a moment, then looked at me, confused.

I imitated the breathing, exaggerating it for effect. She gave me a long, wary look, then shrugged. I let the subject drop, but not before kissing Yao's silky forehead and whispering in his ear that he was trying to scare me, and he should cut it out right away.

Two days later, as Minessi took her daily stroll past the construction site, she stopped and gestured to me. I set down the short pile of cement blocks I was balancing precariously on my head and skipped over. She looked at me for a moment with an anxious, indecisive expression, then whispered in my ear that she would like some money to buy medicine for Yao. Could I bring some to her house tonight?

Sure, I told her, how much did she need?

But she didn't want to talk about it now, in front of everyone. She hurried away before I had a chance to kiss Yao.

When I arrived at Minessi's house that afternoon, she was neither pounding nor sweeping. She was sitting on the front step, quite still, with Yao in her lap. Amoah saw me approach and called out "Sistah Korkor!" as usual. Hearing this, Minessi sprang up and dragged a stool out of her hut for me to sit on. She then disappeared again and returned with a plate of *kenke* and *shitoh*. *Kenke* was another Ghanaian staple, made from fermented cornmeal. It had a grainy texture, which was much more palatable to me than *fufu*'s odd plasticity, and a flavor that reminded me of sourdough bread. *Shitoh* was a sweet, dark paste, like plum sauce with a bite.

Minessi handed me the plate and gestured that I should eat, while Yao reached out his arms to me and gurgled in his throat like a dove. After I'd eaten, I swung him onto my lap. He looked up with a smile of pure delight, then stuck his fingers in my mouth and coughed. Minessi stood watching, not saying a word.

"Minessi?" I said at last. "You wanted some money for medicine?"

She glanced over at Amoah, who was playing with his children and seemed not to hear.

"Yes," she said softly.

"How much do you need?" I asked.

Silence.

"Please tell me, Minessi. I want to help. I want to help Yao."

"Please, you give 1,000 cedis," she blurted.

I looked at her for a moment in astonishment, then exhaled a short sigh of relief. Less than two dollars stood between my darling and his medicine.

"That's fine, Minessi. No problem at all."

I reached beneath the waistband of my cotton skirt for my

money belt and pulled out a small, sweaty wad. Minessi stared as I peeled off two 500-cedi notes, then watched my hands as I replaced the rest. She dropped her eyes.

"Thank you," she said, not looking up.

A week later, our time in Afranguah was coming to an end, and Yao's breathing was no better. It scraped and croaked. I asked Minessi whether she'd gotten the medicine, and she nodded. I told Yao to get with the program and shape up. I hugged Yao and Minessi and Amoah and Amoah's three children. Everyone squirmed and laughed uncomfortably in my embrace. I told them I'd be back to see them after my next project.

✦

Back in Afranguah after a month's dusty labor in the Eastern Region, I couldn't wait to see Yao. I wedged myself into a packed *tro-tro* for the bumpy ride from Saltpond Junction to Afranguah. In Afranguah a cadre of children greeted me with enthusiastic shouts. They accompanied me as I dumped my luggage in the cinderblock house belonging to the town minister, Billy Akwah Graham (his father met the American preacher in person once and was deeply impressed), and ran down the hill to Minessi's mud hut with its corrugated tin roof.

Minessi was in the courtyard, pounding *fufu* with a long wooden pestle. She laughed when she saw me with my entourage and shouted, "Eh! Sistah Korkor! You are welcome!" I ran to hug her. Yao was on her back, and I covered his little head with kisses. Minessi leaned the long stick against the scooped-out wooden bowl and unwound the cloth that held Yao to her back. She handed him to me.

I looked deep into his soulful eyes and was shocked to find them glassy. Then Yao coughed: a wrenching, guttural cough that sent a shudder through his whole body. I looked up at

Minessi in alarm. She started at my expression, taking a step backward.

"Yao is worse, Minessi, he's worse." A shrill panic came into my voice. "What happened to the medicine?" I asked.

"It is finished," she said. "Every day, one spoon."

She went into the hut and brought out a bottle, empty and carefully washed, with the label still on it. Examining it, I saw that it was a kind of drugstore cough syrup, cherry flavored for children.

"Oh, Minessi, who gave you this?"

"Saltpond Junction. I tell him Yao is sick. He says it is the best. From England."

"Minessi," I took her hand. "I want to take Yao to see a doctor. There's a hospital in Saltpond, right?"

She shrugged and looked at the ground.

"I'll pay for it, okay? Whatever he needs. But let's get him there as soon as we can. Can you go today?"

"I must tell my husband."

I'd forgotten she had a husband. Where was he all day? I didn't remember ever seeing him. There were so many more women than men in Afranguah that I'd scarcely registered it. Most of the young men had migrated to the cities, looking for work, while the women stayed in the village, farming and caring for the children and a few elderly parents. While the women carried water, pounded *fufu*, nursed babies, and bent over the millet stalks in the fields outside of town, the few remaining men (with the exception of Amoah, the schoolteacher) spent their days hanging around the bar, drinking *apeteshi*—or so it appeared to me. I was struck now, not for the first time, by how little I knew about the people I considered friends.

❖

When I stepped outside Billy Akwah Graham's house the next morning, Minessi was waiting for me. She was wrapped from head to toe in beautiful printed cloth. The cloth was bright orange and stiff, as though just purchased for a festival. Yao was strapped to her back, asleep. I leaned close and kissed his soft cheek, listening to the low uneven motor of his breath.

The walk from Afranguah to Saltpond Junction, where we could catch a *tro-tro* to the midsized town of Saltpond, took about forty-five minutes. The heat of the day hadn't settled in yet, and I enjoyed the cool silence as we headed down the dirt path through the luxurious greenery. I asked Minessi where she'd learned English, but she didn't seem to understand the question, answering only "yes." I asked her if she wanted more children.

"No!" she said firmly. "Finished. Four children. Enough."

"Four children? I thought you had only Yao!" I looked at her closely, wondering how old she was. Her queenly bearing made her seem older, but looking at her dewy, unlined face I guessed that she was in her early twenties.

"Three girls!" she laughed. "They stay with my sistah. Cape Coast."

"What are they doing there?"

"School. Her husband, he is guide. At the monument."

The "monument" in Cape Coast was a fort, built in the six-teenth century, that was later used as a base for the slave trade. Tourists came from all over the world to bear witness to that grim piece of history, following the guides through the waist-high dungeons where African men, women, and children once lay shackled in darkness, waiting to be shipped overseas. All that foreign income probably provided Cape Coast with better-equipped schools than those in Afranguah, which had neither paper nor pencils nor books.

"You must miss your girls a lot," I said.

"I will go to them. I want to learn." She touched her hair and gestured: twisting, braiding, arranging; her long, tapered fingers moving nimbly through the air.

"You want to be a hairdresser!" I cried, absurdly delighted by this small confidence. For all the laughter we'd shared, Minessi had a kind of detachment, an underlying reserve that I'd never been able to penetrate.

She nodded. "Then I go to live in Cape Coast, too."

At Saltpond Junction we waited for two hours while the *tro-tro* accumulated passengers. While I wandered around outside with Yao in my arms, Minessi preferred to sit in the sweltering vehicle, holding our places. She leaned her head against a window, gazing out.

None of the windows opened, which made the ride to Saltpond a kind of low-grade torture that gathered intensity as the trip progressed. I kept my head down and breathed deeply, trying to ignore the sensation that I was a cauliflower trapped in a steamer. It was past noon by the time we arrived, and the whole town was wilting in the midday sun. We walked to the hospital, the sultry air dragging at our limbs. Yao, strapped to Minessi's back, groaned in his sleep like an achy old man.

The hospital was a modern cement building with bare, scrubbed hallways. A few people waited in the entryway. It was nothing like the hospital in Accra, with its outdoor courtyard crowded with patients from morning till night. Perhaps the people in this region, accustomed to traditional methods of healing, were suspicious of these Western-style doctors and their unfamiliar medicine.

A nurse sat at the reception desk. She discussed Yao's condition with Minessi in Fanti for a while, then wrote "cough" on the sheet of paper in front of her.

"His breathing, too, listen to it," I chimed in. Minessi glanced at me uneasily. The nurse added a few notes to her paper, then told me I should go into the doctor's office with Minessi and Yao to explain the situation to the doctor. I added that Yao already had the cough when I left a month ago. The nurse looked at Minessi in surprise.

"*Bohsom?*" she said sharply, which meant month. Minessi nodded slightly, looking caught out.

The cost of the visit was 200 cedis: astoundingly low by my standards, but what that sum meant to Minessi, I couldn't say. Much of the village business was conducted by barter, and cash was extremely scarce.

The doctor was a young Ghanaian man in a white button-down shirt and wire-rimmed glasses, with a silver cross around his neck. Probably a recent university graduate doing his mandatory public service. He sat behind a broad desk, wearing a stethoscope, and spoke curtly to Minessi. She replied respectfully, her eyes dropped.

"*Bohsom eko,*" she murmured softly. One month.

The doctor brought his hand down on the desk in an impatient gesture, barking a response. I was dismayed to see the proud Minessi cowering now, her elegant posture literally shrinking under this man's rebuke. She unwrapped Yao and set him, naked, on the desk.

"She feeds the baby mashed *kenke*. No milk," the doctor told me in English. "Do you know what is *kenke*?"

I nodded stiffly. Minessi avoided my eyes. I was stunned that he spoke like that in front of her. Did he think she didn't understand? If she was feeding Yao *kenke*, it must've been all she could afford. But wasn't she also breast-feeding? I realized I didn't know; I couldn't remember ever having seen her feed him. For a heart-stopping moment I wondered whether she was guilty of negligence. My mind flitted to her other children, her daughters: why weren't they with her? I quickly pushed away the disloyal thought. She was wonderful with Yao, so gentle and patient. If she'd stopped breast-feeding, there had to be a reason. And cow's milk, which could only be found in tins, was certainly out of her range.

The doctor ordered Minessi to remove a small pouch that hung on a frayed red ribbon around Yao's neck.

"I too have my superstition." He winked at me. "I won't touch the baby while this is on."

Placing the stethoscope against Yao's tiny chest, the doctor looked up and shook his head at me again.

"They feed the babies mashed *kenke* and then wonder why they grow pale and have no energy," his voice rang with disgust. "I tell them and tell them but they won't listen."

He smiled at me ingratiatingly. In my periphery I saw Minessi adjusting her orange cloth, looking sideways at the bare walls of the room. When the doctor turned his attention back to Yao, I tried to catch her eye.

After the examination, the doctor again spoke sharply to Minessi in Fanti. She nodded, expressionless, head down.

He turned to me. "The baby has pneumonia. It is lucky that he is alive. He will have to sleep two or three days here in hospital," he continued in a comradely tone. "One hundred cedis a day to stay here. Not so much, eh? But she is afraid to bring him. Instead she will visit the witch doctor. Then she will sit in her house until the baby dies. They can never find money for the hospital, but they will always find money for the funeral."

Minessi was silent as we walked down the sterile hallway.

"That doctor was a jerk, wasn't he?" I said finally, but she just stared straight ahead.

In the pediatric section, which seemed to consist of a room with eight cots—six empty and two occupied—they gave me a prescription to fill. We walked into town to find a pharmacy.

Twenty-five hundred cedis for ampicillin. Twenty-one hundred for paracetamol. Minessi looked on with an incredulous expression, shaking her head slightly as I fished out the money for the medications. On the way back to the hospital, she repeatedly removed the medicines from their paper bag and looked at them.

"Are you all right, Minessi?" I asked, but she didn't respond.

Back at the hospital, she sat down on a cot with Yao. In a flat voice, she asked me to tell her husband to come tonight with clothes for her and the baby, and some water.

I began to leave, but she stopped me. "Chop money," she said, her face turned away. I gave her 1,500 cedis for food and told her to send word with her husband if she needed more. She took the money without comment and didn't look at me as I walked to the door.

◆

Yao and Minessi stayed in the hospital a week. When they returned, Yao's eyes were clear and bright. His breath flowed unimpeded, a strong sweet column of air.

"I'm so glad he's better," I said to Minessi as she pounded *fufu* in a corner of the yard. She had been distant toward me since her return from the hospital. My feelings toward her had changed, too. I had an agenda now: to keep Yao healthy. Where I once thought Minessi an ally, I now feared she might be an obstacle. I kept my tone cheery, trying to neutralize the tension by ignoring it.

"Isn't it a relief that Yao is back? Maybe we could go together and buy some milk for him. I could set up some kind of a milk fund."

She continued to pound silently, the muscles in her back working.

"Sistah Korkor!" called Amoah, from across the yard. "You

people know so much! Here we thought the boy is fine. He smiles, he looks around, this is a healthy boy. And now we find that the boy was so sick. We know nothing!"

I sensed, more than saw, a bristling from Minessi. The pounding sped up.

"Oh no," I said. "Minessi knows a lot more than I do. She just couldn't—she didn't—"

"No!" Amoah laughed. "She is a foolish African woman. Not smart, like you. Is it not true, Minessi?"

Minessi stopped pounding; her pestle hung midair. "Yes," she said suddenly, loudly. "Before Sistah Korkor and her friend the doctor we know nothing. We do not know Yao is sick, we do not know Yao is well. We know nothing; we can do nothing. We must say thank you to Sistah Korkor." She turned to me, her jaw taut. The veins stood out in her neck and arms.

"Thank you, Sistah," she said, her voice low and shaking. "Thank you for the life of Yao."

She turned her back. The thud of her pestle filled the air like a mournful drum, a rhythmic counterpoint to the other women pounding out their dinners in nearby huts.

5

Musical Chairs

In Apam, every time I step outside the door I attract a following. Foreign visitors are rare here, and people shout "obroni" at me—white person—from morning till night. Mothers bring their youngsters close, point a finger right in my face, and pronounce the word slowly so that the children can learn. Yesterday a group of children trooped after me through the streets, exuberantly chanting, "Obroni / How are you? / I am fine / Thank you!" Toddlers start to cry when they see me, and their mothers seem to find nothing funnier than to drag them toward me, saying in Fanti, "Take him to your country." Even Santana and her family refer to me as "the white lady." I overhear them saying to each other, "The white lady is up; the white lady is hungry; the white lady is taking a bath."

S aturday nights at the Afranguah camp, we took turns sharing party games from our countries. On our first Game

Night, an English volunteer introduced "telephone," in which a whispered message is passed around the circle. First time around, when the last link in our forty-five person chain was asked to relay the message he'd received, he said quizzically, "Fun-dee?"

"How did you hear fun-dee?" shouted Ayatollah, who'd originated the message. "I said, 'The small girl is pounding *fufu*.'"

"I said to him 'fund me,'" said Gorbachev, the penultimate player. "I thought Ayatollah asks us to pay his fees at university."

Everyone laughed at that.

"Let us trace this," said Virgin Billy, the baby-faced home secretary. Though not officially on staff, Billy was in charge when the camp leader was otherwise occupied, and he took his position seriously.

"This can be scientific," he said enthusiastically, "to find how the words underwent mutation, from 'the small girl is pounding *fufu*' to 'fund me.' Ballistic, what is it that you passed to Gorbachev?"

"I also heard 'fund me.'"

"And Okoto, what have you passed to Ballistic?"

Okoto, a lumbering Australian, worked as a marine biologist back home and had therefore been named after the Twi word for crab. He was about to respond, when a large Ghanaian woman seated in the middle of the chain could no longer contain her mirth.

"I said, '*Fuck me!*'" she crowed. "I did not request you to pay my school fees."

The crowd erupted. All the Ghanaian men shouted at once.

"Santana, you have ruined the whole game!"

"You make us ashamed with this language!"

"How is it that you, one person, should spoil it for all the rest?"

Grace Appialeh Odoom, a.k.a. Santana, radiant in a maroon satin dress, surveyed the uproar with delight. Tipping back in her chair, she shouted with laughter.

◆

"Sistah Korkor, this is no good," Virgin Billy told me at the end of the evening. We were cleaning up the dining room, scooting the chairs and tables into place. "Santana should be expelled from the camp."

"Expel her for having a little fun?" I asked. The camp consisted of thirty Ghanaians and fifteen foreigners. Of the thirty Ghanaians on the project, only two were women.

"She has shamed us. It is not natural to talk this way. To be this way."

"Oh Billy, come on."

"The Europeans will get the wrong impression of Ghana women!"

"I think the Europeans are used to women acting all kinds of ways," I said.

He pursed his lips primly. "In Ghana we are not."

◆

Santana took up space. She talked out of order at meetings, served herself more food than was allotted, and mocked the male volunteers mercilessly on the construction site. She called them weak and challenged them to competitions of strength. They declined to participate, declaring it beneath them to compete with a woman. Santana's body was round and firm, her voice deep and gravelly. Her clothes, too, were constantly surprising. She worked all day in a shapeless nightgown or housedress, her hair a frizzy cloud, but in the evening she pulled out the stops.

Her wardrobe contained a seemingly limitless parade of dresses that looked like they belonged at a high school prom—puffy-sleeved, ruffly satins in purples and reds and emerald greens. She had African clothes as well, and occasionally showed up at dinner wrapped head to toe in illustrious cotton batiks and prints, her hair oiled and pressed to her head or wrapped in a tower of cloth. The more flamboyant her outfit, the more delight she seemed to take in wearing it.

A week and a half into the camp, I came down with dysentery. For several days, while the other volunteers toiled at the construction site, I lay prostrate on top of my sleeping bag on the cement floor of a classroom in the village school—out of session for the summer—that provided our housing. By the third day, I felt well enough to read and write and was beginning to enjoy the quiet hours. I was perched on the front steps with my notebook when Santana returned from the site for an early lunch.

"*Eh!* Sistah Korkor!" she shouted.

"Sistah Santana." I smiled; I didn't think she knew my name.

"Three days now, you don't work. They say you are sick, but to me you don't look so sick." She put her hand on my cheek. "You are not hot."

"I don't have a fever," I said.

"Then you must work! Other people, they work harder because you lie in bed."

"I'm having stomach problems," I told her.

Santana laughed. "So is Sistah Mansah, from England. So is Brothah Okoto, from Australia. So am I. Why do you think your stomach is more important than my stomach?"

"I don't!" I said, bridling. "I just think it'd be hard for me to work if I had to run to Chicago every fifteen minutes!"

"Chicago" was our nickname for the camp toilet, a clean-swept room with a chrome-covered hole in the floor.

"It is true that you could not work while you were visiting Chicago, but when you returned from Chicago you could work for fifteen minutes before visiting Chicago again. And so, throughout the day, it is entirely possible that you could work many hours."

I glared at her.

"You think it is something very special when a small insect is living inside you," she continued. "If an African man went to the hospital for a test, he would find thirty or forty different insects living inside him."

"Fine," I said resentfully, "I'll come back to work tomorrow."

"Eh *heh!*" said Santana, giving me an *I'll-believe-it-when-I-see-it* look. "The association is not buying your food so that you may have a rest vacation." She disappeared into the room.

I returned to work the next day, cursing Santana every time I had to drop my shovel and dash to Chicago.

❖

The camp leader requested a fee of 200 cedis each to cover transportation for a weekend excursion to the nearby village of Enyana Abassa to witness a new chief's inauguration ceremony. Many of the African volunteers couldn't afford the fee, so Virgin Billy made an announcement requesting foreigners to sponsor them. Santana was standing next to me with her hand raised, indicating that she needed sponsorship.

"I'll sponsor you," I said.

"You, lazy girl?" She raised an eyebrow.

"If you shut up about that."

"Eh *heh!* I am not very good at 'shut up.'"

"Great, then there's potential for growth."

She laughed a deep, scratchy belly laugh, and took my hand. "You will be my sistah tomorrow. So you do not go missing. This place will be so crowded."

"You're going to look out for me?"

She smiled. "Will you trust me?"

✧

In Enyana Abassa, we were crunched all day long in a joyous welter of bodies. I strained to get a glimpse of the new chief, who was carried through town on a bier. Men walked beside the bier, beating with hooked sticks on the taut, fur-covered heads of enormous wooden drums. The young chief was swaddled head to toe in exquisite layers of *kente*, the traditional hand-woven Ghanaian cloth, its rich blue, red, and gold dazzling in the midday sun. On his head was a colorful hat, shaped like an upside-down canoe. Beneath the hat, his face was round and unlined, its expression oddly impassive, as though his mind were somewhere far away. Beads of sweat glistened on his broad forehead. An adolescent girl sat in front of him, also wrapped in *kente*, with a stern expression on her face.

"Why do they look so gloomy?" I asked Santana.

"They must not smile during the festival."

"Why?"

She shrugged, looking bored. "It is the rule."

A long line of women with painted faces stood waiting, with gifts for the chief balanced on their heads. Their offerings included tall pyramids of oranges, yams, and tomatoes; towering piles of folded cloth; and hand-carved wooden stools. One woman carried a large wooden table upside down on her head, while another toted three antique sewing machines, one on top of the other. I went crazy with my camera, trying to record these astounding feats of balance. In a dusty central square, rifles were fired into the air, and a man in a bird suit danced.

When I asked Santana the meaning of the dance, she just shrugged again.

"Our grandparents knew," she said. "To us, it is just a party."

A man crouched on the ground, covered head to toe in white powder, wearing only a loincloth. A circle of children surrounded him. When I raised my camera, he lunged toward me, shouting.

Santana sprang into motion, pushing him back. She bellowed in Fanti until the man spun around and walked away. Then she turned to me, grinning broadly.

"He wanted you to pay him for taking his photograph."

"All he had to do was ask."

"He expected to frighten you into giving him too much money, but I have sent him away. I have told him that I have a strong family fetish. I said if he bothers you, I will curse his family for three generations to come."

"I didn't know you practiced traditional religion."

She smiled. "Oh, sistah," she said, "I practice everything, when it is useful."

◆

"I want to marry white," Virgin Billy told me the next morning over a breakfast of bland maize porridge, called *koko*, with sugar dumped on top.

"Why?" I asked suspiciously.

"I would like to have half-caste children. I like the color."

"So it's an aesthetic thing?"

"Yes," he nodded. "And I like white people. I like the way they live."

"You mean money."

"Not just money," he protested. "They are educated. I would like my children to go to school in Europe, or the United States. Then they can become lawyers, or write books, or be bank managers, or artists."

I smiled at this unusual assemblage of occupations. "Artists?" I said, "Why artists?"

"Artists are paid very well," said Billy.

"Not in the U.S."

"Here in Ghana they are," he insisted. "You can make one picture, a simple picture, and sell it for 20,000 cedis. Or weave some *kente* and sell it for 8,000. Some artists own five buildings."

"A word of advice," I said. "If you meet an American or European woman whom you want to marry, don't mention to her that you want to marry white. Just pretend that she, as an *individual,* is the kindest, smartest, most beautiful woman you've ever known in your life."

He nodded soberly. "Thank you for these words."

When Billy got up and brought his plate to the kitchen, Santana slid into the seat beside me.

"Sistah Korkor," she said to me, "whatever he tells you, you must not marry this man. He hates himself, and he will hate you even more."

"Billy?" I asked with surprise. "Why would you think that?"

"There are some men in Ghana here," she said, "they hate themselves and love white people. But if a white woman will love them, soon she will become just like a black woman to them. I have seen this before."

✧

"The white man brought us civilization," Billy told me the next afternoon as we stood side by side at the construction site, applying mortar and bricks to a growing wall.

"What do you mean?" I asked.

"Before the white man came, we were living in trees. We were uncivilized. Then when he came we were afraid, and we ran into the jungle." He put down the brick he was carrying and

flailed his hands in the air, imitating a frightened villager running for cover. "It is only unfortunate that we have not retained
better relations with the British. Look at Ivory Coast. They are
wealthier than we are, because they have kept a good relationship with the French. Kwame Nkrumah should not have thrown
out the British so fast. When you leave your mother's house, you
should not shun her. You should keep good relations with her,
so that you can come to her for guidance and support."

I was so stunned that for a moment I didn't know what to say.
Ghana, formerly Gold Coast, had gained its independence from
the British in 1957, making it the first sub-Saharan African nation
to break free of colonialism. Dr. Kwame Nkrumah, leader of the
Ghanaian independence movement, first president of the new
Ghana, and an early African nationalist, was a hero here. It was he
who had given present-day Ghana its name, after a prosperous
West African kingdom that flourished between the fourth and
eleventh centuries. I had thought Dr. Nkrumah uniformly
revered. Billy was the first person in Ghana I'd heard criticize him.

"Africa has the oldest civilization on earth!" I sputtered.
"Look at the ancient universities of Timbuktu! You had elaborate
systems of government long before the British came and carved
the place up. If people ran toward the forest when they saw white
faces, they were smart to do it. Look what the whites did to this
continent! Slavery! Colonization! Generations of exploitation!"

"Yes, yes," he said dismissively, "but it was all for the best."

✧

"Sistah Korkor, I am not happy," Santana told me. "I have not
been happy for some six months."

The camp was over, and I was spending a week in Apam
with Santana's family before heading north to another camp.
Apam was a fishing town on the coast. Before his death, Santana's

father had owned a small fleet of boats there. As a teenager, Santana often took the bus to Accra, carrying batches of smoked fish to sell at the market. Whenever possible, she used these trips to develop her English skills. She had attended six years of school— a lot for a small-town Ghanaian woman of her generation, but not enough to satisfy her curiosity about the world. Whenever she met white people, she spoke to them. She'd heard about the voluntary association from a German woman she met on the bus.

Apam had a peculiar beauty all its own—a dreamy, unruly splendor. Looking down on the town's flat expanse from Fort Patience, the seventeenth-century Dutch fort perched on a hill just outside of town, you saw a jumbled maze of houses built of gray cement or red mud, their sloping bamboo or corrugated tin roofs reaching outward to the slate blue sea. Shabby, brightly painted wooden sailboats and rowboats were jammed together

on a sandbar, which stretched like a tawny arm between the shallows. A few of the small crafts boasted outboard motors.

On the rocky coast outside of town, the ocean foamed and roiled. Pigs played in the surf, and palm trees tossed their tousled heads in the breeze like Rastas at a party. Pygmy goats not more than two feet high roamed the dusty streets, bleating. Walking through town, I was amazed by the range of the goats' voices and by their human-sounding timbre. The kids, some with shriveled umbilical cords still hanging off their bodies, whimpered in plaintive sopranos. The nanny goats scolded in nasal altos, and the billies chimed in with gravelly bad-tempered baritones. Sometimes I'd see a mother goat toddling anxiously back and forth on her short legs, looking for her kid. The call and response between the searching mother and the lost child sounded like a musical game of Marco Polo.

A short hop from the beach was a row of dilapidated colonial mansions, replete with columns, balconies, and balustrades. Santana's extended family shared one of these with several other families. The house was in an advanced state of decay. The floorboards were loose and rotting—you had to be careful where you stepped. Parts of the ceiling were crumbling, and a gust of wind or a heavy stomp could release a small blizzard of plaster flakes.

The outhouse in Santana's yard was filled to the point of overflowing, and no one had gotten around to digging a new one. Every morning we trooped a few blocks to the public toilet, where we waited in line to go in. The women's side consisted of a wooden bench with six holes in a row where women squatted, side by side, like silent crows on a line. The first time we went I lingered outside, planning to enter after everyone else had gone. But either it was rush hour or the place was the hottest ticket in town, because new people arrived as quickly as others left. I finally took a deep breath and plunged in, so to speak. As I arranged myself beside my sistahs, trying to ignore a little girl who gaped at me with unmasked fascination, I waxed philosophical. To squat next to four or five other women, each of you straining in silent (or not so silent) solidarity, is a great equalizer, a uniquely humbling experience. Imagine employer and employee perched side by side every morning before work, I mused. Wouldn't that go a distance toward breaking down hierarchy? Or world leaders, before they go into a conference room to decide their country's fates. Every president and prime minister, I decided, should have to try this at least once.

On my second morning in Apam, after returning from these rather chastening ablutions, Santana and I stood on the sagging upper porch of her family's home, talking. Stacks of tires, piles of wood, and crumbling cement blocks were strewn about the yard below. The scene was a kaleidoscope of motion: children chasing a ball, goats chasing the children, women stirring pots of steaming mush. Two men played cards while others stood around in a circle, drinking and offering advice. Groups shifted and reshuffled as people came and went, walking or pedaling their wide-wheeled bicycles, balancing things on their heads. At the far end of the yard, the words "Cry Your Own Cry" were painted in bright blue letters on a boarded-up shack. Beyond the yard, corrugated tin roofs stretched a few hundred yards to the cape, where the shaggy-headed palm trees leaned toward the sea.

As Santana and I talked, smells of smoking fish and roasting corn wafted up, while shouts, cries, laughter, and the staticky pulse of a radio mingled in our ears. A big-bellied, thin-limbed child in underwear sauntered barefoot across the yard, eating from a can. She looked up at us and shouted *"obroni"* fifteen or twenty times, until I waved to her and called out "Hello!" Satisfied, she continued her stroll.

"Sistah Korkor," Santana was tapping my arm. "Did you hear what I said? I said I have not been happy for some six months."

"What? Why?"

"My man, he has left. He has gone to Italy ten months ago. Then, some six months ago, he has sent a cassette to his parents, and he has told them that I should find a husband. He calls Ghana women a natural resource. Himself, he will find a more costly woman. A Europe woman. Because I have not traveled, I am worth nothing. A natural resource only, like water, everywhere, cheap. Because I have stayed in Ghana here."

"What a jerk!" I said.

"Eight years I was with him. Now I am twenty-seven years old. You see? He has wasted my years. I should have traveled before him. I should have been in Europe long time now."

"What do you mean?"

"I have given him the money to go. Then, some months later, I should have followed him. My father, he had seven fishing boats. Now he has died and my stepbrothers have lost five of them with drinking. But before, I managed the affairs. I saved. I gathered 600,000 cedis, and my brother was bringing this money to Accra to arrange the visa and the plane tickets, when he was in an accident with the *tro-tro* and died. When we went to claim the body, the money was not there. Now my brother has left me with five children to provide. So I have lost my chance. I have lost my chance and my man, too."

I looked at her in surprise, searching for something to say. I'd never imagined such a story, never sensed her underlying despair. "You'll meet someone better," I said, taking her hand. "Someone who values you."

She shrugged. "I don't want them now, these men. I see what they are. Two have betrayed me. Now the other, from before, he begs me to come back. But he has betrayed me last time, with a woman. All his friends say, 'Santana, come back to him,' because I used to cook for them, long time. They all love me; they remember. But I say no, he has betrayed me once, he will do it again."

I nodded sympathetically.

"What about your man?" she asked suddenly. "Your sweet Michael."

"What about him?"

"Why have you left him?"

"I . . . I wanted to travel . . ."

"You will go back to him?"

"Maybe. I don't know."

She lifted an eyebrow.

"I don't know, Santana, I'm not sure." I felt suddenly defensive.

"Does he beat you?"

"No," I laughed. "No, he doesn't beat me."

"He goes with other women, then?"

"No. No. I mean, now, maybe, because I said we should leave things open, but when we were together, no." The thought that he might be seeing other women now brought a painful tightness to my throat.

"So why, then? What is wrong? You think African men are more costly because you must go far to find them?"

"No! I just . . . I don't know. I love him but . . . it's complicated."

"It is not complicated. He is natural resource. He needs to grow rare."

"Stop it, Santana, I—" I stopped midsentence. How did she always manage to drive me nuts? My mind formed the words I might use to explain the situation to a friend back home: *I love him, but I'm not sure I'm in love with him. I'm not sure he's the one.*

The words seemed unbearably childish, mere semantic diddling. I could never say them to Santana, not with that knowing smile on her face. Not in the wake of what she'd just told me.

"*Anyway,*" I continued. "We were talking about *you*. Where can we find *you* a better man?"

She shook her head. "No more man for me. My heart, it has closed." She smiled. "Now I only torture men. I may be Ghana woman, everywhere resource, but I am more strong than they. I have no need of them, and this makes them crazy. All this they want," she turned around slowly, swaying her hips, "but they can never have."

"The woman is the p-property of her husband," said Santana's cousin Ema, short for Emanuel. He was laughing, but he was angry. I was angrier. I'd heard enough of this kind of talk during my time here to build up a reservoir of frustration. We were sitting on the weathered wooden floor around a low table, over the remains of *kenke* and pepper sauce. Santana sat beside me, silent for a change. We had all washed our fingers in a bowl of water and wiped our mouths with our wet hands. My tongue burned from the chili.

"A woman is a human being," I said, fighting to keep my voice even. "An equal human being. Not property."

Ema laughed again. "A woman is not equal to a m-man. See this m-muscle?"

"Physically, women and men are different," I said. "Different strengths and different capabilities. Intellectually, they are equals."

"But if the m-man is stronger, then the m-man must d-dominate," Ema insisted. "That is how it is in nature."

The topic under discussion was whether or not men had the

right to beat their wives. Looking at small, slender Ema, with his gentle hands and slight stutter, it was hard to imagine him dominating anyone.

"Then does a strong man have a right to dominate a weaker man?" I asked. "Should a strong man make a weaker man his slave?"

"We are t-talking about the way things are, not the way they should be."

"No, we're talking about our opinions. You didn't say, 'Many men in Ghana treat their wives as property.' You said, 'The woman is the property of her husband,' implying that you felt that was just fine."

How we'd segued onto this topic from Christianity, I wasn't sure. Ema had spent the entire afternoon trying to save me, a phenomenon I'd grown accustomed to during my time in Ghana. The country was brimming with fanatical Christians of every imaginable stripe. The missionaries had done their work thoroughly, and every vehicle had a religious slogan painted on the side; every business had a name like "God Is Love Beauty Saloon" (sic) or "Blood of Jesus Carpentry Shop." I enjoyed flaunting my agnosticism, driving the faithful to increasingly heroic measures in their efforts to convert me. Throughout the day, I'd maintained a faintly ironic tone while Ema begged, pleaded, cajoled, and railed. Now, with the wife-beating discussion, the tables had turned. He was relaxed, content to disagree, while I was desperate to convert him to my point of view.

"History is against you," I told him angrily. "Women are rising all over the world."

"Ghana m–must not be part of the world, then," he retorted.

Santana rolled her eyes. "Let the man think what he wants," she said, pronouncing the word "man" with visible disdain.

In public, Santana treated me like a pet parrot. She'd taught me a few phrases of Fanti, most of them scatological, and as we made our daily rounds through town, she made me repeat them over and over, eliciting roars of laughter from everyone we met.

"Santana, please," I begged her. "Stop. Just stop for a while."

"Yes," she would say, but within five minutes she'd demand that I do it again. "Why not make some laughter?" she asked.

"Because I'm tired of being a sideshow."

"You are not side. You are the main show in Apam!"

My body was another point of contention. Santana was obsessed with my skinniness. During meals, I sat on the floor around a low table with the adult members of the family, each with our ball of *fufu* or *kenke*, sharing a pot of stew. Santana watched me eat as though it were the most intriguing performance she'd ever seen. If I ate slowly, she berated me to speed up. If I ate quickly, she forced another ball of *kenke* or *fufu* on me.

I'm not a large person, and in the heat, my appetite had diminished. Furthermore, in spite of years of feminist self-education, I have as much body image baggage as the next American female. Being forced to eat past the point of fullness brought up all my adolescent angst. My attempts to explain this to Santana played like a ludicrous cross-cultural Abbott and Costello:

ME: Santana, please don't pressure me to eat more. When I eat too much, I feel bad about myself. Do you understand? *(Santana nods.)* Good. Thank you. *(I finish my ball of* kenke, *sit back, and relax. Santana shouts something to one of the young girls, who brings another ball of* kenke *and sets it on my plate.)*

ME: Santana! Didn't you hear what I just told you? If I eat too much, I start to hate myself. I feel disgusting.

SANTANA: You hate my food!

ME: It has nothing to do with your food!

SANTANA: It shames me to have a skinny guest. We must make you fat and beautiful.

ME: (*voice rising in panic*) I don't *want* to be fat and beautiful.

SANTANA: They will say I am starving you. That I am a bad hostess. Eat!

ME: I can't eat another bite. I refuse to eat this *kenke*.

SANTANA: (*shouting*) Thank you for refusing what I give you!

Meanwhile, the children hovered silently, eyeing the *kenke*.

But the biggest issue was money. Santana liked to keep me guessing. Here I was, staying in her family's home, eating their food, going everywhere with her. When I offered direct compensation, she always said no. To make up for this, I went out and bought things—large bags of rice, tins of milk, packages of sugar—and brought them to her home as gifts. Periodically, however, she spontaneously commanded me to pay for something: a *tro-tro* ride, a shopping trip, a visit to the hairdresser.

This irritated me beyond logic. I wanted consistency. The seeming arbitrariness of it made me feel off-balance, out of control. My feelings ricocheted wildly. One moment I was sure Santana was the most generous person I'd ever known. The next I had the distinct feeling she was taking advantage of me.

One day we dropped in on the local dressmaker. It turned out Santana had already chosen fabric and engaged the woman to make matching outfits for us. The patterns were drawn up; we had only to be measured.

The gesture moved me deeply. The fact that the material she'd selected was a neon green print with swirling yellow vines on it did nothing to dampen my enthusiasm. But when we went to pick up the finished dresses, Santana ordered me to "pay the woman."

Again the agonizing litany: Was Santana my friend, or was she just trying to get things from me? Had she ordered the dresses as a means for us to bond, or because she wanted a new dress?

The day after the incident with the dressmaker, we shopped for the ingredients for a garden egg stew, dressed in our twin outfits. A garden egg is a popular Ghanaian vegetable that resembles a small, ovoid zucchini.

"I want to learn how to make the stew, so I can cook it for

my friends back home," I told Santana with excitement. "And I want to photograph every step of the process, to document it."

In the cheerful chaos of the market, Santana knew everyone. She knew which woman to buy the garden eggs from, which the peppers, which the *kenke*, the palm oil, the small cube of bouillon to add flavor to the stew. We picked our way among spread-out blankets piled high with brightly colored vegetables. Women grabbed at our skirts and called out to us in passing, "Santana, buy this! *Obroni*, nice, nice."

The shopping trip took hours. With each vendor Santana bartered endlessly, shouting, haggling, cajoling, shaking fistfuls of tiny red peppers, tomatoes, or rice in the seller's face. Santana and the saleswomen played out a complicated drama, in which they sometimes seemed like bitter enemies, sometimes best friends. Even after an agreement had been reached, Santana would cop a coy look and ask the seller to add a few extra of whatever it was, as a bonus. The woman usually complied, a rueful expression on her face. They parted, finally, shouting half-humorous threats.

"Next time you pay me right away or I call the police!"

"Next time you give me fresh vegetables or I steal your husband!"

"She owes me much," Santana said of the woman she bought the peppers from. "I have given her fish many times."

When we purchased tomatoes, Santana said again, "Pay the woman."

"Why the tomatoes?" I asked suddenly. "Why not the rice, or the bouillon cubes, or the chili peppers? Why the tomatoes and only the tomatoes?"

"Why not?" she laughed.

"Because it doesn't make sense," I said. "Why don't you let me pay for all of it? Or let me give you some money. Or let me decide myself what I want to buy."

"Because today," she shouted, "I want you to buy tomatoes!"

Carrying the ingredients up the rickety stairs, she asked me, "Do you shop like this at your end?"

I flashed on an image of Santana at Safeway, trundling around a cart piled high with packaged goods, Sarah Lee and Kellogg's and Kraft. The image made me sad.

"No," I told her. "Shopping is very different at my end."

Later, I sat down at the coal port to fan the flames beneath our bubbling stew. A fixture in many Ghanaian kitchens, a coal port was a small iron structure, about sixteen inches tall. Coal went in the bottom, and the top was a funnel with an airhole in it on which to place a pot.

"Will you take a picture of me doing this?" I asked Santana, handing her the camera.

"So you can lie to your friends at home?" she asked.

I nodded.

"I will take this photo," she said. "But when they ask me, I will tell the truth. I will tell them that you are lazy and will not work. Also that you come to my house and fight with my cousins. That you insult me. That you refuse to eat." She smoothed her bright green dress. "But it is also true that you choose very nice dresses for your Sistah Santana and yourself."

A flash lit the stew.

"Will you send me this photo?" Santana asked, after a pause.

"Sure," I said.

"You will forget."

"No I won't," I snapped, "I'll send it. I said I'd send it and I'll send it."

"Say what you want," she said, "You are my sistah, but I know what is true." She took the palm leaf from my hand and began fanning.

"Look," she said softly, "so many delicious tomatoes."

Game Night again. My turn to share a national pastime. In the cement-floored dining room, we pushed the tables against the walls and placed the chairs in a wobbly circle. There were no electric lights, only the orange glow of kerosene lanterns and the pale moonlight flooding in through the windows and doors. I called for a volunteer to operate the radio. Virgin Billy raised his hand.

We counted the number of players and the number of chairs. There had to be one less chair than there were players, I explained. Each round, one person would be eliminated. Each person's sole object was to stay in the game.

Three rounds in, the Ghanaian volunteers became convinced that Virgin Billy was cheating. Instead of cutting off the sound randomly, they said, he intentionally left certain people stranded. In the last two rounds, the odd men out were both Ghanaian volunteers with whom Billy had recently quarreled. The Ghanaian volunteers would only allow Billy to continue operating the radio if he turned his back while we circled the chairs. That way he couldn't intentionally influence the outcome.

A dozen rounds later, it was down to four people: two Ghanaian men, the Australian called Okoto, and Santana. The music began, and they started circling. The men stuck rigidly to the rules, their steps stiff and regular. Santana played by her own rules. She hovered over each chair as long as possible, swiveling her enormous bottom above it as though stirring a cauldron, her body in sync with the twinkling, bubbly highlife music that forced its way through the thick foam of the radio's static. Then, just as a rival approached, she'd sashay to the next chair and begin the whole process again.

The music stopped. Okoto was left stranded. He exited gracefully, without fuss.

Virgin Billy scooped up a chair and set it aside.

The music began again. The two men watched each other like lions. They ignored Santana to the extent that it was possible to ignore such an ebullient presence, their eyes flickering unwillingly toward her from time to time. The two chairs were placed far apart, and the men stayed close on each other's tails. They practically ran between the safety zones. Santana played this round as though she'd lost interest. Flaunting her indifference like a cunning lover, she sauntered between the chairs with a bored expression on her face: all the time in the world.

The music cut out. The two men dove for the same chair, their chests colliding in the air above it. While they struggled for dominion, Santana moved laconically toward the empty chair and slid into it.

The play-offs. Two contenders remained: Santana and the skinny young man we called Castro. Though a woman, Santana could no longer be ignored.

Santana and Castro circled the lone outpost. Santana performed her sensual shimmy above it until Castro gave her a light shove, forcing her to circle behind. He then remained beside the chair, swaying from foot to foot, until Santana bumped him with her prodigious hip.

Music. No music.

Castro was squarely above the chair. With a smug grin on his face, he slowly bent his knees and began to lower his rangy frame into it. At the last possible instant, just before his bony bottom made contact with the wood, Santana whipped the chair out from under him. Castro crashed to the floor, his legs stretched out before him, a stunned look on his face. Santana brought the chair down beside her with a loud *thwack*. She straddled it, her arms raised high in the victory sign, magnificent as a queen in her outrageous satin, laughing like a woman with nothing to lose.

6

Telegram

*The power is out in Accra, and except for a sliver moon and a few
kerosene lamps illuminating the odd food seller, the streets are very dark.
I am walking back to the hostel from the Wato Bar, when a group of
young Ghanaian men comes toward me. They are laughing and shouting, deep in conversation. As we pass each other, one of them sees me
and nods, grinning.*

"Hello, obroni," he says.

*"Hello, obibini," I respond, returning his salutation "white per-
son" with the Twi term for "black person." He laughs appreciatively
and repeats it to his friends.*

*Later, lying on a lower bunk beneath a snoring German volunteer, I
realize that this is the first time in my life that I've passed a group of
young black men on a dark, deserted street without feeling afraid. In the
U.S., if we'd spoken at all, our exchange would've been acutely charged,
both with my fear and their inevitable awareness of it.*

◆

I rushed out of the hostel barefoot to meet the new American volunteer, anxious for news of home. I was back in Accra, hanging out for a few weeks between projects. I'd been the only American on the two camps I participated in, and I was eager to connect with another.

She stood on the gravel path with a letter in her hand, gazing with an abstracted expression in the direction of Dr. Nkrumah's mausoleum and, if you veered right, the ocean. She was a light-skinned black woman in her early twenties, small and delicate-boned, wearing wire-rimmed glasses, a white UC Berkeley T-shirt, and artfully faded jeans. Her hair was pulled tight in a thousand tiny cornrows decorated with red, green, and gold beads.

"Hi! I'm Tanya," I said, extending my hand.

"Nadhiri." Without meeting my eyes, she offered a cool, limp shake.

"Are you from Berkeley?" I asked.

She turned her head in my direction. Her eyes slid slowly from my buzzed hair and sunburned face down the voluminous faded T-shirt and dusty olive drab skirt, finally coming to rest on my bare feet, the negative image of sandals bright white against the tan.

"No." She turned deliberately back toward the path, as though expecting someone.

I stiffened, but continued in a cheerful tone, "Oh, I just thought, because of the T-shirt . . ."

"I go to school there," she said curtly.

"Oh cool! I live in the Bay Area!"

"Which part?" she asked, after a drawn-out pause.

"Excuse me?"

"Which part of the Bay Area are you from?" she overarticulated. Her voice was high-pitched and nasal. It sounded brittle and unsupported, weightless as a dry leaf.

"Oh. Richmond."

Without bothering to glance in my direction this time, she said, "Richmond's not the Bay Area."

I laughed incredulously, "It's right on the Bay."

"The people I know there don't consider it the Bay Area."

"Huh. Well, I don't know. I just live there. Most of the time I'm over in San Francisco."

She snorted, "Well, if you're not involved in your community."

"I've gotta meet someone." I took the path toward the ocean quickly, tripping over a piece of exposed pipe, stubbing my toe. I blinked a few times to clear my eyes of impending tears, and kept walking, feeling a familiar tightness. After four months in Ghana, it surged through my body like a telegram from home.

✧

A couple of weeks before Nadhiri arrived, I'd decided to splurge on a phone call to Michael. I was feeling sick and lonely, and I craved the goofy intimacy of our conversations, the sense of being known. Calling at around 10 P.M. his time, I'd found no one at home. I tried again at eleven, then at midnight, one, two, and three. Again the next morning. Finally, I left an icy message, something to the effect that finding him gone all night was a surprise not unlike finding a knife twisting in the base of one's spine. Ten days later I received an outraged letter, asking what the hell I thought I was doing, guilt-tripping him? I was the one who'd set the terms! He'd begged for monogamy, but no, I'd insisted we be free, because I wasn't sure I wanted to come back to him. I had one hell of a nerve. One fucking hell of a nerve.

I cried all day and then responded with as conciliatory a tone as I could muster. Yes, of course, he was right, I'd given him a raw deal. I had no right whatsoever to expect anything of him. *But welcome to the world of feelings,* I couldn't help adding. *They aren't logical. They don't always play by the rules. Your saying that I have no right to be hurt is like my saying that you have no right to be angry. Words.*

I put the letter in the mailbox. For the last week I'd had my eye on a new Ghanaian volunteer called MC Brown. I decided to pursue his acquaintance.

❖

In the hot white beams of rented floodlights, you could see steam rising off the grass. Tinny highlife music zinged and crackled through the air, a gentle, mocking xylophone under-scoring the cranked-up guitars. I was at the center of a pulsing crowd, dancing with MC Brown. We were toying with each other, savoring the thrill of possibility. As we danced, I admired the compact curves of his body in Levi's knockoffs (the label said "Leevy's") and African print shirt. Inches apart, without touch-ing, we enacted a cagey sensual drama of coiling fingertips and jolting hips. I breathed deeply, taking in the sweet, acrid mix of sweat, cocoa butter, mosquito repellent, and cut grass. My bare feet kneaded the earth; my arms and legs were slick.

We were on the expansive lawns of Legon University, one of the few places in the Accra area that you could easily confuse with the U.S. Among the manicured lawns, neatly trimmed shrubs, rows of palm trees, and geometrically shaped buildings, you might think you were on a college campus in Florida, say, or Southern California.

Today we were celebrating the birthday of Marcus Garvey, best known as the founder of the Back-to-Africa Movement.

Born in Jamaica in 1887, Marcus Garvey came to the U.S. at the age of twenty-eight and established the largest mass movement in African American history. At the height of his popularity, membership in his organization, the Universal Negro Improvement Association, numbered over a million. He believed that Africa was the spiritual home for all people of African descent, and that blacks would never achieve equality in countries where the majority of people were white. He encouraged blacks from all over the world to emigrate to Africa, with the goal of reclaiming it from European domination and establishing an independent, united Black Nation. I was one of a handful of whites attending the party, our faces spots of pink neon among the hundreds of Africans gathered for the event.

"She's gone, but I'm still dancing," the singer wailed, following up with an extended riff in Twi. MC Brown was singing along, his mouth next to my ear, husky and off-key. I moved a fraction of an inch closer, condensing the force field between us. He turned his head, his lips hovered near mine—

The music cut out. Static. The microphone squeaked. I looked at the stage and was surprised to see six people dressed in full African regalia, with draping layers of *kente* and other precious cloth. There was something incongruous about them, even beyond the formal dress. Perhaps it was the way the women stood side by side with the men, their stance at once righteous and timid. Dreadlocks emerged from beneath one of the men's circular hats—a style I'd only seen in Ghana on a couple of Rastas selling beads at the beach—and two of the women wore glasses. I knew immediately that they were Americans.

A small, thin young woman stepped forward and began fiddling with the microphone. Behind her, the others raised their fists in the freedom salute. She wore round, John Lennon glasses, and her skin was golden in tone. She was wrapped in a rich indigo cloth. As the squeal of the microphone died down, I removed my hands from my ears.

"My brothers and sisters. I am speaking to you today on behalf of the African American exchange students of Legon University, who helped to organize this event." She spoke in careful, measured phrases, as though reciting a prepared text. With a jolt, I recognized Nadhiri's reedy voice. *Is she a student?* I wondered. *I thought she was a volunteer.*

"Marcus Garvey was not Martin Luther King," she continued nervously. "Marcus Garvey was not Malcolm X. Marcus Garvey was a man who believed in places *of* black people, *by* black people, and *for* black people, throughout his entire life."

A murmur of confusion. Heavy shouts of "Order! Allow!"

"We came to Ghana as African Americans to discover our heritage and to get to know our African brothers and sisters. It has been a moving reunion. However, in coming here tonight to celebrate the vision of our brother, the late Marcus Garvey, we are disturbed to see a violation of his principles taking place."

A louder buzz this time, punctuated by angry discourse in a multiplicity of languages. I was beginning to recognize the sound of the different Ghanaian tongues, and now I caught snatches of Fanti, Ewe, and Ga. Again the cries of, "Allow! Allow!" Slowly the commotion died down. I glanced sideways at Brown, who stared intently at the stage, fists clenched, jaw set in a rigid line.

"Marcus Garvey was a black nationalist and a black separatist. That doesn't mean he hated white people, only that he felt that blacks and whites should lead separate lives, in separate places. Therefore, in the interest of respecting the memory of the deceased, we ask that those present who are not of Black African descent please leave the premises. Thank you."

Nadhiri replaced the microphone in the stand, where it

screeched in resistance. She joined the others in a line, and they once again raised their fists.

Chaos. All around, fierce arguments erupted—arms gesticulated wildly, voices strained to be heard. Brown shouted at the stage in Twi. Beside me, two men leaned into each other, engaged in passionate conference.

"They were never Ashanti," I heard one man say, and the other nodded.

"They are *weak!*"

Onstage, the band had gathered around the group of Americans. The men strained toward each other, near blows. Nadhiri placed her hand on the shoulder of one of the American men in a calming gesture. My stomach alive, I began to make my way through to the edge of the crowd. A hand circled my wrist. It was Brown's.

"No," he said. "You must stay. They must not insult you like this. I will beat them."

The crowd pressed in. I fought for air among the ripe bodies, the rising heat.

"Sweetie, I have to get out."

"You have not to be scared," he shouted in my ear. "The students, they are not angry with you. They are angry with these lazy, these no-good people who insult our guests."

Headrush. Turning in the tightening crowd, searching for an opening, I put my hands in front of me like a blind woman, pushing. The crowd thinned, and I emerged at the side of the stage beside a palm tree. A breeze picked out my sweaty body like a breath of heaven. I leaned back against the scaly bark. The microphone squealed again.

"My brothahs! My sistahs! Order! Order!" From where I stood, I saw the partial profile of a slight, bookish-looking young man in a blue oxford shirt and dark, pressed pants. He removed the microphone from its stand. The African American students and the band members paused in their argument and turned slightly toward him.

"Brothahs and sistahs, I am president of students at Legon University here, and I am deeply saddened by what I have just heard. I beg of our white brothahs and sistahs present that you have not taken offense."

Shouts of "Here! Here!" from the crowd.

"I beg you, it is not our custom in Ghana here to tell our guests that they are not welcome. I beg you, you are welcome. Then, if there are those people at this party who must ask other people to leave, I must ask those people that they themselves might leave."

Cheering. Scattered applause.

"Now, as this is a party, and the band has not yet finished playing, perhaps we may once again dance."

Loud cheering. The young man moved away from the microphone. There was a moment of silence, the African Americans and the band members face-to-face. Then, slowly, the drummer sat down on his stool and pulled a *djembe* between his knees; the marimba player picked up his mallets. A signal passed between the Americans. They turned as a unit and walked down the steps at the side of the stage. As Nadhiri passed me, our eyes met and held. She saw that I was afraid. And I saw that she was crying. As she turned her head sharply away, her face darkened, and I saw there the same thing I felt rising in my own chest. Hot, leaden, inescapable shame.

✧

"They have brought the troubles on themselves," Brown said to me the next day, sitting on the wooden steps outside the volunteer hostel. "They are lazy, I know this for a fact. They could be rich, living in America, but instead they take drugs, and steal, and shoot people with guns."

"That isn't true at all! Millions of black Americans are working themselves to the bone every day." I scratched around an enormous bite on my leg. Insects didn't usually go for me, which was fortunate, because I didn't much care for repellent. Last night, however, an itinerant mosquito had found its way inside my net and covered my ankles in angry red spots.

"I have read it," Brown insisted. "They are criminals, they are all in jail."

"Not *all*, a small percentage—"

"I have read. *Time* magazine. All the black males are in prison."

"Oh Brown," I sighed. His attitude was not uncommon. I'd encountered a surprising amount of prejudice among Africans against black Americans, gleaned mostly, I supposed, from the news media and the blockbuster movies that made their way here. African Americans visiting Ghana rarely got the kind of special treatment whites got. A black Peace Corps volunteer I met at a bar in Accra told me that when she arrived in her village for the first time, the villagers looked at her with dismay.

"They thought they'd been shortchanged," she said, shaking her head ruefully. "One lady wanted to know if their village had lost some kind of lottery. She said her cousin's village had gotten a white one!"

She told the story lightly, over a beer, but I sensed the heartbreak behind it. She'd come here, like so many black Americans, expecting to find home. To be treated as a second-class citizen in her ancestral homeland produced a desolation I could scarcely imagine.

How strange, I thought, not for the first time, that Ghanaians had such affection for white people, given their recent history of colonization. But then, perhaps the very nearness of that experience provided the explanation. The effects of colonial education were so fresh that the majority of Ghanaians still esteemed their former colonizers rather than resenting them. The absence of a significant white population also helped. There was no European aristocracy in residence, lording its wealth over the local people. Almost all the *obroni* to be found in Ghana were aid workers, students, or volunteers.

I sighed again, trying to collect my thoughts.

"It's true there are a disproportionate number of black men in American jails," I told Brown, "but the reasons for that are very complicated. Generations of economic oppression, racism, the police, the courts . . ." I scratched the bite fiercely, drawing blood.

"But look how they behave," he said. "They are rude."

"It's . . ." I sighed, abandoning the insatiable itch. "It's complicated. There's a lot of anger built up. But this group isn't representative, either. Most black Americans aren't separatists."

"I will beat them," he said.

I looked at him, and we burst out laughing. I picked up his hand, pressing his calloused yellow palm against mine. "My hero, defending my good name."

❖

The jovial guard at the gated American Embassy compound refused to believe there were homeless people in the U.S.

"No!" he shouted at me. "No one begs in America. It is not possible."

"I'm sorry," I told him, "but it's more than possible. It's the truth."

"I will never believe it."

"Okay," I shrugged and moved to enter the building.

"You must marry me and bring me there, and then I will see for myself," he called after me. I didn't respond and he tried again, "Why not?"

I turned back to him, grinning. "You want to marry me? I'd make a horrible wife. I barely cook; I hate to clean . . . And when you got to the U.S. and saw all the homeless people, you'd divorce me and head straight back to Ghana."

"Never! Others will cook and clean; no problem."

I laughed, shaking my head helplessly. "And what if you didn't like it there? What if you couldn't find a job?"

He laughed and laughed, calling out something to the other guard in Twi. They were handsome in their dark blue uniforms, their faces shiny from the heat. "I will have no trouble in America," he said, wiping his eyes. "Do not worry. My brother is in America. He writes me, he has two cars. He lives in Dallas; he is married with a white lady. His name is Atineku. You have met him?"

"I don't think so. I've never been to Dallas."

He laughed again. "Good. When do we go?"

My daypack passed inspection, and I entered a low-ceilinged room filled with yellow plastic chairs. The air-conditioning iced my bare arms, and I shivered. At one end of the room, separated by a glass partition, a U.S. official sat behind a counter listening to Ghanaians plead their cases for visitors' visas to the U.S. Their task was to persuade him that they would return to Ghana once the visa expired. Unless they had a secure, well-paying job in Ghana that could reasonably tempt them back, their chances of getting a visa were slim. This ruled out 98 percent of the population. All the same, the room was full of people, dressed in festival clothes, clutching letters of recommendation from American friends.

The counter for American citizens was on my right as I entered the room, and there was only one person in line: Nadhiri. I hadn't seen her since the Marcus Garvey event, a week ago.

"Hi," I said, approaching the counter.

Her face went blank when she saw me. She nodded slightly. I felt an obstinate desire to push the connection, to force her to acknowledge me.

"What are you doing?" I asked her.

She indicated the form she was filling out.

"Registering? That's smart; I never bothered to do that. I'm adding some pages to my passport." I flipped it open, displaying the pages filled with stamps. "I'm thinking of going to Mali."

She finished filling out the form and handed it to the woman behind the desk, thanking her.

"Goodbye," I said, as she headed for the door.

She didn't want to answer. She wanted to keep going, but something, some law of politeness drilled into her from an early age, caused her to turn slightly and nod in my direction before she pushed through the heavy glass door.

⚜

Over the next few weeks in Accra, I watched for her. Sometimes she hung out on the wooden steps in front of the hostel, chatting with the Ghanaian volunteers. With them she was a different person, laughing, putting her arms around them, slapping their legs. She had learned a bit of Twi, and they laughed at her pronunciation, teasing her. Watching her with them, I felt a nameless longing, an ache so strong I had to turn away.

Without exactly trying to, I discovered her habits. I bumped into her now at least once a day—buying pineapple on the street corner, inspecting printed cloth in the bustling Makola Market, standing in line at the post office, waiting in the crowded car park for a *tro-tro* to the beach. Each time I saw her, I said hello. Just that: "Hello."

I'd discovered her weakness. I took perverse glee in watching her fight and lose the inner battle over whether or not to respond. It was a short-lived, joyless rush. I could make her nod at me, but I couldn't make her see me, or recognize our bond.

And then one day she was gone.

I dawdled around Accra too long and arrived a week late for my next work camp in Kaleo, Upper West Region. MC Brown was there, and I was looking forward to seeing him. I hitched a ride from the regional capital of Wa on a tall truck, bouncing along painfully with metal implements of all sizes grinding against my sides. My legs were somewhere down below, sandwiched between two heavy metal poles with prime potential to roll. I had the uncomfortable sensation that in the event of an accident or even a particularly ill-timed stop, I could be sliced neatly in half.

I tried not to think about that, but instead focused on chatting with Katie, an Englishwoman I'd met in Afranguah who was also catching a ride. When I boarded in Wa, the men on the truck had shouted, "*Obroni*, your friend, your friend!" and parted to reveal a slender figure with light, stick-straight brown hair sitting in the bed of the truck.

"Katie!" I'd said in surprise, and the men had roared with glee. Ghanaians are under the impression that all white people know each other, and they take great delight when this idea is confirmed. I'd been on many buses in which the people around me had excitedly called my attention to some hapless *obroni* riding in the back. They were always extremely disappointed when I claimed not to have met the person before.

The Upper West Region of Ghana was drier than the coastal areas where I'd previously spent time. It was almost October now, too, and the rainy season was drawing to a close. Though still very hot, the air was less muggy here, and therefore more bearable. As we drew closer to the Sahara, the tropical landscape gave way to flat, grassy savanna with scattered clumps of trees. The huts here were round, rather than rectangular like the ones on the coast. They had conical thatched roofs and were often grouped together in extended family compounds surrounded by smooth mud walls.

The most conspicuous trees in this region were the baobabs. Comical and monstrous, a single baobab often stood alone in a field or on the crest of a low hill. No two looked alike. Their enormously thick trunks resembled either a single bark-covered cylinder or multiple cylinders welded together. They could grow up to sixty feet tall and twenty-five feet in diameter, though many were much smaller. Their short branches stuck out from their trunks like deformed arms and radiated off the tops like bad haircuts. Legend had it that the baobab complained so many times to the creator about where it wanted to live, moving gradually all over the African continent, that the creator got fed up with its whining and stuck it in the ground upside down, with its roots in the air.

The men in our truck were boisterously good-natured and soon began teaching us songs. By the time we arrived at the camp, we were belting them out at the top of our lungs. Katie and I waved and shouted as the truck clattered away, its tires spraying us with pebbles and dust.

Katie had been at camp for a week already. She had gone into Wa that day to mail a letter and purchase some supplies. While she went to store her supplies in the kitchen area, the camp leader, a heavyset man from Accra called Facts ("Fats?" *"Facts"*), told me that the other volunteers were at the construction site and would be back in about an hour. If I would like to set up my bed and wash, he said, I could greet them when they returned. I nodded, eyeing the rain barrel full of greenish water with distrust.

"Be quiet when you go inside," Facts cautioned me. "Our sistah is recovering from malaria."

I groaned. Malaria had hit almost all of the volunteers in the camp, picking them off one by one like ducks in a shooting gallery. Because of mosquitoes' aversion to me, I'd so far been spared.

I saw Nadhiri as soon as I entered the tiny unfurnished church where the volunteers stayed. She was curled on a mat in the corner, fast asleep. The sight of her sent a painful jolt of adrenaline through my bloodstream. I felt like a gunslinger in an old Western, grimly anticipating a showdown. *Out here,* I thought, *there's nowhere to hide.*

✜

When Brown returned from the work site, sticky with sweat, I threw my arms around him and kissed him on the cheek.

He returned my hug stiffly and pulled away first.

"How's camp?" I asked.

"Fine, fine." He looked at the ground.

"Yeah? What's going on?"

"Camp is very nice. Excuse me please, I must bathe now. Tonight I cook the dinner."

I stared in disbelief as he headed into the church and emerged again moments later, carrying a bucket and towel. He gave me a small, perfunctory smile, dunked the bucket into the rain barrel, and disappeared behind the reed screens. He avoided me the rest of the evening, but I noticed him going in and out of the church several times, carrying food and water. Once I peered in and saw him kneeling by Nadhiri's mat, placing a cloth on her forehead.

"So you and Nadhiri became friends?" I asked him as we piled shovels and picks into a wheelbarrow the next morning.

"She is a very brave girl."

"That's great," I said, forcing a smile. "Because from what you said before, it seemed like you had a lot of ideas about black Americans that . . . well, it seemed like the media had given you a false impression."

"Yes," he looked at me for a moment, then looked away. "My ideas have changed."

✧

A European and American night was declared, in which we were to prepare a typical European or American dish for dinner. Jan from Germany, Katie from England, and I volunteered to cook. After much discussion about the menu, we decided on pancakes. They were simple to make, we reasoned, the ingredients were readily available, and they resembled Ghanaian food enough that we felt confident that people would like them. As the day approached we grew excited. Jan thought he'd seen a stand in town that sold small jars of jam. Could we create syrup by mixing the jam with water and sugar? How about melting down some chocolate bars for a real treat? We planned to mix bananas into the batter and have oranges on the side.

There was a slight ruckus with Facts over the request for extra eggs.

"Usually the campers fund this European night themselves," he said.

"On my last camp the association funded it," said Jan.

"Yes, mine too," said Katie. "I assumed it would be that way this time as well."

Facts grunted and scowled. He'd been in a surly mood lately.

"Well," he said at last. "The camp may perhaps provide you with some eggs, but such things as chocolate you must surely purchase yourselves."

On the day itself, we tried to get a buzz going around the camp.

"Pancakes tonight," we announced eagerly at the construction site. A couple of local people who were working with us seemed excited about the prospect.

"You must not invite these people to partake of our food," said Facts. "It is prohibited. Soon we must feed the entire village!"

At dusk I mixed batter beneath a baobab whose enormous trunk was actually four trunks joined together. We'd tried once to encircle it with our arms and found that we needed four people before our hands could touch.

Katie and Jan fried the batter in two iron pans. What emerged were crêpes, really, thin and slightly dense, not the fat cakey pancakes we eat in the U.S. Katie and Jan competed with each other over degrees of thinness. Jan was the professional— he and a friend had hired themselves out in Germany to make pancakes at children's birthday parties.

I ran to the church to make the announcement: "Pancakes ready! Come get your red-hot pancakes!" then hurried back to stir the chocolate.

No one came. I returned to the church and poked my head in again. Several foreign volunteers lay crashed out on their sleeping bags. Nadhiri huddled in the corner with a group of Ghanaians.

"Come on, everybody!" I shouted. "Pancakes getting cold!"

"I guess I'll set an example," said a Danish girl, lazily setting down her book.

Ten minutes later, despite multiple trips by Katie and myself to promote our cause, not a single African had partaken of the food. Several Europeans sat around eating crêpes with chocolate and commenting nostalgically on the ones they'd had in France.

Nadhiri emerged from the church, set up a coal port, and began to heat up some leftover goat stew from the previous night. She didn't even glance in the direction of the pancakes. Next to the stew she set a pot of rice.

Slowly the Ghanaians emerged from the church and made their way toward the stew.

"Castro!" said Jan eagerly. "Surely you'd like a pancake. Just one pancake?"

Glancing guiltily at Nadhiri, Castro accepted a pancake on his plate. The three of us were giddy with excitement.

"Would you like chocolate? Or jam? An orange?" Katie and I buzzed around him with pots and spoons, offering things. Looking down, he shook his head. He headed for the stew.

"Good idea—a savory pancake!" said Katie. "I'm sure they'll go quite well with the stew."

"Except for the bananas," I murmured.

"Let's make some batter without banana," said Jan, "so they can eat them with the stew. Perhaps eating sweet things for dinner doesn't seem right."

While the pile of banana pancakes attracted flies, we hastily made up a savory batch, holding off on the sugar and adding a bit of salt. A couple of Ghanaians tasted them, but no one came back for seconds. Soon the savory pancakes too began to pile up.

"Perhaps I could invite some villagers?" I said to Facts, who hovered nearby, frowning. "We don't want the food to go to waste."

"The Europeans will eat it," he said grimly. "If not today, then tomorrow."

The Ghanaians sat aside, in a group, sharing the rice and goat stew. On my way to the bathroom, I overheard a snippet of conversation.

"See how they treat us?" said Nadhiri. "Like children waiting for a treat. They act like we've never seen a pancake before!"

Who's us? I wondered angrily. *You're a girl from D.C. You have more in common with me than you do with the Ghanaian volunteers.*

"Yes," said MC Brown, sitting at her side. "They come here thinking we live in trees, and they return home with the very same thought."

After the disastrous dinner had been cleared away, Katie, Jan, and I lay on our backs on wooden benches, gazing up at the astonishing layers of stars and fighting off mosquitoes.

"She's turned the Ghanaians against us," I said bitterly. "A true gift, to inspire hatred and distrust."

"Aren't you being a bit dramatic?" said Katie. "Perhaps we simply served the wrong food."

I cast her an arch glance.

"Really," said Jan. "Maybe they thought it was cheap of us to prepare something without meat. Perhaps they were expecting McDonald's hamburgers."

"I'm surprised I haven't seen a McDonald's here," said Katie.

"Oh, I'm sure it's just a matter of time," I said sardonically. "American culture is conquering the world."

"You mean poisoning the world," said Jan, and we laughed.

From the darkened doorway of the church, a high-pitched voice said, "American culture. I don't think there is any such animal."

I looked up in surprise.

"I guess it depends what you mean by culture, Nadhiri," I said carefully. "Obviously the U.S. is a blend of many cultures.

But if you define culture in terms of a common mythology, common symbols—"

"What is an American?" she asked suddenly.

"What do you mean?" asked Katie, after a short silence.

"What do you think of, when you think of the word 'America'?"

The condescension in her voice irked me, and I answered sharply, "A lot of things. An imperfect experiment. A military-industrial bully. I don't know! Baseball, hot dogs, apple pie and . . . oh, whatever." I was suddenly tired. "What are you even asking? It's not one thing. You know that. Culture, counterculture. It's a dance, an exchange. Just like anywhere."

"And 'American'?" she said to the group, ignoring my response. "What is the image in your mind when you think of an American? Do you picture someone like me?"

"I picture a person with a United States passport," I said. "In case you haven't noticed, we come in all shapes and sizes."

"I guess you want us to say we think of a white male," said Jan.

"The only real Americans," she said, with the exaggerated patience of a teacher speaking to a particularly slow student, "are the Native Americans, most of whom were massacred."

Well, no shit, I thought, stung by her tone and the elementary political point. Was this supposed to be news?

"But when they teach us 'American' history in school, it's all about white men."

Breathe, I told myself. *She doesn't know you. This is your chance to show her you're not the enemy.*

"That's right," I said. "It's disgusting."

"We were speaking about McDonald's hamburgers," interjected Jan. "That's what we meant by American cul—"

"I don't recognize any United States," said Nadhiri, still

sounding like a lecturer. "I see only Divided States. I am part of a Black nation that intends to establish its autonomy within the territory that claims that name."

"Within the U.S.?" I asked incredulously. "How's that gonna work?"

"We will create two or three Black-only states."

"Which ones?" I sputtered. "And how do you plan to get the current residents to leave?"

"Why do you white liberals always get so hostile when you talk about race?"

"Me, hostile?" I was flabbergasted. "What about you? And from the word 'go'!"

"I try to mind my own business, but you're like a stalker, in my face, in my face . . ."

"I was trying to connect with you, but you're so full of hate—"

"Hate? You think I hate you? I don't care enough to hate you. I didn't come here for you. What is it with your egos?"

"And I'm not liberal, I'm . . . progressive." I heard how stupid it sounded as it came out of my mouth. "Radical," I added, feebly. "I believe in radical change, from the root."

"Radical?" she snorted. "I bet you believe in integration."

I paused for a moment, then said uncertainly, "Yes, I do."

"When are you love-and-peace hippies gonna figure it out? Integration doesn't work. Shit's worse than it ever was. At least under slavery they fed us."

Jan and Katie had gone, though I didn't notice them leave. I looked at Nadhiri's face, half in shadow, half glowing pale, reflecting the pregnant moon.

I was so flustered, my tongue caught in a thick net of rage, that I could barely speak. "That kind of thinking's just . . . Who— who can it benefit? That—it—you're working against . . . the future, what is actually . . . It's not a choice—races are mixing. That's what's true. If you like it or . . . If we don't . . . If we don't learn to deal with each other, it'll all just explode in violence."

"Get it," she said coolly. "It's already happening."

◈

The foundation for the women's center we were building was uneven and had to be redug. A nearby baobab had spread its brawny roots farther than expected, forcing us to move the whole structure a few feet farther away. We spent the morning knocking down bricks we'd painstakingly laid the day before. Itchy with sweat and sticky red mud, we stood, panting, surveying our loss.

Facts approached us on a path through the high grass, the flesh of his heavy arms shaking as he ran. His forehead dripped; his white T-shirt was plastered to his skin. He held a folded piece of paper in his hand.

"Sistah Nadhiri," he said. "Telegram from home."

Facts's round face glistened. He moved the paper away as she reached for it.

"Come," he said. "We will read it back in camp."

But Nadhiri grabbed the paper and scanned it. All expression dropped from her face. She stared, frozen, at the document in her hand.

"Sistah, what has happened?" asked Brown.

"Uh," she said, a funny, pedestrian sound, as though she were clearing her throat. "Uh." She turned and walked away from us, down the path through the yellow grass. She walked about four steps, then stopped for a long moment, stood absolutely still. Then she broke into an awkward, loping run.

"Keep working," said Facts, going after her.

Brown threw down his shovel and followed.

The rest of us stood, looking quizzically at each other. Finally Castro, the home secretary, said, "The camp leader has said 'keep working,' therefore let us continue to work." So we picked up our shovels and worked.

◆

I heard from Katie, who heard from Jan, who heard from Facts that Nadhiri's father was killed the night before in a random stabbing on the streets of Washington, D.C. "Stabbed in the neck," Katie said. Facts accompanied Nadhiri to Wa and put her on a bus to Accra. Brown offered to go with her, but she said no. She left for the United States the next day. None of us heard from her again.

◆

Castro said to me, "This bad thing happened to our sistah Nadhiri because she does not like white people. She is a racist. So, she is punished."

Jan said, "I did not like her, but I would not wish such a thing on anyone."

Katie said, "It's terrible, isn't it? Just terrible."

Brown stared at me, but moved away when I approached.

And me? I wanted to lose myself in Brown's smooth body, catch myself up in the touch and smell of him, where everything might make sense. But that fantasy was gone. Nadhiri stood between us—a raging, sorrowful ghost. Before she left, I'd pursued her relentlessly, though I scarcely knew why. Now I wanted to be free of her, but I couldn't make her go.

Somebody's Heart
Is Burning

Many months later, I lie on a hardwood floor in Katie's cold London apartment, looking at pictures of Ghana. I'm wearing one of her sweaters, a thick Shetland wool that still smells like sheep.

"These!" Katie says. "These! Two entire rolls. I don't get it."

I flip through the pile, nostalgia tightening my chest. Amid hundreds of perfect shots—faces so crisp you can see the pores, mud huts with each blade of thatch standing out in sharp relief, silver waves caught on the crest—twelve blurry photos. Two girls in pink dresses skid by, baskets on their heads, a shimmer of motion. A plain cinderblock building slides sideways out of the frame. Elongated cars, unreadable storefronts, and more skewed women, always in motion, wrapped in bright cloth. Several times, a dark blurred face hovers large in the corner of the frame, as though someone had taken his own photo, holding the camera at arm's length.

"I don't get it," Katie says again.

I shrug. "You left the lens cap off?"

We look down at the photos spread across the floor.

"What town is it?" I ask.

"Wa."

"What did we do in Wa?" I shuffle through for other Wa photos, and find one of myself sitting with freshly cropped hair amid a gaggle of grinning Ghanaian children. I'm holding up a ridiculous 8 x 10 glamour shot of myself, backlit and soft, taken a year before in another life—a photo within a photo. Behind me stands a bright-eyed young woman with a smile at once exuberant and demure.

"Christy," I say, and Katie groans with recognition.

"Of course! Christy." She reflects a moment, smiles, shakes her head sadly. "Sweet Christy."

We met Christy in Wa, capital of the Upper West Region, on a humid night after a blistering November day. Nadhiri had left the Kaleo camp, and though she wasn't forgotten, things had settled down considerably.

Meanwhile, Katie and I had become fast friends. She was a gangly artist with a dry sense of humor and an impish grin that sparked intermittently, utterly transforming her sensible English face. On this particular day, the two of us had escaped the afternoon's labor in Kaleo for an unapproved romp in the Big City. We'd spent the guilty hours sitting at a wooden picnic table in a shady open-air mineral bar, pressing frosty Pee Colas (the Ghanaian version of Coke) to our flushed foreheads, writing in our journals and reveling in our truancy.

We were standing on the dusty road out of Wa, waiting for transport back to Kaleo, when a girl jumped off a crowded *tro-tro* and headed straight toward us. The sun was setting, and everything was bathed in an orange glow. She was dressed in a red Western skirt and red and black striped blouse, impeccably clean and crisp. She looked like a cheerful employee in a Burger King commercial, only her smile was bigger, brighter.

"Friends!" she called. "Remember me? One week ago I showed you the post office."

"What a coincidence," Katie said.

In the two weeks since I'd arrived in Kaleo, Katie and I had come into Wa, the regional capital, four or five times. Each time, people approached us on the street: *Remember me? I offered to carry your bags when you got off the bus. Remember me? I sold you nice bread.* It had become a running gag we teased each other with, inventing new ones: *Remember me? I chased you down the block with a stick of fried meat. Remember me? I almost ran you over with my bicycle.*

"You are in Kaleo, yes?" Christy asked. "I know the white lady there. Sharon. Peace Corps. She said you would come today."

"How could she know?" I asked lightly.

"Yes," said Christy, cryptically. "I know so many white people. This man, Mac. VSO. He was one year in Wa here." She reached into her bag and pulled out a photograph. It showed her, beautifully dressed in an intricate blue and gold African print, standing beside a short, scruffy young man in T-shirt, glasses, and dusty khaki pants.

"Mac," she said proudly. "My friend. He has promised to send a letter."

I smiled encouragingly.

"Please. I can help you," Christy continued. "You will come to my house and greet my mother."

"Oh, we'd love to," said Katie, "but I'm afraid we've got to get back. They're expecting us at the volunteer camp."

"Yes," said Christy, smiling sweetly. "There is never another lorry tonight. Tomorrow."

"We thought we'd get a taxi," I said, and miraculously, one appeared. Christy stepped onto the dirt road, waving her arms.

The car pulled up in a cloud of dust. Peering through the window in the fading light, I saw it had no control panel, only a mass of wires. Two men shared the front seat with the driver, while two women with babies on their laps argued in the back. A young boy was sandwiched between them. Christy stepped to the window and began speaking to the driver in Wala. Soon she was shouting and gesticulating, her speech punctuated by cries of *"Eh!"* Finally she stepped back, waving her hand disdainfully at the taxi, which drove away.

"He will rob you," she said. "Because you are white, he will charge you 3,500 cedis."

Katie and I looked at each other. About five dollars—a fortune, in Ghanaian terms, for a half-hour cab ride.

"We do need to get back," said Katie.

"He is a thief. My brother has a taxi. He will send you to Kaleo for 600 cedis. Come," said Christy. She took my backpack, swung it onto her back, and reached for the camera that hung around Katie's neck.

"Oh no, it's okay," said Katie, stepping back.

"Come," Christy repeated. Laughing, she grabbed the camera strap and hoisted it over Katie's head. She set off down the dusty road. We followed.

✦

One thing about Africa: at night, it's dark. In a village, if there's no party going on, a twinkle of candlelight after 10 P.M. is a rare sight. You could walk right by a village and never know it was there. Even in a small city like Wa, which has electricity, many neighborhoods depend on kerosene lanterns, which disappear into the huts after dark.

On this occasion, the moon was a delicate sliver. As we moved outside of the central area, paved roads gave way to dirt ones, then narrowed to paths. Cinderblock houses were replaced by group-ings of round mud huts. Lulled by the motion of my feet and the gentle caress of the cooling air, I followed Christy down the dirt paths, through high grass and over puddles. A gentle breeze had arisen, and the night air was pleasantly cool. I had no idea where I was going, and after a few minutes I forgot to care.

"Are we almost to your brother's?" Katie's voice startled me. We'd been walking a long time and seemed to be outside of town. It had been awhile since we'd seen a road, and I wondered vaguely how a taxi could get out here.

"Yes," said Christy.

Soon we entered a compound of four or five round mud huts with thatched roofs that looked freshly trimmed, sur-rounded by smooth mud walls.

"Here," said Christy proudly. "I have brought you to greet my mother."

"I thought we were going to your brother's," said Katie.

"Yeah," I chimed in, slightly alarmed.

"Yes," Christy said. "First we chop rice. Here is my mother."

A woman in traditional dress, with a leathery, smile-creased face, came out of the house. She was holding a baby, which she quickly passed off to Christy. She grasped our hands warmly and shouted, "You are welcome." We responded with the word *anola*, "good evening" in the Wala language, which pleased her so much she repeated it several times, laughing loudly. I saw where Christy had gotten her brilliant smile. Four children, ranging in age from about two to twelve, hovered around the circle of light cast by her lantern, pointing at us and giggling. Katie and I looked at each other.

"You know—" I started to say, but Christy cut me off.

"We chop rice!" She gestured to a table.

I glanced at Katie again and shrugged. We sat down. Christy's mother sat beside us. She didn't eat, but watched closely as we consumed the rice balls and spicy groundnut soup. Whenever we slowed down, she smiled broadly and gestured for us to keep going.

"This is really trying," Katie murmured in my ear.

"Christy," I said, after we'd finished eating and a polite interval had passed, "we really do need to get going. People at the camp will worry about us."

"Yes," said Christy, smiling and making no move.

"Really," I said.

"Really," said Katie.

"Yes," Christy said again. Reluctantly, she stood up, spoke to her mother in Wala.

"Thank you," I said to her mother, also in Wala. She crowed with delight. I said to Christy, "Please tell her it was delicious."

"Yes."

Underway, I again lost myself in the rhythm of the walk. Lost in thought, I was only dimly aware of the neighborhoods we passed through, mostly made up of decoratively painted mud huts with glimmers of kerosene lamps coming through the windows. Occasionally we'd pass a small group of men gathered beneath a thatched overhang talking and laughing, with bottles in their hands. After about twenty minutes, Katie looked at me and raised her pale eyebrows to the hairline.

"Ah, Christy . . ." I began.

"Very soon, sistahs," she said with such gentleness that I felt reassured.

We came to another walled compound, where a snarling dog kept Katie and me very much at bay. I'd decided against investing $300 in rabies shots before leaving the United States, and that decision haunted me now.

"It is okay," Christy laughed. She made a calming gesture toward us, "Small, small."

She entered the courtyard while Katie and I hovered outside, clinging to each other's hands in solidarity. Next to the house stood a rusty vehicle.

Christy came back out. "My brother has traveled to Bolga for books. He will not return for some days."

Katie threw me a "now what?" look, as though the whole thing were my fault.

"Christy, we're getting really tired," I said, suddenly feeling it. "I think we're ready to invest in that taxi ride. Can you please direct us to the taxi park?"

"Taxi?"

"Yes, we're willing to pay the 3,500 cedis."

"Oh no, no, they will rob you," she said. "Do not worry. We will visit the pastor. He will drive you."

"Thank you," I said firmly, "that's very kind, but I think we'd rather pay. I'm afraid the people at the camp will be concerned about us. We weren't even supposed to leave the camp in the first place!"

Christy stared at me.

"They'll worry," I repeated, with some urgency.

"No. No. Do not worry. Come." She started off again, purposefully.

I scampered after her.

"But if the pastor's not there," I said, "you'll take us back to the taxi park immediately, right?"

"Yes," she said seriously, looking straight into my eyes.

The walk to the pastor's house took us back to a more populated area, with cinderblock houses and dirt roads wide enough to accommodate cars. I took this as a positive sign and glanced hopefully at Katie, but she stared resolutely forward, avoiding my gaze.

The pastor's house was dark. When Christy knocked, a woman came out of an adjoining house, calling to her. Four children of various sizes followed her and, seeing Katie and me, began calling out, *"Tubabu! Tubabu!!"*—white person in yet another tongue—all the while screaming with laughter.

"Don't tell me," Katie said, when Christy approached. "The pastor has traveled."

"Yes," said Christy, smiling sweetly.

"Now we go to the taxi park, right, Christy?" I asked.

"It is late. The taxis have gone home. You will sleep at my house."

A band of frustration tightened around my temples. "Let's at least look, okay? That was the deal."

"Yes," said Christy. "We will visit the forest manager. He has a car. He will surely send you to Kaleo."

"The forest manager," Katie said dully.

"The forest manager," I started to laugh. "Of course. Why not?"

Christy looked from one to the other of us, uncertain of our mood.

Katie began to giggle, too, and soon we were both laughing helplessly, holding our sweaty bodies against each other. I lifted my heavy hair from the back of my neck. The cropped look I'd left the U.S. with had grown into a straggly mass.

"I need a haircut," I said.

"Good," said Christy eagerly, back on firm ground. "I will cut your hair. I have cut white men's hair before. Mac, VSO. And Eric, Peace Corps."

"But not now!" I said.

"No, no, sistah," she laughed. "It is nighttime! Now we go to the forest."

When we reached a paved road, Christy flagged down a passing car, and after a brief consultation with the driver, indicated that Katie and I get into the back seat.

"He will take us to the forest manager," she said.

"To the forest!" I murmured, starting to giggle again. I was definitely slaphappy at this point.

"This is a fairy tale," I told Katie, as we drove down a narrow road, through thick trees. She seemed to have fallen asleep, her head lolling against my shoulder like a child's. "The forest manager will make everything well," I whispered into her tangled hair.

✧

"You are lucky to find me in."

A portly man with glasses emerged from the darkened cinderblock house in slippers and *bou-bou*—the full-length cotton robe worn by men in this area. He switched on an electric light. "I have just today returned from Accra."

True to Ghanaian hospitality, he made no comment on our

late arrival in this secluded spot, but ushered us into his home, offering minerals as though receiving bedraggled white visitors were his nightly custom. The front room was simple and bare, as in most Ghanaian dwellings I had visited. A clean-swept cement floor, a plastic table and chairs. A low maroon-colored couch against one wall. The only decoration was a placard on the wall, which read, "I am covered in the blood of Jesus," with a drawing of a thorny crown tipped with bright scarlet blood. A television sat on a table in the corner. Beside it was a small stack of books. Through an open door I glimpsed a narrow second room with a single bed.

After ten minutes of small talk, I leaned over to Christy and whispered, "Please tell the forest manager why we're here."

❖

Back in Kaleo, we thanked the forest manager profusely. As we climbed out of his air-conditioned car, Christy leaned over and said to me, "Tomorrow you come for your haircut."

I was about to tell her that we had other plans, but before I could get the words out, Christy and the forest manager had disappeared in a puff of warm exhaust.

❖

When we didn't appear in Wa the next afternoon, Christy made her way to Kaleo to find us. Against the wishes of Facts, who was still annoyed about our absence the previous day, she worked beside us all afternoon and spent the night stretched out on a grass mat beside Katie's sleeping bag. The next day Facts insisted that she leave.

"We cannot be housing the entire village," he said huffily. It took a great deal of cajoling before he gave his permission for us to visit Christy on the weekend for my haircut.

We met Christy at the taxi park. With a flock of appreciative children in tow, we walked to her sister's house for the scissors and then to her mother's compound to perform the operation. The distance seemed much shorter in daylight.

I'd brought my theatrical headshot from the previous year, to show Christy the haircut I had in mind. My brother is a hairdresser, and back in the U.S. he always cuts my hair. This particular haircut was short and hip, with wispy bangs, a sprouting top like a cactus, and a zigzagged line shaved into the side. When I showed it to her, she smiled cheerfully and nodded.

"Yes," she said.

Christy, whose manner up to this point had been sweet and self-effacing to the point of subservience, became a warrior goddess with scissors in hand. Brow furrowed in fierce concentration, she cut from all angles, moving up and down like a dancer, leaning over the top, barking at the children to stay out of her way. Grabbing chunks of hair, she chopped swiftly and decisively, while Katie gasped, "Oh!" and "Wait!" her hands flying to her mouth.

"What?" I asked repeatedly, but Katie simply brought her hands back to her lap and smiled weakly.

"Nothing," she squeaked. "Never mind."

Finally a mirror was brought. Uneven tufts stuck out all over my head. Most alarmingly, a parade of very short bangs trooped across the top of my forehead in a severely straight line.

Getting control of my breath, I took the scissors and showed Christy how to make the bangs "fringy," as my brother would say. Then I pointed to various tufts and asked her to snip here and there.

"Oh! You've made a bald spot!" Katie cried.

I grabbed the mirror and inspected the damage. I demanded that Katie take an active role in the process, instead of heckling from the sidelines. Soon it became a group effort. The children screamed and pointed, making snipping motions with their fingers.

By the end my entire head was buzzed close, like a Buddhist nun. Katie took a photo of Christy and her shorn client, with Christy holding up the scissors and the headshot. Her face wore a wide innocent grin.

✦

Christy claimed Katie and me as her own. She came to the camp almost every afternoon, and stayed until Facts kicked her out.

"What does that girl want?" he asked repeatedly. "She should go home and stop loitering about."

Though Katie and I weren't entirely sure we wanted Christy around, we felt compelled to defend her.

"She's not hurting anything," I told Facts.

"Well, she cannot stay overnight again," he said. "For her own sake. If something goes missing, it is her they will blame."

What *did* Christy want? We couldn't figure it out. She never asked Katie or me for anything, not money, not clothes, not to take her to our countries. She seemed simply to enjoy our company. She would sit near us for long stretches of time, watching us closely, scarcely participating in the conversation. At first we tried to include her, asking her about herself, but she never seemed to understand what we were asking and always turned the questions back to us. After a while, we almost forgot she was there.

She was very solicitous of us and would do things like straighten our sleeping bags or bring us our food at dinnertime. This made me uncomfortable. When I asked her if she expected to be paid for her work, she just laughed.

"Never, sistah."

"Then please don't do it," I said.

The next day I caught her taking my laundry out to wash.

"Stop, Christy," I told her.

"What, sistah?"

"Don't do my laundry for me. I can do my own laundry."

"Yes," she said, and continued walking.

"No!" I stopped her. "Please, I mean it."

With a dainty sigh, she put the laundry down.

Christy was fascinated by Katie's camera and my tape recorder. She was constantly pushing the buttons on the tape recorder and opening and closing the camera's lens. When I asked her to stop, telling her she was wearing out my batteries, she always gave me the sweetest possible "yes," but the next time I looked, she was at it again.

Sometimes I wondered if she was mentally disabled, but looking into her eyes, I knew better.

"She understands what she wants to understand," I said to Katie one evening, after Christy had left.

"What do you mean?" she asked.

"I mean that she pretends not to follow what we're saying in order to gain more information. Even that night, when she was leading us around. She knew we wanted to get in a taxi and head home, but she pretended not to grasp it."

"So who's she gathering information *for?* The CIA?"

"That, my friend, is the million dollar question."

She rolled her eyes. "Wake me when you've worked it out."

✦

When the camp ended, Katie and I planned to spend a few days in and around Wa, then a week traveling in the Western Region before we headed back to Accra. We'd just arrived in Wa with our backpacks when we ran into Christy. She was hovering out-side the *tro-tro* park, as though she'd been waiting for us.

"Please, you stay at my mother's house," she said.

Katie and I had anticipated this offer and decided against it. Sweet as Christy was, her constant attention was beginning to creep us out.

"Next thing you know she'll be wiping your nose," Katie had said on the *tro-tro* into Wa.

And now, as if on cue, Christy stepped forward with a tissue.

"Christy!" I was alarmed. "Don't!"

"Your face is dirty," she said, spitting on the tissue as my mother always had.

"Don't!" I shouted, and moved back. Christy looked gen-uinely wounded. Curious passersby turned to see what was go-ing on.

"You are not kind, sistah," said Christy.

"I–I'm sorry. It's just . . . you're . . . invading my space."

"Invading?"

"I . . . We . . . We need some privacy," I said.

"It's been terrific spending time with you," said Katie, "but Tanya and I would like to be on our own now."

Christy stood absolutely still for a long moment, looking at us. Then she turned around without a word and walked away.

"Bye!" I called after her. "Thank you for everything!" But she didn't look back.

❖

A few days later I was flipping through my journal, and I noticed that several pages at the back of the notebook were covered with penciled writing. As I began to read, a shock ran through me. The words were mine, but the handwriting was not. Someone had copied a series of pages from the front of the notebook, word for word, in a careful, even hand.

Katie, too, discovered a number of drawings in the back of her sketchbook, close imitations of sketches she had made in the front.

Other small messengers appeared over time. One of my books had pencil markings in the margins—certain words copied and recopied up and down the sides of the page.

"The pencil goblin," we said each time we found something new, but we felt shaken, exposed. What did she want? we asked each other again and again. Was she, in fact, a being out of fairy tales, looking to steal not our possessions but our souls?

I thought the blurry photos were the final breadcrumb on Christy's trail, but I was wrong. It wasn't until I was back in the U.S. that I discovered the tape. I'd recorded about fifteen cassettes over the course of my time in Ghana, mostly of music. Periodically I mailed a few of them home to lighten my pack. One day I was going through them, writing up labels. I popped one into the tape recorder and heard a high, thin voice with a heavy Ghanaian accent. It sounded like a young woman reading, forming each of the words slowly, mispronouncing some, occasionally going back and trying one again.

"Michael said he holds me in his heart like the love that holds the stars in place. He believes the stars are held by love."

I sat down on the bed, my heart racing. The voice continued.

"'What else could hold them?' he asks. 'What else could keep them from jiggling wildly in their spheres, colliding like a mad game of asteroids?' And what else holds me, keeps me from scattering, shattering . . .'"

A deep heat rose in my face. My words. My unconsidered, intimate words. Bad enough she'd copied them down as a penmanship exercise, but to speak them out loud, to broadcast them! When could she have done it? During the day, while we were at the construction site? I pressed the fast forward button. The voice continued, slowly, painfully, reading, reading.

". . . moving away from political work, simply because it affords so little hope in a day-to-day way . . ."

Fast forward.

". . . Facts says he wants comments but when you make one he jumps on you . . ."

Fast forward.

". . . from a stagnant pond, green and murky . . ."

". . . and Nadhiri—is this fucking high school?"

". . . crying dream: Michael and I were running through an empty . . ."

". . . graves, tributes to the ancestors . . ."

Fast forward. Fast forward. Fast forward.

"Christy is scaring me. I don't know what she wants."

My breath caught. Would she react in some way? Comment? Respond? But no, the voice continued, struggling, picking its way through the thicket of words.

And then the reading stopped. A long pause. Then the voice began to sing, sweet and high and pure. A familiar melody. Something I heard her humming once, as we walked through the streets of Wa. A song she said her mother had learned in school:

I hear a robin singing, singing
Up in the treetop high, high
To me and you he's singing, singing
The clouds will soon roll by.

Somebody's heart is burning, burning
Somebody's heart is burning, burning

Somebody's heart is burning, burning
Because he sees me happy.

And then new words, finally, blessedly, words not mine, but her own. I held my breath. An answer now? But all she left me with was this:

"Sweet sistahs, goodbye, I will miss you so. When you hear this record, remember Ghana here, remember me. Remember Christy, your special friend."

8

The Man in the Cave

It's hard to reconcile the world I left with the one I find myself in now. I feel as if I cheated fate and got a whole other life in my allotted span. In my imagination two scenes unfurl, as if on a split screen. On one side, an experimental theatre troupe is performing a new piece. In the piece, onstage television monitors display video clips of prostitutes working the streets interspliced with congressional hearings, while actors speak Shakespearean text in bland, cheerful voices, and dancers shuffle across the stage, performing gestures both pedestrian and obscene.

On the other side of my imagined screen, a Ghanaian woman pounds fufu in a village with neither running water nor electricity. Beside her, two little girls sit on the packed earth, shelling groundnuts. One of the girls has a baby strapped to her back. The baby starts to cry, and the woman interrupts her pounding to nurse it. The girls start singing, their clear sopranos mingling with the baby's cries and the faint percussion of the splintering shells.

⬥

"You ladies have some small gift for the chief?" asked the chief's interpreter. He was a young man, tall and skinny, dressed in a blue-and-white woven dashiki top with white pajama pants beneath. He stood beside the chief's bench, beaming and fidgeting. The skin of his face bore a grid of razor-thin scars, as though a burning spiderweb had been laid across his face. Facial scarring was common in this region. It was a form of familial and tribal identification, done in infancy.

Katie and I were on our way to visit the Tongo Hills shrine in the Upper East Region, one of Ghana's leading tourist attractions. When the host at our guesthouse in Bolgatanga told us we'd need to offer gifts to a couple of local chiefs in order to gain permission to visit the famous shrine, I knew just the thing.

Before coming to Africa, I'd read Chinua Achebe's *Things Fall Apart* and learned about the ceremonial role of the bitter kola nut in West African culture. Ever since, I'd longed for an opportunity to make use of this knowledge. Katie and I finally located the pyramids of glistening nuts hidden behind a sea of tiny red chili peppers in Bolga's chaotic marketplace. We wrapped them carefully in banana leaves, tying them with a slim rope of braided vines.

"Some small gift?" the interpreter repeated, a look of concern crossing his face.

I stepped forward. "Kola nuts," I proclaimed, loosening the knot, and the leaf opened outward like a flower.

We were in the village of Tongo, at the base of the hills. The shrine we intended to visit was located high above us, among the Whispering Rocks. These bleached boulders were said to be visually stunning, piled atop each other by a mighty unseen hand into formations that resembled every element of creation, from trees to human bodies to birds in flight. The rocks got their name from the shushing sound you heard while walking in their midst, as though the creator himself were whispering in your ear. This whispering was said to be most audible between the months of November and March, when the strong dry wind called the *harmattan* blew in from the Sahara, carrying with it a fine coating of pale dust. Lodged in a cave on a rocky pinnacle was the fetish priest, an oracle whose job was to communicate praise, pleas, and concerns to the powerful ancestral spirits that watched over the surrounding villages.

The walls of the chief's hut were lined with animal bones and skins. A framed photo of the chief shaking hands with then Ghanaian president Jerry Rawlings graced the wall behind the low bench where the chief sat, draped from head to toe in indigo fabric. Heavy tribal scarring marked his wizened, papery cheeks, and his lively eyes danced with mischief. Two little boys about four years old sat on either side of the bench.

When I proffered the kola nuts, the boys snickered, hiding their mouths with their hands. The interpreter chuckled uneasily.

"Nobody brings the chief kola nuts," he said in a low voice. "Even Jerry Rawlings," he indicated the photo, "brought some small money for the chief. It is not the chief himself. It is the elders. They will expect the chief to buy some *pito* to share. Otherwise they will say he has been greedy, and kept all for himself." *Pito* was the preferred beverage of the region—a weak, sweet wine made from fermented corn or millet.

"American dollars are fine," he continued, very low. Then, glancing at Katie's pale face and bermuda shorts, "Or pounds sterling."

"How much in cedis?" I whispered.

He pursed his lips. "Whatever you want to give."

I pulled out a crumpled 500-cedi note and handed it to the interpreter, who smoothed it and presented it to the chief.

The chief mumbled a few words.

"The chief wishes you a safe journey."

Outside the hut, our guide crouched in the shade of the thatched roof. He was a skinny man of about sixty with rotten teeth, baleful eyes with pouchy skin beneath, and ragged pants with a bright floral patch on the seat. He wore a teepee-shaped straw hat, the top half of which was covered in leather, with a leather tassel hanging from the tip. He carried a walking stick. The huts in this region were round, with conical thatched roofs that mirrored the shape of our guide's hat. Clustered together beneath the giant baobab trees, they looked like fat brown mushrooms.

"We never agreed on a price with this guy," I muttered to Katie as we trudged along.

She shrugged, "I'm sure he'll let us know what he'd like in due time."

The heat pressed down on us like an iron as we followed his bobbing hat through the sleepy town. I felt flattened beneath it, drained of all moisture. Every day Katie and I vowed to start our adventures at dawn, to avoid the midday heat, but when the time came, we never managed to get ourselves out of bed.

"We're just bone idle," Katie often said, with a laugh.

We plodded through pale, dry hills, the grass and shrubs prickly as the quills of giant porcupines. Occasional piles of stones blocked our path, like trail markers left by overzealous Girl Scouts.

Suddenly our guide turned to us.

"You dash me two thousand," he said.

"Two thousand!" said Katie.

"I am an old man. The sun is hot."

We stared at him.

"How much you want to pay?" he asked.

"A thousand," I said.

"Yes," he said instantly, and kept walking.

Then guilt. The ever-present guilt. What the amount meant to me as opposed to what it could mean to him.

"He expected us to bargain," said Katie, as though reading my mind. "If he didn't like the price, he wouldn't have agreed."

As we ascended, the vistas opened out, revealing wide fields of brown grassland dotted with rocky outcrops and occasional clusters of trees. Sometimes we'd see a village, its round huts huddled together like bodies around a fire.

"I wonder why they're so close together," said Katie. "You'd think there was a shortage of space."

It was puzzling. Perhaps the vastness was just too over-whelming—all that space and light. A line from T. S. Eliot sprang to my mind: "Humankind cannot bear too much reality." We press together for comfort, clinging ever tighter, like a child digging his knuckles into his eyes, trying to forget the largeness, the terrifying domain of rock, tree, dust, and bush, all brimming with powerful, unfathomable life.

Caught up in the somnambulistic rhythm of the walk, I fell into a reverie. I'd gotten a very sweet letter from Michael recently, forgiving me for the phone call incident and then some.

"Forget the guilt when you think of me," he'd written. "Life's a big mess. Know that I love you and that means what-ever you need it to mean to be happy."

His generosity of spirit floored me. My thoughts drifted to a hike we'd once taken in Colorado. We were almost to the mountain's peak when he remembered he'd left his wallet back in the tent. He wanted to go straight back for it, but I said, "Come on, we're almost there. We've been going for hours—we might as well check out the view before we rush back." I kept telling him to let it go, and he kept getting more and more frustrated. Finally he stripped off all his clothes and threw them and his daypack off the side of the trail, shouting, "Take me as I am!"

What a drama queen he was! I smiled to think of it, but it left a melancholy aftertaste. The one thing he asked of me was the one thing I couldn't give him: simple acceptance. The very thing he gave so naturally to me. The very thing I was never quite able to give myself.

A few hours later, we came to a dusty clearing where gnarled old men leaned against equally ossified trees, shelling groundnuts and popping them into their mouths. Their shirts were in shreds, strips of fabric hanging on their bony frames. Their faces lit up when they saw us.

We had arrived at Tenzuk, the mountain village that the

famous shrine protected. This village had a chief as well, but he was away on business. His nephew, a soft-spoken young man of about eighteen dressed in immaculate Western clothes, offered to show us around the family compound before we climbed up to the shrine.

"You like to make snaps?" the chief's nephew inquired politely, flashing us a shy smile. "You get a nice view of the shrine from here," he added in carefully articulated English.

We stood on the roof of a granary. Like the villages we'd seen earlier, the compound was a miniature city of about twenty huts, surrounded by a circular mud wall. Inside was a teeming warren of narrow passages and archways so short that people had to bend nearly double to enter them. Women sat in the low doorways, weaving hats from dyed grass, crushing chili peppers on flat stones, nursing babies. Children barreled down the slender corridors, chasing each other. This chief had quite an extended family.

"The shrine is there," the young man said, pointing at an impossibly steep cliff directly behind us. He smiled at the look of panic on our faces.

"Do not worry, we will help you," he said kindly. "You snap here first? You snap with me?"

We took turns posing, our arms around the smiling young man.

"You send me the snap?" He turned to us with disarming eagerness.

"Of course," said Katie. "Why don't you write down your address?"

"Sure you will," I murmured in her ear.

"You give me a gift for the snaps." He extended his hand.

"How much?" I sighed.

"Please," he seemed surprised. "You give what you want."

I ungraciously forked over 200 cedis. He looked at Katie, and she did the same.

After our brief tour, we returned to the clearing outside the compound.

"Myself and these men will accompany you to the shrine," said the chief's nephew. The old men were rousing themselves for the journey. Our guide was sound asleep under a tree.

"The shrine belongs to the fetish," the nephew explained gravely. "The fetish protects the village."

"What's a fetish?" I asked bluntly. I'd heard the word so often, yet I was never completely clear as to what it meant.

"The fetish is only a statue, but the spirit of a very strong ancestor, a chief, speaks to us through it, through the fetish priest," he explained. I pictured an elaborate carving, perhaps a giant totemic mask, with froglike features and a head of wild, fleecy hair.

"People offer fowl to the fetish, and then they ask it for something," he continued. "For example, if your daughter is sick with malaria, or if your mother's feet have swollen up, then you can ask the fetish to cure them. Unless it is their time to die. If it is their time the fetish can do nothing. You too may ask for something. But first you must purchase a fowl."

"Oh, I don't think we'll do the fowl," I said.

"You must sacrifice!" His eyes widened in surprise.

"We just want to look," I explained. "We aren't going to ask it for anything."

"We don't want to watch a fowl being killed," Katie chimed in, with a note of distaste.

"You don't want to watch?" The young man looked perplexed.

"We'll give some money instead," I said.

"Really," said Katie, holding out another 200-cedi note, "won't money be enough?"

We set off on the steep trail. The air was filled with fine dust, which clung to our hair and clothes, got in our eyes, and made us cough. After a half-hour or so, we came to a clearing that looked out on an enormous valley. Scrub, rock, and a few scattered villages stretched out beneath us as far as the eye could see. In the sudden quiet that arose in the wake of our crunching feet, I heard doves shurring deep in their throats and another bird repeating a three-note hiccuping tune.

Panting and red-faced, Katie and I collapsed on the rocks, while the old men chuckled.

"Here you remove shirt and shoes," said the chief's nephew.

"What?" we squeaked in unison.

The men began unbuttoning their frayed cotton shirts, hanging them delicately over the rocks.

"It is the custom," he said, smiling at our amazement. "To respect the spirit and show that we are humble. All tourists do this," he reassured us. "Many white ladies. No problem."

"Excuse us a moment," I said.

We turned our backs to confer.

"Breasts are desexualized here," I whispered to Katie. "You've seen the women in the villages. Besides, what's gonna happen?"

She glanced over her shoulder at the old men. "True."

I raised my eyebrows. She shrugged.

"Carpe diem," I said, pulling my T-shirt over my head.

"How California," she said dryly.

I stood for a moment in my newly unclothed state while a light breeze raised the hair on my arms.

"What about this?" asked the nephew, indicating our bras.

Katie stared at me.

"No," I said.

This hung in the air a minute.

"As you wish," he said coldly.

"What happened to 'carpe diem'?" Katie whispered as we scrambled upward, avoiding thistles and scree. Our toes clung to the bare rocks. Soon it was so steep we were forced to use our hands. I imagined the spirits looking down with amused tolerance on our band of pilgrims: two skinny white girls in sensible brassieres, a clean-cut African youth, and a gaggle of ancient men.

"Is it much farther?" I gasped, pausing to stanch some blood that was dripping from my knee.

"Shhh," said the nephew. "You must crouch here." He indicated an overhanging rock that led into a deep cavern, gaping like the mouth of some petrified beast. "He is there."

On hands and knees, we crawled below the lip of the rock. We blinked in the sudden shadow, trying to make out the shapes.

Then I saw him. An emaciated man, wearing only a loincloth, crouched deep in the crevice like a bird jealously guarding its egg. Next to him were piles of bones and feathers higher than his head. His bloodshot eyes locked with mine. I looked around for a statue.

"Where's the fetish?" I whispered to the chief's nephew.

"The fetish is underneath the offerings." He indicated the pile of debris. "This man is the fetish priest, the spirit's human contact."

"He's so thin!" I said.

"The spirit takes all his energy," he replied. "Anything he eats, it takes most."

I gaped at the man. I'd expected artifice, ceremony—a symbolic connection to the spirits, not a literal one. Not a tiny, fragile human being, staring at me with the ravaged gaze of a prisoner of war.

"Would you like to snap?" the nephew asked.

I asked, taken aback, "He won't mind?"

"Please. You are our guests."

I hesitated. The man's eyes held mine, and their expression seemed to change every moment: now accusatory, now curious, now sad. Yet as intense as his gaze was, I wasn't sure he really saw me. At times he seemed to look through me, as though connecting with someone who stood just behind. Was I witnessing madness, or was he genuinely channeling an otherworldly force? Goose bumps rose slowly and acutely all over my flesh.

"Please," the nephew said impatiently, gesturing toward my camera. Slowly, I raised it.

The little man winced at the blitz. Afterward he looked stunned, shaken. His eyes found mine again, and this time his expression was clear and personal. Betrayal. A powerful sense of shame flooded through me, as though I'd been caught hiding in someone's closet, watching him make love. I'd intruded on an intimacy and cheapened it with my gaze.

"Please, some small money for the fetish priest," the nephew said. He glanced at his watch, a gesture I'd rarely seen in Africa.

Katie handed the nephew a bill. He handed it to the man in the cave, who snatched it hungrily, his lips still moving.

"We go now?" said the nephew.

◈

"Are you all right?" Katie asked me, as we made our way down.

"Sure," I said. But I wasn't. Sure, that is.

After a few minutes back in the hard sunlight, it was easy to persuade myself I had imagined the look of betrayal. I told myself it had all been part of the show.

When we reached the clearing, the men retrieved their shirts, threadbare but neatly hung, while we picked the thorns out of ours, which lay in a careless heap.

"Please, some small money for the elders," said the nephew sweetly.

"Oh, come on," said Katie.

"They climbed all this way to assist you. They must have money to buy kola nuts, and—"

"Kola nuts?" I said, jolted out of my reverie. "Why, it just so happens that we have some kola nuts!"

"And tobacco. They must also buy tobacco."

But I was busy pulling the bundle from my daypack. A few nuts had fallen out, and they rattled loosely in the bottom of the pack. "Kola nuts," I crowed, handing him the banana leaf. I fished around in my pocket. "And 200 cedis."

"You must give 1,000 cedis. You see we are many. You didn't even bring a fowl." He looked genuinely annoyed.

"I need to save something for the *tro-tro* to Bolga," I said. This may have been true—without going through my pockets, I couldn't be sure.

Disgruntled, they conferred briefly, in low tones. We waited uneasily for the verdict.

"We go now." The nephew's face was blank.

"They keep springing it on you," I said to Katie as we descended. "It's not so much the amount. Because if you convert it . . ."

"If you go converting things, your holiday will last weeks instead of months," she said firmly.

Just then I stumbled over a rock, pitching forward.

One of the old men spun around with amazing agility, catching me in his ropy arms.

"Sorry!" he exclaimed.

"Thanks," I mumbled gruffly.

Back at the compound, we woke our guide. The sun was dropping fast, and we didn't want to miss the last transport.

"Safe journey," the nephew called after us as we left.

When we reached the public square in Tongo, I handed our guide the 1,000 cedis we'd agreed upon. His face lit up as though he'd witnessed a miracle. Had he thought we wouldn't pay him?

"God bless you. God bless you," he said.

"Thank you," I said. "We had a good time."

The sun hovered on the horizon as we watched our guide disappear nimbly up the trail. In the square, a man sat at a table displaying three packs of cigarettes and a few pieces of chewing gum and hard candy. A woman fried triangular chunks of yam over a small fire. When we asked about transport back to Bol-gatanga, they shook their heads.

"Gone," they said.

"Well," I said to Katie, "what should we do?"

"We could try to spend the night here," she suggested doubt-fully.

We looked around at the cluster of mud huts. I'd enjoyed Ghanaians' extraordinary hospitality countless times over the six months I'd been here. So many people had opened their homes to me unquestioningly, asking nothing in return. But tourism had changed the Tongo Hills area. Too many foreigners had walked through with their cameras, snapping up pieces of the villagers' lives. Now they wanted something in exchange for what they gave.

The image of the tiny man flashed through my head. Some-where above our heads he crouched, gazing through stone with those raw, tormented eyes. Whatever was going on around him, his was no performance.

"We could walk to Bolga," I said quickly.

Katie protested, "It's nineteen kilometers."

"What doesn't kill us makes us stronger?"

"Unless it maims us," Katie said. "Carpe diem, cliché queen."

We started down the dirt road. The view looked just like Africa in the movies: low, flat-topped trees silhouetted against an enormous red disc. But this wasn't a movie. Happy endings were not guaranteed.

"Katie," I said, "did we do something wrong?"

"I don't know," she said, putting a hand on my arm.

A tiny lump at the bottom of my pack bounced against my spine. I took the pack off and removed the shining globe. It glowed orange, reflecting the dying light. I pulled out my Swiss army knife and split the nut, revealing pinkish innards. I handed Katie half and took a small nibble myself. It was dry and bitter.

"Delicious," I said.

"Yuck," said Katie. "I see why the chief prefers cash."

9

Appetite

On the bus to Kumasi, we meet a university student. I ask him what he thinks about Ghana's future—whether things will get better or worse. He tells me it depends on whether or not the college graduates stick around and develop new industry. The vast majority of educated people want to leave, he says, because they can get a better job and make more money elsewhere, but there will only be more and better jobs in Ghana in the future if they stay and create them. They need to have a vision for the country that goes beyond themselves and their families. They have to be patriotic, to sacrifice.

"What about you?" asks Katie. "Would you leave the country if you had the chance?"

"Myself, yes," he says, without hesitation.

"Even though you think the only hope for the country is if educated people such as yourself stay?" I ask in surprise.

He nods, slightly sheepish.

I ask him if he'd look back from his life in the U.S. or Holland or England. Would he lobby for better policies toward Africa? Work for fair trade?

"Yes," he says quickly, happy for the chance to redeem himself. "Yes, I would be an activist." He pauses. "Do you like that?"

Peter J. Obeng, nicknamed Bengo, was the hungriest man I'd ever met. Bony and brilliant, fingers drumming, knee bouncing, he pulsated like a scrappy star, sucking in every shred of light from those around him and muscling it out again, blinding hot. Circling in his orbit was a slight, smooth-faced young man named Kojo, handsome to the point of beauty, who matched Bengo's rapacious incandescence with a slow-burning charisma of his own.

Katie and I were spending a few days in Kumasi, capital of the Ashanti region and the second city of Ghana, on our way back to Accra. Once the seat of power for a vast Ashanti kingdom, Kumasi is now a modern city with a population of 1.5 million people. Surrounded by lush wooded hills, it is a center of culture and learning. One bright yellow morning, while Katie headed for the museums and the *kente* weavers, I dropped by the University of Science and Technology to visit Gorbachev's cousin Stephen, whom I had met, briefly, at his family's home in Accra. I had been in Stephen's dorm room less than five minutes when two faces appeared in the open doorway.

"*Ko ko,*" said Kojo politely, voicing the Ghanaian equivalent of "knock knock."

"How do you know her name?" Stephen asked.

"Pardon?" said Kojo.

"This is Sistah Korkor," said Stephen, indicating me. "So you must say, '*ko ko, Korkor.*'" He giggled at his own joke.

"Is she Ghana born?" Bengo broke in, incredulous.

"She is not Ghana born, but she has received a Ghana name," said Stephen, smiling. "Is there some problem?"

Now it was Bengo's turn to laugh. "Surely there is no problem, brothah. Only you surprised me. We have heard that you have a visitor from the United States of America."

"Information circulates so quickly," said Stephen. He turned to me. "Sistah Korkor, I present to you my brothahs of the university. Brothah Bengo studies economics and development planning and will one day be president of Ghana here, if not of the whole world. And Brothah Kojo, who studies language and literature, will one day be a learned professor and writer of books."

"I'm honored." I extended my hand.

Bengo's long, knobby fingers grasped mine with surprising force. His eyes were conspiratorial, as though we shared a thrilling secret.

"Sistah Korkor! This will be a very profitable friendship for the two of us."

As it happened, Stephen was on his way to class. With effusive apologies, he explained to me that I had come on the one day of the entire semester on which he had no time to spend with me. He had classes and appointments scheduled back-to-back and would not return to his dorm until nine o'clock that night.

"If you have some hours to spend on campus here, Kojo and I will be very pleased to be your guides," said Bengo.

❖

The Kwame Nkrumah University of Science and Technology occupies a luxurious seven square miles of land, a quick twenty-minute *tro-tro* ride from Kumasi. The campus is elegantly laid out, with vast green lawns and brightly flowering tropical plants.

The buildings are sleek and modern. We strolled through the botanical gardens, the air rich with the musky aroma of blooms just past their prime. As we wandered the tree-lined paths of the campus, taking in a sculpture garden, a science lab, and an art studio, Bengo kept up a running commentary on the university's history: when the buildings were constructed, illustrious gradu-ates, visiting professors and dignitaries. I nodded and smiled, paying scant attention, enjoying the sensation of the sun on my arms and the nearness of these two handsome men.

After my tour was completed, Bengo invited me back to the dormitory for conversation.

"I would like very much to air my views on many subjects, and to have an opportunity to learn yours," he said.

On our way back to the dorm we stopped at a stand selling minerals. I selected an icy Pee Cola, and Bengo and Kojo got orange Fantas. When I tried to pay, Kojo spoke up for the first time, insisting that I was their guest. We carried our icy drinks up to their bedroom, where they turned on an overhead fan. I sat in a corner chair in the cramped space—similar to my own college dorm room, but slightly smaller—while they perched on their respective twin beds.

"Now," Bengo said eagerly, as soon as we were seated. "Tell me every single thing about the United States of America. Omit no item, large or small."

I laughed. "That's a daunting task."

Bengo did not laugh with me, but simply gazed at me like a scientist observing a chemical reaction, his eyes alert with expectation.

"Well," I began, "it's a large country, very diverse . . ."

Time disappeared in their room. I sat talking with the two of them while outside the small window day turned to dusk turned to night. Sometimes it felt like I was being pounded by a heavy shower, an unrelenting flow. Bengo had a vast inner storehouse of Americana that ranged from the trivial to the profound. This included entire memorized speeches by Martin Luther King Jr., Abraham Lincoln, and John F. Kennedy, as well as the populations, geographic features, and chief industries of all fifty states. There were few facts about the United States of America he didn't already know, and none he didn't want to learn.

But as broad as his interests were, there were certain questions he kept returning to; they nagged at him like mosquito bites.

"What about the black man there?" he asked me at least five times over the course of the day. "Are things improving for him, or are they actually getting worse?"

"That's a big question," I'd begin, and we'd be off and running: Martin Luther King Jr., Marcus Garvey, Malcolm X, Louis Farrakhan, James Baldwin, Muhammad Ali, Mike Tyson, Michael Jackson, Mumia Abu-Jamal, Clarence Thomas, Rodney King, the gains of the civil rights movement, rumors of the CIA planting drugs in poor neighborhoods, black separatism, affirmative action. The breadth of his knowledge took my breath away. How had he gleaned all this information? Even in Accra, the capital, I'd had trouble staying on top of the most basic current events. He must have spent every waking moment searching out reading material and devouring it.

Bengo's politics were eclectic. He was willing to consider any perspective: left, right, or center—consistency was no object. He liked to try opinions on for size. He argued strenuously for the virtues of creating an independent black nation within the U.S., as Nadhiri had done, then turned right around and declared it impractical. In discussing the rights of racist groups to march and organize, he made an eloquent case for uncompromising adherence to the First Amendment, then contended that certain types of speech did not deserve protection.

"But what do *you* believe?" I asked him again and again. "You've just effectively argued both sides. What's your actual opinion?"

He grinned mischievously. "I would not be a good politician if I told you, eh?"

"Come on."

"I have not yet perfected my views on these subjects. I am gathering evidence."

"Do you really want to go into politics?"

"Oh yes."

"Why?"

"Because I trust that when I do form opinions, they will be sound and well-balanced. I am a reasonable man, and reasonable men must govern if Africa is to move forward in the new century. I will never let my personal emotions stand in the way of my judgment."

"You mean you are ruthless," said Kojo quietly.

"I mean I am capable of doing what needs to be done. I have every confidence in myself."

But despite his avowed openness, Bengo had a strong streak of the bootstrap conservative in him. His father was a wealthy merchant with more than twenty wives. At nine years old, Bengo had gotten sick and missed so much school that he was held back a year. His father considered this a disgrace and refused to pay his school fees from that time on. In order to continue studying, Bengo became resourceful, growing vegetables behind his mother's hut and selling them in nearby villages. He cultivated his running skills and delivered messages for the village women, sometimes over great distances. In this way, he paid his own school fees until he finished high school and was awarded a scholarship to the university.

"You see?" he said to me. "I did it all myself. Why do people need handouts? When I hear those in Ghana here who say they can find no means to educate themselves, I think they are simply lazy."

I groaned. "Bengo, look at yourself. You are not an average person. You're not even an above average person. You're a phenomenon. You have the intellect of a Nobel scientist and the stamina of an Olympic athlete. Someone shouldn't have to be you to get an education. And besides, you did have certain advantages. You had to pay your own school fees, but you didn't have to sell gum on the street corner to eat, like some of these kids. You didn't suffer from malnutrition. As it stands now, the main factor in getting a decent education, both here and in the U.S., is money. It's ridiculous. Everyone deserves a shot."

Bengo thought about this for a moment, then he began to chuckle. "He shouldn't have to be me, eh? Well, perhaps you have a point."

Bengo was the first true atheist I'd met in Ghana. In his commitment to atheism he reminded me of my mother, a statistician so convinced of the absence of God that she smirks at the suggestion of belief. Although Kojo claimed to be an atheist like Bengo, he did feel that there was more to Ghanaian life than met the eye. Committed as most Ghanaians were to Christianity, he said, every village still had a fetish priest, and these men wielded a great deal of power.

"If someone is in line for a promotion ahead of you," said Kojo, "and you want to stop him, the fetish priest can help you to do this. Many of them will use their power for evil as well as good, if you pay them enough money."

"How could he prevent the promotion?" I asked.

"He can cause the man to drop dead."

"Surely he cannot do this," Bengo scoffed, "unless he spices the man's soup with poison."

"He can do it by calling out the demons," said Kojo.

"So you believe there are demons?" I asked.

"I don't believe in them," said Kojo quickly, "but they exist."

"Eh!" shouted Bengo. "Stop with all this. You will give a bad impression to our American friend."

"You cannot tell me what I have and have not seen," said Kojo, flaring. "I have seen a small girl vomiting frogs."

"This is a trick," said Bengo angrily. "Primitive superstition. Something that civilized people cannot accept."

"I said I do not believe in it myself," said Kojo, backing down beneath Bengo's stare. He remained silent for a long moment, his mouth and forehead working as though he were engaging in a strenuous inner dialogue. Then he added, with quiet dignity, "But the fact remains that I have seen it."

"Why is there so much divorce in your country?" Bengo asked me later. This question had come up so often in Ghana that I'd developed a fairly elaborate response. I delivered my spiel about the individualism inherent in American culture, the way our families and communities didn't hold couples together the way they did in Ghana. I talked as well about the Hollywood-style expectations of love I'd grown up with.

"We don't get into relationships expecting to have to toil over them," I told him. "We expect them to come ready-made. When things get too rough, we just persuade ourselves we've picked the wrong person and start looking for someone else."

"Eh!" said Bengo. "You must be a sociologist! You understand this phenomenon very well."

I smiled wanly. Ah, irony. I knew the ills of my society like I knew the smell of my own sweat. But at twenty-seven years of age, my longest relationship by far was the one with Michael, and we'd lived together for exactly two years. No matter how I might rail against rugged individualism and overblown romantic expectation, I was a prime example of both.

"What do you think of these interracial couples?" asked Bengo.

"I think people should marry whomever they want," I said.

"I wholeheartedly agree," he said. "Whichever woman a man wishes to marry, he should do so." He paused for a moment, then asked pointedly, "Don't you think so, Kojo?"

"I think that in marriage, a person should choose among those who understand him best," said Kojo, staring at him evenly.

"There are still some small-minded villagers who feel that a man must stay within his tribe, that Ashanti must marry Ashanti," said Bengo.

Bengo and Kojo were both Ashanti, as were a high percentage of Ghana's political and economic elite. Although I was light-years from understanding Ghana's complex tribal histories, I saw that the Ashanti as a group garnered both respect and resentment. Long ago, they had sold other tribes into slavery.

"This attitude is small-minded," Bengo continued. "I myself will marry an intelligent woman. I do not care whether she is Ashanti or not. I do not even care whether she is black! I care only that she is educated and that we can talk to one another as equals." He looked at me with those laser-bright eyes of his, and I felt my face grow hot. Kojo, too, was watching me with an unpleasant expression on his face.

"What do you think, Sistah Korkor?" Bengo asked.

"Well, it's complicated," I said, stammering a little. "As I said, I think people should marry whomever they choose, regardless of race or nationality . . . or gender," I added. Kojo looked startled. He glanced at Bengo, whose face was blank.

"But I do think cross-cultural marriages can be challenging," I continued. "If I were to marry a Ghanaian, for example, we would each come to the relationship with certain expectations about what a partnership between a man and a woman means—anything from who is expected to do the cooking and cleaning to how we handle our finances to how we raise a child. My boyfriend in the U.S. is Chicano—his parents are Mexican, but he grew up in the States—and even there, there are challenges. I'm not saying it can't work, just . . ." I stopped, feeling a pang of emptiness. I'd called Michael my boyfriend. But what should I have called him? My former boyfriend for whom my feelings remained suspended in a state of hellish limbo?

Bengo started to say something, but Kojo interrupted.

"Gender, you say," he said cautiously. "Is it true that there are those in the United States who believe that two males or two females should be permitted to marry each other?"

"Oh, sure," I said. "Lots of people. Not the majority yet, but more and more. Certain employers are already providing bene-fits to partners of the same sex who live together."

"This is not wise," Bengo said sternly. "It will cause the breakdown of the social order. It is against nature." He looked directly at Kojo as he spoke the final sentence.

"Now you sound like the Pope," I said lightly, looking from one to the other. Their eyes were locked in some kind of stare-down, which Bengo broke to respond to my remark.

"This is not religion; this is science. If men married men and women married women the human race would die out. Charles Darwin has shown that our instinct is to continue the species. If you go against nature, things will not go well for you." His tone was hard.

"I might argue that all human behavior is natural," I said. "We are, after all, animals. So anything humans do comes from our own natural urges. We don't manufacture our desires." I paused and glanced at Kojo, who appeared to be examining his navy blue bedspread with intent interest. "Isn't there a movement for gay rights here in Ghana?" I asked.

Bengo shook his head vigorously. "No. There is never a movement. There may be some rumor of a young boy, in school, who has made some experiment with another boy, but he will never boast of it. He will deny it every day."

Later on, Bengo briefly excused himself and left the room. Kojo and I sat for a couple of minutes in a deepening silence. Suddenly he drew in his breath and spoke, in a soft, furtive tone that was almost a whisper.

"You live in San Francisco?"

"In the area, yes."

"I have heard . . ." his voice trailed off. He glanced quickly at the door.

"Yes?" I said encouragingly.

"I have heard that there are very many, very many of . . . of those men and women who . . ." he swallowed, closed his eyes, pressed his palms tightly together.

"Yes," I said, "There are. Very many. A whole community."

His eyes met mine, then, for a quick moment. "And they can live there, as they are, openly?" His tone was querulous, disbelieving.

"Yes, they can." I looked at Kojo's smooth face, struggling to contain my curiosity. "You and Bengo," I said suddenly, "are you lovers?"

Kojo looked at me in terror. I was immediately sorry I'd asked. I heard Bengo's step in the hallway.

He shook his head violently. "Please," he whispered.

I shook my head too, to reassure him, placing a finger to my lips.

We had returned from our campus tour at noon. Now my watch said seven o'clock. Other than Bengo's brief departure, we hadn't stirred from our perches in many hours. I was dizzy and exhausted. My stomach was growling so loudly I was sure they could hear it. Kojo, too, appeared drained. Since our conversation he hadn't spoken a word, and in fact seemed to have sunk into a kind of catatonia, staring blankly into space. Bengo, however, showed no sign of tiring. His eyes gleamed as he pumped me for details about the U.S. He was debating the highs and lows of Richard Nixon's career when I finally spoke up.

"Bengo—" I interrupted.

"Yes?"

"I'm hungry."

"What?" Kojo stirred from his lethargy.

"Please . . . I'd like to get something to eat. Is it time for dinner, do you think?"

Bengo started laughing. "Oh, my goodness," he gasped. "Our guest, we have overlooked. We have forgotten to feed her."

Kojo looked at him reproachfully.

"This is not funny," he said. "This is shameful. We must apologize. We were simply so eager for your words that we have forgotten everything else."

"Oh, no, it's no big deal. I was just thinking, you know, maybe we could get something . . . before the stands close down."

"Oh," said Kojo, "This is terrible. We become so absorbed. We forget entirely what is right."

He went to a shelf and pulled down a tin of fish from a small stack.

"This we have," he said. "We have only to buy some *kenke* and pepper sauce to accompany it."

We walked a couple of blocks to where a lone man stood at a table beneath a streetlight. Once back in the room, Kojo opened the tin of fish while Bengo brought out a small folding table.

"Is this okay?" said Kojo, anxiously. "Will you have enough?"

"Oh sure, plenty," I said, although I wasn't sure at all.

There was a momentary silence as we pulled apart our balls of *kenke* and dipped the pieces into the pepper sauce. I ate slowly, trying to stretch out the experience.

"Do you guys normally eat dinner later, or . . . ?"

"We are not so conscious about food," said Bengo. "Sometimes we will eat twice in a day, and sometimes only once. For myself, I try to conserve funds, for books. I am not so concerned with hunger. I have more important concerns," he smiled. "Like talking to my new American friend."

"Of course," said Kojo. "Why should you be concerned for her stomach? You have no concern for anyone's appetite but your own."

Bengo looked at him coldly. Then he gave me an uneasy smile.

"I am sorry for your hunger," he said

"Oh! Not at all," I said, embarrassed. I looked quickly from one to the other, wiping my mouth with the back of my hand.

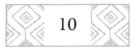

The Children of Afranguah

I'm sitting on a step watching a three-year-old boy play in a muddy yard. He is a perpetual motion machine: jumping and spinning, shirt over his head, chubby tummy exposed. He falls to the ground, rolls around, climbs the steps and jumps off again, stomps his foot in a puddle. He's been playing on his own for almost an hour now, with no sign of slowing down. Everything is exciting to him, every action a science experiment. If he stands on a step and inches backward, how far can he go before he tumbles off? How small a part of his foot will support him? How high can he get the puddle to splash?

I can't help thinking of a three-year-old boy I knew in California, the son of a friend. The last time I was at their house, he ran through the living room in his cowboy suit brandishing toy guns, then ran out into the yard and drove his plastic car around a toy filling station, came back in and colored with his magic markers, changed into his Ninja eye patch and cape, and then cried that he was bored and needed something to do.

❖

Bengo and Kojo were eager to take me sightseeing, but Katie and I wanted to get on the road. As compelling as my time with the two men had been, I wasn't sure I had the stamina for another day in their presence. Later, back in the States, I received a letter from Bengo, proposing marriage. He was in graduate school now, he said, and would soon be moving into a government job that would allow him sufficient income to begin a family. He said he'd never forgotten our conversation that day in Kumasi. He longed for a wife he could hold such frank discourse with, on so many topics. Ghanaian women, he complained, thought only of their hair and their clothes. I wrote him back, saying I was honored that he'd thought of me, but I was hesitant to start an involvement at such a distance. I couldn't see myself making it back to Ghana anytime soon, I told him, and I wasn't ready to commit based solely on the information we already had. I asked him how Kojo was doing, whether he was in graduate school as well.

Bengo responded graciously to my letter, saying that he'd always known I was practical and wise. Kojo, he said, had married a German girl and moved to Berlin. He had not written to Bengo, but Bengo had heard from a mutual friend that Kojo had abandoned his studies and was selling African beads on the street.

After leaving Kumasi, Katie and I decided to take a detour before returning to Accra. We wanted to spend a week in the village of Afranguah, the site of our first work camp. We missed the children there. There had been other villages, and other children, but these particular kids remained sharply etched in our memories. There was Yao, of course, but also Essi, Abba, Baba, Kwesi, Kwabena, Efuwe, Kukue, Mansah, and countless others. They danced in my mind: their skinny legs and radiant faces, their tiny hands clinging to my fingers, tentatively stroking my inner arm to see what white skin felt like. At once shy and bold, impossibly eager, achingly open, they darted and danced and laughed and sang, parroting English words and teaching me Fanti ones. Katie and I wondered aloud whether they would remember us. They were children, after all, and several months had passed.

The moment we stepped off the *tro-tro* from Saltpond Junction, a swarm of little bodies engulfed us, all of them hugging and cheering and jumping up and down. How had they gathered so quickly? I wondered. It seemed impossible, unless someone from the junction had run ahead to tip them off. The village minister, Billy Akwah Graham, had extended an invitation to the foreign volunteers to stay in his home whenever we chose to visit. Now the children insisted on carrying our luggage to Billy's house. Our overstuffed backpacks rode above their heads, hoisted by six or eight little arms like chief's palanquins. As we walked through town, women stood in doorways, shouting their salutations. Ama Akrabba, the village grandmother, ran from her house, beaming a toothless smile, to crush me in her leathery arms. Even the slacker men who hung out streetside, drinking *apeteshi* all day long, called out *"Eh! Obroni!"* grinning and waving.

Billy Akwah Graham had the largest and nicest house in town. Made of cinder blocks and stucco and painted a clean white with blue wooden shutters, it sat on a hill at a slight distance from the other houses. While extended families often shared a single room, Billy's home actually had extra rooms, entire unoccupied spaces surrounded by walls. He was a Ghanaian anomaly: a financially solvent rural bachelor in his thirties. He shared the house with his adolescent nephew Kofi. When recent college graduates came to Afranguah from Accra or

Kumasi to fulfill their national service requirement by teaching in the school, they, too, stayed in Billy Akwah Graham's guest rooms. Someday they would stay in the teachers' quarters our association had begun to build, but for now they remained with Billy, sometimes for as long as a year or two.

Billy was a dapper, bird-boned man, always impeccably dressed in Western clothes. Although I had stayed in his house once before, when I returned to the village to visit Yao, I had never developed a sense of ease with him. He'd spent a fair amount of time around our construction site, conversing with the camp leader and the home secretary, but I'd never seen him lift a brick. He moved in the world with the practiced, sunny air of a politician, smiling and shaking hands, spouting vague, optimistic statements.

It was unclear to me whether Billy had a prior arrangement with the association or had simply befriended the camp leader. In either case, it was soon established that he would oversee the completion of our project by the villagers once our group had left, and that he would communicate any additional need for supplies to the office in Accra. It was he, as well, who would administer the sponsorship of children's school fees, a project which originated with our brigade. Twelve or fourteen of the foreign volunteers, Katie and myself included, had agreed to take on the yearly fees of a school-aged child through the completion of high school. The fees were nominal to us, along the order of forty dollars a year, but enormous to the villagers. Billy chose the families and matched children to volunteers. The yearly checks would be filtered through him, since most of the families had neither bank accounts nor post office boxes, and he would supply the volunteers with updates and photographs of the sponsored children.

When we arrived at Billy's house, he stepped outside the door, extending his arms in welcome. His nephew, Kofi, stood slightly behind him, smiling shyly. Kofi was fourteen years old and, like his uncle, always perfectly groomed. He had occasionally accompanied Billy on his visits to the construction site, but I'd never heard him speak. He'd simply stood there in his school uniform, watching.

Billy gestured for us to enter the house, shooing the children away. They backed up twenty or thirty yards and remained there, wide-eyed, bearing witness. He shouted for them to be gone, and they backed up a little farther and settled down to play in the dirt. Exasperated, he was about to shout again, but abruptly changed his mind and ushered us inside. The living room was simple and spare—a couch and a low table on a bare cement floor, no decoration of any kind.

"You must stay as long as you like!" said Billy effusively, "one month I hope, maybe two."

"You're very kind," said Katie.

"Yes, thank you," I added, "but we'll be here four or five days at the most. We really just wanted to see everybody again. How's the construction going?"

"Oh . . . very slow," said Billy. "I try to make these people work, but for no money, they do not want to do anything. I tell them, this is for you, so that your children may be educated. They think that if they wait, the foreigners will return and finish the job."

I nodded and sighed. Afranguah was one of the few places where I'd felt reasonably confident that the work we began would eventually be finished. I didn't envy Billy's role in the process, though. Getting people to donate their labor was a difficult task anywhere in the world, whether it was in their own interest or not.

Kofi showed us to our room. He stood by as we began to unpack, watching our every motion with a shy, eager look.

"Are you in school, Kofi?" Katie asked.

"Yes, in Saltpond. I finish in two years."

"And what would you like to do then?" I asked.

"I would like to attend University," he said, "if only I could find the funds."

"Surely your uncle will help you," I said.

"It is too great a cost for him. He wishes me to acquire a foreign sponsor," he said demurely, looking at his hands.

◈

The days went quickly. We spent them with the children, sitting on the steps of Billy's house when he was out, playing clapping games, braiding hair, trading Fanti and English words. One of our favorite activities was a verb game in which we took turns giving each other orders in Fanti. The children would call out words like "cry," "laugh," "dig," or "dance," and Katie and I would act them out, prompting wild laughter. Then we'd switch and have twenty criers, dancers, and laughers going at it with gusto in response to our commands.

Every day I dropped in to see Yao. He was crawling now, and he'd acquired a couple of single syllable words, which he shouted upon occasion. It was wonderful to see him healthy, his extraordinary eyes alight with intelligence. Although he didn't remember me, we soon renewed our friendship, and he would climb straight into my lap when I arrived.

Repairing things with Minessi was not so easy. Although the tensions between us had eased, our relationship lacked the camaraderie of our early days. I tried to initiate a conversation with her about the hospital, asking her if I had done something to make her angry, but she either didn't understand or didn't want to engage. I soon abandoned the effort. Because of the strain, my daily visits were much shorter than they had once been.

The other children followed Katie and me around every moment that they were not in school or asleep, which for the littlest ones meant every moment of daylight. Among the company were Minessi's neighbor Amoah's three children: Baba, Kwesi, and Essi, and his niece, Mansah. Eight-year-old Baba had a smile that could light a dark cave to its unknown corners. With her laughing eyes and wide, flexible mouth, her entire face reflected an irrepressible joy that was absolutely contagious—you had to smile back. She was quick, too, remembering English words with astonishing precision. She never seemed to forget anything, from songs and phrases to hand gestures and dance steps.

Baba was the primary caretaker of her one-year-old sister Essi and her three-year-old brother Kwesi. Essi rode most of the day in a sling on Baba's narrow back, while grave-eyed, dimpled Kwesi toddled beside her, hanging onto her arm as though it were a life buoy and the world a lake. Ten-year-old Mansah was more reserved. She was upright and slender as the millet stalks in the fields outside of town, her face long and foxlike, with the kind of elegant bone structure that telegraphs the shape of the adult face to come. She supervised her younger cousins like a cautious mother, the sober counterweight to Baba's bubbling exuberance.

Also among our youthful entourage was thirteen-year-old Essi Abokoma, my personal sponsoree and language instructor. Essi Abokoma had luminous almond eyes and a deep, resonant voice, which consistently surprised me when it emanated from her small frame. Whenever she shouted I jumped a little, and this soon became a running joke between us. When she wasn't at school, she spent hours pointing things out to me, patiently repeating their Fanti names, then painstakingly copying them out for me in my notebook.

At the end of a child-filled day, Katie and I were usually exhausted. A woman came in to prepare Billy's meals, and we got into the habit of eating with him. Afterwards Katie and I would retire to our room to read and rest. On the second night, Kofi followed us, standing silently in a corner of the room.

"Can I help you with something, Kofi?" I asked, after a minute or two had passed.

He picked a pair of pink-framed plastic sunglasses from the top of my open backpack.

"You give me these," he said.

"I'm sorry, Kofi, but I need those."

He then picked up my straw sunhat, which was perched on the floor beside the pack. "You give me this."

"Kofi . . . I need that too."

"You give me this," he said, pulling out a T-shirt.

"Kofi, I'm not comfortable with you asking me for things in

that way," I said. He nodded, then stood staring down at the backpack, saying nothing.

"Korkor and I are very tired, Kofi," Katie said after another awkward moment had passed.

With a small, strange smile, he left the room.

◈

Kofi hovered around us whenever we were at the house together. He carried the water for our baths, heated it on the stove, made tea for us, poured the milk and sugar, sliced the bread for our breakfast. As with Christy, we asked him to stop, to allow us to do things for ourselves. Katie and I felt much more at ease in the house once he had left for school. Every evening when he returned, he followed us into our rooms and began the low, steady litany: *You give me this, you give me these.* He pushed us to the limits of our patience, then slipped away.

As usual, I was in a complete emotional tangle about how to respond to Kofi's demands. We were guests in his home, and the objects were certainly replaceable. But though I knew it wasn't my job to teach Kofi manners, I couldn't help resenting his demeanor. I thought of the way people in the U.S. complained about homeless people who were aggressive in their requests for change. "They're *hungry*," I'd often responded. "If you were hungry, you might not be so pleasant either."

But Kofi wasn't hungry. He wasn't even poor, by Ghanaian standards. He was just . . . Well, he was Ghanaian, and I was American. And an above-average Ghanaian enjoyed a vastly different level of wealth than a middle-class American, even a downwardly mobile one like myself.

Billy began to unnerve me as well. His mouth was locked in a perpetual smile that never seemed to reach his eyes, which were watchful and shrewd. One morning as Katie and I sat on the step outside his house, eating white bread and drinking tea, he came and sat down next to me.

"I want to come to America," he said.

"Eh *heh,*" I said noncommittally, offering the familiar Ghanaian exclamation.

"Will you welcome me?" he asked, watching me closely.

"Yes, of course," I answered mildly, looking away. I felt a twinge of apprehension. Ghanaian hospitality was so complete. All the people I'd stayed with had encouraged me to remain in their homes as long as I liked. They had provided meals and seemed to have limitless time at their disposal for my entertainment. Billy would undoubtedly expect the same treatment from me.

He continued watching me for some time while I stared straight ahead, chewing, trying to ignore the hot beam of his eyes. At last he turned to Katie. "What will you do when you return to England?" he asked.

"I'd like to go back to school and get a teaching certificate," she said.

"You are a teacher already, no?"

"Well, yes, I've been teaching art to mentally ill adults, but if I get certified, I'll be able to go for better jobs, at colleges and things."

"When you get that expensive job you will send me money," said Billy.

"Billy," Katie said gently, "that puts me in a difficult position."

"I simply meant that when you have more money, it will be more possible for you to help people," said Billy quickly, backpedaling. "That's how we are here in Ghana. If we have anything at all, we share it. We are very much interested in sacrificing ourselves to help our fellowman."

After being with Billy and Kofi, the company of the children was a positive relief. They seemed to genuinely want nothing more from us than to spend time in our presence. Unlike children in the cities, who grabbed at our clothing and possessions in much the same way Kofi did, they never asked us for anything at all.

◆

The day before we left, Katie and I went into Saltpond to purchase parting gifts for our cadre of kids. After looking around the market, we settled on brightly colored pencils and tablets of drawing paper. For Essi Abokoma, who had spent so much time teaching me Fanti, I bought a pair of sunglasses, since she had often admired mine. Reluctantly, we picked up a pair for Kofi as well. His behavior still drove us around the bend, but we didn't see how we could exclude him, given the lengths he and Billy had gone to for our comfort. For Billy we stocked up on foodstuffs both ordinary and special: bags of rice and tins of fish and condensed milk, palm oil and chilis and tomatoes.

That evening we gathered the children ceremoniously around us on the steps of Billy's house. Billy stepped outside to act as our interpreter.

"You know we're leaving tomorrow," Katie told them. "We've really enjoyed the time we've spent with you, and we wanted to give you a small gift to remember us by."

The children stood still and eager as Billy translated her words. They seemed to hold their collective breath. Katie pulled out the colored pencils and the tablets.

"There are enough of these for everyone to have five or six different colors," she began.

She was about to ask them to line up and make their choices, but before she could get the words out, the children flew into a kind of frenzy, grabbing at the pencils and the small notebooks.

Billy exhorted them to be calm, to no avail. The bigger ones intimidated the little ones, grabbing pencils from their hands. The mayhem continued for several minutes until Billy raised his voice in a deep, throaty shout. They settled down then, clutching their pencils and notebooks possessively, some of them glaring at others who seemed to have gotten more or better colors. A few of the littlest ones stood on the sidelines, wailing. Three-year-old Kwesi waved his empty fists furiously in the air. Katie and I exchanged alarmed glances.

"Maybe this wasn't such a good idea," I said.

"They are badly behaved children. It is shameful," said Billy fiercely, giving them the evil eye. "They only wish that I will not tell their parents how they behave."

"Oh, please don't," said Katie with alarm. "It was our fault."

Billy sniffed, frowning severely at the chastened children. He then commanded them sharply, in Fanti, and they began to disperse. I called to the older Essi to remain. I hadn't yet given her her present.

She followed me into the bedroom. When I handed her the sunglasses, she gave a little shriek of delight, then looked down in sudden shyness.

"Thank you, sistah," she said.

She turned, then, clutching her sunglasses, pencils, and notepad as if they were gold.

As I opened the door of our bedroom to let Essi out, Kofi came in. When he saw the sunglasses in her hand, his hand shot out to take them. Essi snatched them away, bellowing at him with her extraordinary voice. She ran from the house. Kofi strode over to my suitcase and began grabbing things, one after another: camera, T-shirt, notebook, hat. He recited his usual mantra, but faster now, more aggressively: *"You give me this, you give me this."*

"Stop it, Kofi," I said. "Stop it!"

He looked at me with a taunting expression, as though daring me to make a move. He continued methodically tucking the entire contents of my backpack under his arms.

"You give me this, you give me this."

I looked around for Katie, but she was not in the room. We'd planned to give Kofi his sunglasses tomorrow, just before we left, to surprise him.

"Kofi," I said, in a slow, even voice. "You put every one of those things back right this moment, or you will get nothing, do you understand me, nothing."

He stared at me defiantly.

"Are you challenging me?" I said, though I knew he didn't understand. "Because you will not win." I paused a moment. He stood frozen. Some things fell to the floor. "Do you want me to call Billy? What do you think he will say?"

Slowly, insolently, he lifted his arms. All the items tumbled down. He stepped over them and walked out of the room.

We got up early to finish packing. I asked Billy where we should toss our garbage.

"I will take care of it," he said. As I turned away, I saw him throw the tied-up plastic bag out the front door, into some low bushes at the side of the house.

When everything else was packed, Katie and I debated whether or not to give Kofi his sunglasses.

"We gave Billy all that food," said Katie.

"Yeah," I said. "But still . . . Billy knows we gave gifts to the other children. We've got to give Kofi something. I just can't stand to see him win, that smug little—"

"I know," Katie said. She sighed, "Well, let's leave the glasses with Billy. He can pass them on to Kofi after we've gone."

Fortunately, I didn't see Kofi that morning. He was already at school by the time we made it to the door, loaded down with our backpacks. We hugged Billy and thanked him profusely, promising to return someday.

"I will visit you!" he said, smiling his peculiar hollow smile. "And you will welcome me, my beloved sistahs."

We opened the door to an unexpected crowd. Our usual entourage of children had quadrupled in size. There were faces I recognized from the village and some that I didn't recognize at all. As we stepped out the door, a thicket of slender arms reached toward us, fingers outstretched.

"Pencil, pencil!" they called, a chorus of high, plaintive voices.

"Paper!" called a single voice. It sounded like pay-pah. They all took up the cry. *"Pay-pah! Pay-pah!"*

"Oh, God," I said to Katie. "What have we done?" A cliché sprang to my mind, something about the road to hell.

"Look," said Katie. "Some children are going through the rubbish."

I looked. At the side of the house, a cluster of children was ripping apart the plastic bag that held our trash, grabbing frantically at the contents. Bits of paper were scattered about the ground. Baba and a slightly older boy had their hands on an empty insect repellent bottle and were pulling back and forth, shouting furiously at each other. Little Essi was on Baba's back, and Kwesi sat on the ground, screaming. Then the boy Baba was struggling with saw a package of stale cookies and immediately let go of the bottle. He grabbed the package and ran, stuffing the cookies into his mouth. Several other children were examining some used sanitary pads.

Baba began rubbing the insect repellent onto her thin arms.

"Tell her that's poisonous," I said to Billy. "She shouldn't get it near her eyes or mouth."

Billy strode over and grabbed the bottle from Baba, speaking sharply to her.

"If you use this and something bites you it will have no effect on you?" he called to me.

"It's supposed to keep bugs away," I told him distractedly. "They don't like the smell."

He chuckled and shook his head, then rubbed a few drops onto his own knuckles.

"Goodbye, sistahs," he said absently, examining the plastic bottle. "Come again."

❖

The children followed us down the hill to the dusty road. We threw our backpacks on the ground and sat on them while we waited for a taxi to arrive. We didn't look at the children, or at each other. Their voices filled the air around us, *pencil, pencil, paper, paper.* They were still keening half an hour later as we climbed into the taxi and rode out of sight.

11

Another American

On each bus or tro-tro, there are two staff people: the driver and his assistant. The assistant acts as a barker, calling out the destination and enticing passersby, then shepherding the passengers onto the vehicle, collecting the money, and overseeing the baggage. These assistants are efficiency incarnate. Without a moment's hesitation, they assess your baggage and proclaim a charge: 200 cedis, 400, 1,000. With a flick of the finger they tell you it's your turn to pay up. A glance at the driver says, This van is full, let's go; another glance says, Slow down, there's a man running to catch up. They glide on and off the moving tro-tro, collecting passengers, paying tolls, making room.

I admire these fluid men: the grace of their ascents and descents, their willingness to hang halfway out the door to accommodate more passengers. In my imagination, they are not skinny, overworked youth in dangerous dead-end jobs, but high priests of the roadways, following a sacred calling passed down from father to son. They've caught the rhythm of the tro-tro, *and like any good artist, they make it look easy, like laughter, like rain.*

The day began with a sharp 5 A.M. rap on the door. Katie moaned from beneath her mosquito net. I stumbled out of my sleeping bag and through the door, clutching my gut. When I returned from the latrine, she was still lying there.

"Rise and shine, girlfriend," I said. "Bus leaves at five-thirty and look at this room."

As a final detour before returning to Accra, we'd spent a single night in the lodge at the Mole Game Reserve. There we'd exercised our unique talent for demolishing a space. Clothing, books, water bottles, and packets of malaria pills were scattered haphazardly across the cement floor. Our backpacks sat in opposite corners of the spacious room, spread-eagled and overflowing. The room looked as if a giant had picked it up and shaken it to make it snow.

Katie moaned again. "My stomach feels squidgy."

"You too? What'd we have last night?"

"Groundnut soup with rice balls." She stared at me flatly. "Seemed fine at the time."

"Should we stay another day?" We'd planned to arrive in Accra tonight, a journey that would require a host of bus and truck connections.

"Nooooo," she said, heaving herself into a sitting position. "Let's take this bus, anyway. Later we can decide if we want to keep going. This place is too dear."

Bleary-eyed, we picked our way toward the bus in the predawn darkness. We'd spent the previous day tromping through the dense undergrowth of the Game Reserve with a guide, looking for animals. It had rained a lot over the past week, and we inhaled the restorative scent of clean, wet earth. Our guide, Kwame, was a polite, self-effacing young man barely out of his teens. He had a round, dimpled face, large soft eyes, and a voice so quiet you had to lean close to hear his words. He seemed to feel personally responsible, both for the dearth of animal appearances and for the fact that an hour or so into our trek the sky saw fit to douse us with another downpour. Although we assured him that no one blamed him, he continued to apologize, disarming us with his dimpled grin. We withstood the rain as long as we could, then retreated to the lodge for tea, having seen exactly three long-legged antelope, two elephants (from so far away they look like rocks in my photos), and a plethora of colorful birds.

The bus out of Mole turned out to be one of the nicest buses I'd seen in Ghana. Its interior was shiny and clean, with cushioned vinyl seats. It was empty except for a few Ghanaians and another white woman sitting toward the back. Katie and I took separate seats and lay down to nap the trip away, roads permitting.

The bus began to roll silently, as though a handbrake had been released. Just as I began to wonder when they would fire the motor, I heard a man's voice shouting from outside the bus. The driver braked sharply, nearly throwing me off the seat. The driver opened the door, and Kwame boarded the bus, dressed in his Game Reserve uniform. He whispered something to the driver, who simply shrugged.

"Hi there," I said, smiling sleepily as Kwame walked past my seat. He nodded to me in a perfunctory, distracted way. Continuing to the back of the bus, he stopped at the second to last row, where the other white woman sat slumped in her seat.

"Miss," he said softly.

She remained motionless. He lightly placed a hand on her shoulder, to rouse her.

"Miss," he said again, slightly louder. Abruptly, she jumped back, knocking his hand away.

"Hey!" She let out a startled sound, somewhere between a shout and a snarl.

"I'm sorry to disturb you, miss," Kwame said gently.

"Then don't," she said, turning toward the window. Her accent was distinctly American, hard and flat.

"I don't wish to disturb you," he began again, "but I'm afraid you have not yet paid for your last night's room."

"I paid for it," she said, without looking at him. "Ask the guy at the desk."

"It is he who requested that I speak to you, miss," said Kwame.

"Why didn't he come himself?"

"He is still bathing."

"Well, he's a goddamn liar. I already paid for my fucking room."

Our small community of passengers, which had hitherto been too sleepy to take much of an interest in these goings-on, perked right up when it heard that. The five or six Ghanaian passengers scattered throughout the bus swiveled in their seats, sliding toward the aisle for a better view. The driver shifted uneasily. Even Katie, who'd seemed dead to the world, hoisted herself to a sitting position and shot me an anxious look.

Back in the U.S., I'd rarely dwelt on the fact that I was American. I might rail against the government and the emptiness of popular culture or ruminate with guilty gratitude on the freedoms and privileges I enjoyed, but I seldom reflected on the fact of my citizenship as a central part of who I was. Instead, I drew my identity from the things that made me other: Jewish, female, artist, etc. Traveling in Africa brought my Americanness acutely into focus. Everyone I met had such strong ideas about the U.S. that I found myself adjusting my descriptions to counter each individual's perceptions. Since most Ghanaians imagined a promised land, I was quick to paint for them a troubled nation, rife with injustice. For the Europeans who believed all Americans were fervid imperialists, gung ho to impose our brand of corporate capitalism on the world, I hastened to explain that the American people aren't the government—that there is, in fact, a vibrant counterculture within the U.S. that rejects our role as global bully.

With the exception of Nadhiri, I experienced an easy kinship with other American travelers. In addition to sharing a native language, Americans were friendly, gregarious in a way that European travelers often were not. My European friends found American mannerisms superficial, even phony. They mocked the cheery *Have-a-Nice-Day* attitude with vapid smiles and puppet-like bobbing of the head. I, on the other hand, found it reassuring. In my view, encounters that happened during travel were often brief and superficial. If I was going to have a superficial encounter anyway, I'd just as soon it be a friendly one.

But the sense of connection with American travelers went beyond that. I felt implicated by their behavior, even responsible for it. So when Katie whispered, "What's going on?" on the bus that morning, I felt oddly defensive.

"How should I know?" I mouthed.

"I'm afraid you are mistaken, Miss," Kwame said to the young woman, hovering above her seat. "The records show that you have not paid."

At that, she launched into a furious stream of invective: *"I paid 5,500 cedis to stay in this fucking pisspot shithole; I paid that motherfucking cocksucker at the desk yesterday, but he didn't write it down in your shitass books . . ."*

Kwame stood impassively as the foul torrent continued, toxic as an oil spill. My stomach turned over uneasily.

"Katie," I whispered, "I feel sick," but she didn't hear me. She was transfixed. The entire population of the bus was watching the scene with the avid curiosity of accident-mongers at the site of a mangled truck.

It was impossible to tell what the young woman's face looked like in repose. It was a mask of rage, her features scrunched and contorted, pale skin splotched with red, puffy eyes leaking tears. Her voice, too, was barely human, shrill as the call of a ravening bird. Watching her, I felt first numb, then horrified, then acutely, violently ashamed.

"You're gonna have to drag me off this fucking tro-tro . . ."

Kwame flinched, barely perceptibly. The bus was the pride of the Game Reserve. For her to call it a *tro-tro* was a patent affront. Amid the sea of generic obscenities, the word jumped out, sharp and specific. The whole bus reacted subtly, as if drawing in its breath.

"That's right, you cunt-lickers are gonna have to drag me off this fucking thing . . ."

Kwame turned his head and made eye contact with the driver, who gave a slight shrug. Adjusting his round hat on his balding head, the driver began to rise, a grim expression on his face.

The young woman's eyes darted sharply from one man to the other. Then the outburst stopped, midsentence, as abruptly as it had begun.

"All right, all right!" she shouted. She reached down beneath her seat and pulled out a small woven purse. Thrusting her hand into it, she extracted a wad of bills.

"One thousand, two thousand," she counted in a taunting voice. When she reached 5,500 she threw the handful of bills at Kwame. A couple landed in his hands, while several others fluttered to the floor. Keeping his eyes on her, he crouched slowly to pick them up. She made a sudden motion, causing him to start slightly. She laughed harshly. Kwame silently recounted the money. Then he nodded, folded the bills neatly and put them in his pocket.

"Thank you. Safe journey," he said. He walked down the aisle and off the bus. The doors swung closed, the engine purred gently to life, and the bus glided out through the trees into the graying dawn. Ten minutes later I was at the side of the road, expelling the contents of my stomach in a patch of coarse grass.

❖

In the weeks to come, our story spread through the ranks of volunteers like a flu in a kindergarten. At each telling the American woman became more hideous and the Ghanaian man more saintly.

"He was the absolute picture of dignity," Katie said. "He just let her rave."

"I felt ashamed to be American," I told a Danish friend. "Ashamed to be white. I wanted to cover my body, to hide."

Soon the story joined the ranks of volunteer legend, forming a cautionary trilogy with the tales of the Swede who nearly drowned in a toilet pit and the Brit who visited a fetish priest and subsequently suffered a nervous breakdown, growing paranoid and delusional, hiding from the Africans, eating only prepackaged foods after inspecting the packaging for holes. These weren't moralistic tales, exactly. They were more like ghost stories—nightmarish anecdotes traded for shock value. They inspired personal rituals of self-protection: wood-knocking, finger-crossing, whispered prayers.

"Please don't let me fall into a toilet pit," I'd whispered over and over when I first arrived. *"If I get out of here without falling into a toilet pit, I won't kill bugs, I'll call my parents regularly, I'll never complain about anything ever again for the rest of my life."*

In much the same way, I tried to immunize myself against the American woman's fate by telling her story in as distancing a manner as possible. Secretly, she terrified me. Her condition seemed contagious, something that could happen to you, as random and inexplicable as the Swede's fall to earth. You could catch malaria. You could get a sunburn. An Ugly American could move into your body and inhabit it. You could be Ugly without knowing you were Ugly. You could be Ugly to everyone around you, all the while thinking you were Right.

◆

Katie and I were busy preparing for an extended trip. We planned to take off for one to two months, traveling through Burkina Faso to Mali and back again. Our first order of business was to obtain reentry visas for Ghana. Although it was possible to leave the country and simply apply for a new visa at the Ghanaian Embassy in one of the countries we planned to visit, it was less expensive to do it here. And since we both had airline tickets out of Accra—hers back to London, mine onward to Nairobi—we figured we'd be more relaxed during our travels if we didn't have to worry about getting back into Ghana.

We composed a brief letter to the immigration office, explaining that we'd recently finished working as volunteers and wanted to explore other parts of West Africa. We figured that mentioning our volunteer status would expedite the process, which was rumored to be quite protracted. We hoped to get on the road again within a week.

Armed with our paperwork, we boarded a *tro-tro* to the immigration compound, a squat series of buildings located in a dusty, fenced-in yard in a remote section of Accra. Once inside, we made our way down a dim hallway to a fluorescent-lit classroom where a cluster of connected chair and desk units faced a wooden partition with a line of small windows cut into it. They were marked "Officer in Charge," "Commonwealth Section," "Middle/Far East Section," "African Section," "American Section," and "Western European Section." A handful of people stood before the various windows, waiting. All were shuttered except the Middle/Far East Section, where a beleaguered civil servant was assisting a Japanese man with some forms. Katie and I positioned ourselves before the American and European Sections, respectively, and waited. An African man sitting in the room said *"Eh!"* to get our attention, and gestured that we should knock on the windows. We did so, tentatively, with no result.

About five minutes later, the same man who'd been assisting the Asian applicant appeared at my window, sliding back the wooden cover. He was fortyish and puffy-faced, the whites of his eyes yellow and watery. He gazed at me with a haggard expression.

"Can I help you?" he said.

"I'd like to apply for a reentry visa."

He disappeared without a word, sliding the window cover back into place. I waited a few minutes, confused. Had I said something wrong? Then his face appeared at Katie's window.

"Can I help you?" he mumbled.

Katie requested an application for a reentry visa as well, and again he disappeared. Five minutes passed. Ten. Katie and I looked at each other. I raised my hand to knock again, and the window slid back. The man thrust some papers into my hand.

"You will return these papers to that window," he said, indicating the cubby marked Officer in Charge.

"D'you think this guy's the Wizard or just the gatekeeper?" I mumbled to Katie, when the same face appeared at the Officer in Charge window. We handed him our forms and he told us, in a flat tone, to sit down and wait. Half an hour later he materialized behind the Commonwealth window and summoned us to the counter.

"The two of you must bring a letter from your association," he said.

"What kind of letter?" I asked.

"A letter in support of your request to leave the country," he said, a touch of annoyance momentarily animating his face.

"When should we return?" asked Katie timidly.

For a moment he stared at her as though this were the single stupidest question he'd ever heard. "When you have the letter," he said at last.

"Do we get our passports back?" I asked.

"When you return." He closed the window with a thud.

"Okeydokey," I said to the piece of wood. "You have a nice day."

We returned to the hostel, grumbling. Francis Awitor, the president of the association, had an office right next to the room where we all slept. I knocked on the door.

"Yes?" he called out.

"Ko ko," I said, sticking my head in. "It's Korkor and Mansah."

"Come in, sistahs," said Mr. Awitor, giving us a polite smile. He was a formal, cautious man who lacked the exuberance of most Ghanaians. Although his office was right next to the place where we all slept and spent long lazy days between projects, we saw surprisingly little of him. On the few occasions when I'd had cause to knock on his office door, he'd always worn the same expression on his face, an expression that said he expected the worst. Katie and I filed soberly into his office and sat down in two metal folding chairs directly facing his paper-cluttered desk.

"How can I help you?" said Mr. Awitor, adjusting his glasses. "I trust you are enjoying your experience here?"

"Oh, yes, absolutely!" I said. "I've gained so much from volunteering here, I can't even tell you . . ." I paused awkwardly. "Anyway," I continued, "we were thinking of exploring some other parts of West Africa—you know, Mali, Burkina Faso—for a couple of months."

"Well, your contributions have been most appreciated by the association," said Mr. Awitor. "Please come back and see us when you return." He gave us a small smile, and made as if to return to the papers in front of him.

"Well, thanks," I said, "but, um, the reason we wanted to see you, actually . . ." I swallowed, feeling inexplicably nervous. Katie, who sat beside me picking at her cuticles, was no help.

"Yes?" He looked at me coolly over the tops of his wire-rimmed glasses. I explained about the man at the immigration office, the request for a letter from the association.

Mr. Awitor smiled then, and I relaxed. I shot Katie a glance: *What were we worried about?*

"Unfortunately, sistahs, I cannot help you with this," he said after a moment's pause. "You see, in the past I have written letters for volunteers, requesting the reentry visa for them. Then the immigration office has phoned me, here," he tapped the telephone on his desk, "and requested that I come and speak to them. They have asked me, 'Is it necessary to their work that your volunteers must leave the country?' and I have told them, 'No, it is not necessary that they leave the country for their work.' Then they have said to me, 'So why is it that you request a visa for them?' I said, 'I request the visa only to help them out.' He then told me I must not request the visas any longer. So you see," he spread his hands out on the desk, "It is not possible for me to assist you." He smiled benevolently, and returned to his papers.

"But they specifically told us we needed a letter from you," I said.

He looked at me as though he was surprised I was still there.

He shrugged, smiling again. "Perhaps you have not spoken to the right person."

✦

The immigration office was hopping when we arrived the next day. A tall, blond Viking stood pounding on the wooden square covering the Western European Section.

"You've given me the wrong form!" he shouted. A small claque of equally Nordic-looking women stood behind him, softly kvetching in a lilting Scandinavian tongue. Behind them a couple of long-haired young German men in heavy metal T-shirts ranted loudly, waving passports and forms in the air for emphasis.

"What's going on?" I asked.

"I think the man has gone to lunch without informing us," said one of the Germans, "He went to collect some forms over an hour ago and has not returned."

"Oh, that is simply not on," said a middle-aged British woman who had entered behind us. "Dreadfully incompetent," she muttered, sitting down in one of the desk chairs and wiping her brow with a handkerchief. "Dreadful heat."

Katie and I exchanged rueful grins. We took seats, amused by the spectacle of the other visa-seekers' despair. About forty-five minutes later, the familiar haggard face appeared at the Western European window. The Vikings had given up and departed. The British woman had fallen asleep, her head on the plastic desktop. The German youths, who had been leaning against the wall, charged the window like bulls.

"What took you so long?" one of them demanded.

"Here are your forms," the man said, not dignifying the question with a response. "Return them to this window when you have completed them." He was just about to close the window when Katie stuck her hopeful face in his line of vision.

"Hello," she said, full of false cheer. "I don't know if you remember my friend Tanya and me. We were in to see you yesterday."

"Yes," he said, with no flicker of recognition.

"Well, you see," she went on, "yesterday you told us we must bring you a letter from our voluntary association."

"Have you got it?"

"Well, here's the rub." Katie smiled an ingratiating smile I'd never seen her use before. "When we spoke to Mr. Awitor, the president, he told us that your office had expressly forbidden him to write letters on behalf of volunteers! Because, you see, we aren't traveling with the association. We've actually finished our work, and we're traveling on our own, as tourists, you see. Our work is done, so our comings and goings no longer concern the association." She flashed the kaka-eating grin again.

"Your names?" he said.

We told him.

"Please wait." He closed the window. We sighed and returned to our desks. He reappeared a couple of minutes later, holding our passports and letters. "It says here," he said, holding up our letter, "that you were volunteers. Therefore, we must have a letter from the voluntary organization."

"But Katie just explained to you—" I began.

"Perhaps they are still in need of your services. Perhaps they do not permit you to go."

"It's a *voluntary* association," I said, biting off my consonants. "We were there *voluntarily*. We can leave any time we want!"

"You must bring a letter—"

"But you see—" Katie began.

"You must bring a letter!" His voice remained level, but his eyes blazed with intent.

I've been known, on occasion, to have a bit of a short fuse. I once got into a screaming fight with an elderly woman who worked in a pay toilet in France, when she berated me for not bringing the toilet paper roll back out of the stall. On top of that, I have never done well with bureaucracy. If I could be said to have a pet peeve, it would be people who blindly enforce regulations without ever stopping to question their efficacy or common sense. Friends had warned me, when I left for West Africa, to prepare myself for administrative hassles, but up to now I'd dealt with surprisingly few. Two, to be exact. Once at the post office I'd been put through an hour-long rigmarole of forms and questions in order to collect a package. Just as I completed them, the young woman decided to leave for lunch, and refused to get the package for me until she returned. The second occasion was similar, except it took place in a bank. In both these instances I'd remained calm and ironic, congratulating myself inwardly on my increased maturity. I therefore surprised no one more than myself when I marched out of the visa application room in a burst of fury, slamming the door behind me.

"Robots! Fucking robot people, rules, rules, rules, they don't listen!" I shouted in the echoing hallway. A couple of doors cracked and curious faces peeped out, but I was too incensed to care. I strode out of the building and through the courtyard to the side of the road where I sat down in a patch of grass and began to cry. "Robots!" I shouted again.

I'd been crying for a few minutes when I heard sounds of hilarity coming from across the street. Three men were gathered around a stand which sold chunks of fried yam. They were looking at me and pointing, half-chanting, half-singing, "One . . . Two . . . Three . . . Cry!" They burst into laughter and applause, then began the chant over again. I stared at them for a moment, incredulous. Then I began to laugh. Laughing even harder, they gave me a thumbs-up, cheering.

Ghanaians, I thought, shaking my head. *Gotta love 'em.*

Katie joined me a few minutes later.

"Did you make any headway?" I asked.

She shook her head dejectedly. "Though I can't say it helped, your flouncing out like that."

"I know, I know," I said dejectedly. "I thought I had it under control. I just get so . . ." I paused, at a loss. "Well, it won't happen again. What do we do now?" I asked.

✥

I let Katie go first this time. She stuck her head through Mr. Awitor's door, smiling her special smile.

"Please come in," said Mr. Awitor. He raised his eyebrows in a look of tolerant surprise. Though the corners of his mouth turned upward in the semblance of a smile, the tightness of his lips said that the surprise was not a pleasant one. "What can I do for you?" he asked, before we'd had a chance to sit down.

"Yes, well," Katie began. We'd agreed to let her do the talking.

"Yes," said Mr. Awitor briskly.

"It's this matter of the reentry visa," she said, pausing slightly to clear her throat.

"I explained to you—"

"You certainly did explain the difficulty. And we tried to explain it to the gentleman at the immigration office. But you see, unfortunately, he persists in saying that he requires a letter from you. Not a letter stating that you want us to go to Mali, you understand, simply a statement that you have no *objection* to our going to Mali—"

But Mr. Awitor was shaking his head sadly.

"I'm very sorry, ladies, but as I told you—"

"You told us," I interrupted, "that you couldn't ask for our visas. And we don't want you to! If you could just say that we're no longer working for you and you don't *care* if we go to Mali or not . . ."

He laughed and made the same gesture, palms up on the table. "I cannot so much as *mention* Mali in a letter," he said.

"Fine!" I said, my voice rising. "Fine! Don't mention Mali. Not a word about Mali. How 'bout I just type up something that says you don't care where we go one way or the other, and you sign it? How about that?"

"Tanya . . ." Katie placed a warning hand on my arm.

"Sistah Korkor, there is no need to shout," Mr. Awitor said. The polite smile now made me want to wring his neck. "As I have already made clear to you—"

But I was off the chair and out of his office, back into the hostel, raging and banging doors. Every ounce of my hard-won self-control was gone. It was as though, all at once, the accumulated months of heat and nausea and frustration with the work had rolled down a hill like a giant magnetic ball, picking up scraps of rubbish as it went.

"God*damn* it!" I shouted. "God fucking damn it! Idiocy! Total, brainless, robotic . . ."

"Sistah, what is it?" said Ayatollah, who'd been out in the yard behind the hostel, washing some laundry.

"Don't concern yourself," said a new French volunteer, before I had a chance to answer. "She has a high temper."

That stopped me. "How would you know?" I asked. The girl had arrived yesterday. We hadn't exchanged ten words.

She shrugged, flapped a hand at my behavior, smiling. "I know Americans."

❖

There were no applicants in the visa room when we arrived. The American Section window was open, and the familiar jowly face was behind it, staring glumly at some papers on the counter in front of him.

"You must speak to this lady," he said as soon as he saw us, jerking his head toward the Officer in Charge window.

To our great surprise, we saw that the window there was also open and a cheerful young woman's face peered out. She beamed as we approached.

"Friends," she said warmly. "How can I help you?"

"Well," I said, a spark of hope igniting painfully in my chest. "We put in applications for reentry visas several days ago . . ."

"Your names, please?" Her smile was radiant, beatific. It illuminated her entire face.

We snuck a look at each other as she disappeared into the recesses of the office. Could she be as golden as she seemed?

When she returned, she actually opened a door next to the windowed panels and joined us in the room.

"Please, ladies, have a seat," she said. She held our passports, applications, and the fateful letter in which we'd exposed the fact that we'd once been volunteers. "I understand that you were working here, and now you would like to leave the country and travel. I understand as well, that you would like a visa so that after your travels you may return to Ghana. We are happy that you find Ghana so sweet that you want to return." She paused, glancing down at the papers. "Yet surely you understand that we require a letter from your association to back up your request." She raised her eyebrows and smiled directly into my eyes.

The flicker of hope in my chest died instantly, leaving a cold lump. "Miss . . ." I began wearily.

"Mrs. Oppong," she said.

"Mrs. Oppong, perhaps your compatriot has explained to you—" and then abruptly, I stopped. Why was I putting myself through this? To save fifty bucks? I could leave the country and apply for a new visa from the Ghanaian embassy in Mali. If that didn't work I'd try the one in Burkina Faso. Sooner or later somebody would let me back in. I looked at Mrs. Oppong, who was gazing at me with an expression of consternation, a slight furrow in her brow.

"Is there a problem, sistah?"

"No problem at all," I said, making myself breathe normally. I even managed a smile. "I've just decided not to pursue a reentry visa at this time. I'd like my passport back."

"Oh, sistah! Surely you would like to reconsider. If it's not possible for you to provide the proper documentation, we could take a few more days to determine—"

"Thank you, sister," I said firmly. "You're very kind. But I'd like my passport back, please. How 'bout you, Katie?"

"I'm not sure," she said, in a small voice. Katie was on a tighter budget than I was, so the extra fifty or so dollars for a new visa were more significant to her. She also had a more cautious personality than I did—she would worry terribly about whether or not we'd be able to get back in once we'd left.

"If you could just bring us a letter," Mrs. Oppong said gently. Her eyes were bright, luminous. I was certain that she was a siren. She would lure us here again and again, each day, to discuss the state of our reentry visas. The process would be drawn out for weeks, months, until the time we'd allotted for our trip had completely evaporated. It wouldn't be the first time such a thing had happened. I'd heard stories. Cautionary volunteer legends.

"But I'm afraid we can't," said Katie. "We can't get you a letter." She was on the verge of tears.

"Well, then, I'll just hold onto this a few more days and reconsider." Mrs. Oppong held Katie's passport aloft.

"Not mine," I said emphatically.

"Not yours, Miss Shaffer," said Mrs. Oppong, and a slightly unpleasant note came into her voice. Frowning, she placed my passport in my outstretched hand.

"Come on, Katie," I said. "If you change your mind you can always bring it back."

"Oh!" said Mrs. Oppong, alarmed. "But then you would have to start the process all over, from the beginning."

"Yes, I'll take it, please," said Katie, sighing.

"But—" Mrs. Oppong began.

"Please," I said sharply, "give her the passport and let us go. We've spent enough time in this room."

Mrs. Oppong handed Katie her passport.

"Safe journey," she said angrily. Then she turned and disappeared through the door she'd come out of. She slid the wooden cover across the window with a bang.

On the *tro-tro* back to the hostel, a man stood next to the driver selling an English ABC book for tots. He went through it laboriously, page by page, reading aloud each letter until he came to the last: "Zed, Zebra, a Zebra is a beautiful animal."

As a middle-aged man beside us leafed through his new acquisition ("For my granddaughter," he told me, beaming), Katie suddenly doubled over, clutching her stomach.

"What is it?" I said.

She looked up at me, her face very pale.

"I don't know," she said. "A pain."

By the time we got off at the *tro-tro* park nearest the hostel, Katie could barely walk. She leaned on me for support.

"I'm ill," she whispered.

"Let's get a taxi to the hospital," I said. She nodded. Her legs buckled and she collapsed there, at the side of the road. I commandeered a taxi, and we squeezed into the backseat with three women and two babies.

"What is it, sweetie? What is it?" I crooned, holding her hand.

"Terrible," she murmured.

Katie spent the night in a hospital cot on a crowded ward, an IV dripping into her arm. She was dehydrated, the nurse told me, dangerously weak. The next day the verdict was in. Typhoid . . . and malaria. I thought of the faces at the immigration bureau, one diabolically cheerful, the other haggard and withdrawn. I couldn't help feeling there was some connection between our experience there and the sudden onset of Katie's illness. If nothing else, it had weakened her defenses.

I discussed the events with Elise, the irritating but insightful Frenchwoman who had recently arrived. She'd been to Ghana twice before, volunteering both times.

"Why would the immigration people behave that way?" I asked her. "Wouldn't it be to their advantage to cooperate, to be helpful to volunteers?"

"Do you know what Ghanaians go through when they try to travel to Europe or America?" she asked.

I thought of the U.S. Embassy, with its hordes of Ghanaians waiting in their best clothes, clutching all kinds of documentation, only to have their visa applications rejected, month after month, year after year.

"This is the one way they have power over us," she said. "A very small payback for all that humiliation."

"And Mr. Awitor?"

"He's tired of white volunteers treating him like a servant."

"But I never—"

"Well," she said, her eyes narrowing suspiciously, "maybe you never, but someone else did."

❖

Katie was recovering, but slowly. She stayed in the hospital for four or five days. Afterwards, back in the hostel, she moved slowly, shuffling around in her socks. She borrowed paperbacks from the other volunteers and spent the long stuffy days lying on her bunk, reading. I waited ten days, half-impatient, half-fearful, to broach the subject of our departure for Mali. When I finally did, she shook her head.

"What?" I said.

"I'm not up to it."

"Come on! You're getting better every day! I don't mind waiting another week or two."

"Can't do it, Tanya. It's not just my body—I feel afraid. I mean, what happens if we're on that riverboat up the Niger that you're so keen on taking, and I get sick out there, in the middle of nowhere? They told me flat out that if I hadn't gotten treated I could've been dead within a couple of days."

"We don't have to—" I began, but she cut me off.

"I wasn't as bold as you were to begin with. And now . . . I'd hold you back. What's the good of that? We traveled together because it worked out; we wanted the same things. It's not working out anymore."

❖

A week later, about fifteen of us crowded into two taxis to take Katie to the airport. We stood in a circle in a far corner of the airport parking lot, holding hands. The sun was setting, and the western edge of the sky glowed a deep rose. At my suggestion, we went around the circle, voicing our hopes and wishes for

Katie. ("How American," she said dryly, but she smiled at me tenderly.) We wished her a safe journey, and that she wouldn't forget what she'd found here, that she would always carry a part of Ghana in her heart.

"The sweetness," I said. "The exuberance, the dignity. Not the bureaucracy."

"Not the immigration office, please God," she piped up. "But dignity, yes. I've seen Ghanaians respond to difficult situations with extraordinary grace. I wouldn't mind catching a bit of that."

I hugged her, pressing her skinny body to mine. She had always been slender, but wiry, strong. Now, after a couple of weeks of illness, her body felt intensely fragile, a brittle cage of bones. I pulled back and looked into her hazel eyes. Their expression was wry, at once amused and embarrassed, with an unexpected glitter of tears.

"Stop it," she said, laughing. She ducked her head, wiping at her eyes with the back of her hand.

"I love you, Katie," I said. "I'll miss you."

"Prove it by writing me." She flashed her impish grin.

"I will."

We escorted Katie as far as the airport personnel would permit, all of us waving to her from the other side of a metal gate as she disappeared into the welter of bodies. Afterwards, our group drifted slowly back to the parking lot, where we stood talking amid the taxis and *tro-tros*, the carts loaded with luggage and the families clasping each other in greeting or farewell. The night air was cool and delicious, and we were in no hurry to get back to the hostel. The airport made us nostalgic; we were reluctant to part with the feeling of tender melancholy it evoked. For most of the foreigners, this nondescript expanse of asphalt was their first image of Ghana. They'd arrived here and would depart from here as well.

We stood in a kind of group hug for many minutes, then someone started singing, "I Want Somebody to Carry Me Home," a Ghanaian song we'd learned at camp. We all joined in, singing at the top of our lungs:

Oh, to see my mothah once more, baby
I want somebody to carry me home
Oh to see my sistah once more, baby
I want somebody to carry me home

When we finished the song, we broke apart and began searching for a taxi. It was then that I saw the young American woman. It had been several weeks since the incident on the bus out of the Mole Game Reserve, but I recognized her immediately. She stood a few feet from our cluster, her body turned at a diffident angle, half toward us, half away. Although she was motionless, her presence had a hovering quality, a kind of *leaning*, as though our group were a fire that offered crucial warmth.

Just then Gorbachev spotted her.

"*Eh!* Sistah Laura!" he cried. "What are you doing here?" He pulled her next to him with one hand. She submitted, grinning shyly.

"This is my friend Laura," he said. "We met at the Wato Bar some two months ago. She had just arrived in Ghana, and we had such a fine conversation."

"Hi, you guys," said Laura. Her eyes darted around the group. A timid smile played on her lips.

I scanned her face intently, looking for signs of the hellion I'd seen on the bus. She was younger than I'd realized, barely out of her teens. Either she'd lost weight in the last few weeks, or I simply hadn't looked at her closely before. She was all angles—shoulders and elbows sharp in her yellow cotton sundress, skin stretched tight over cheekbones and chin—much as Katie's had been in these final days. Her nose and cheeks were burned and peeling beneath tufty reddish hair. Sunglasses had drawn wide circles around her pale eyes. She gave an impression of elaborate, almost melodramatic frailty, as though at any moment her eyelids would flutter and she'd fall backward in a swoon.

"What are you doing here?" Gorbachev inquired again.

"I'm going home," she said ruefully, indicating a large backpack propped against a pole.

"I thought you were staying here for a full year. You were going to study Twi language in Kumasi, wasn't that it?"

"Yes, yes, I was, but . . . I got sick." She coughed, as if to illustrate her point.

"Oh!" said Gorbachev. "That is so unfortunate. The same thing has happened to our friend Katie. Is it malaria?"

Laura shrugged slightly. "I actually don't know what it is," she said and began to cough again, her whole body shaking with the effort.

In a few minutes she drifted away from Gorbachev. I moved toward her, my heart pounding. She turned her pale eyes on me without recognition.

"We've met before," I said.

"We have?" She smiled uncertainly.

I nodded. "On the bus out of the Mole Game Reserve."

She started slightly. A deep flush rose in her sunburned cheeks.

"I was embarrassed," I said.

"You know," she said, "I thought I'd paid the man. I really did. Only later that day, I realized I hadn't." She shrugged her shoulders and began to back away.

I felt a surge of adrenaline. I needed to tell her, needed to get it out of myself.

"I was so embarrassed," I repeated, more loudly, "humiliated, in fact."

"Don't worry about it." She shook her head once, sharply, as if to clear it. Then she laughed nervously, cocking her head like a bird. "It's not your problem."

"Yes, it is—" I began, but at that moment she started coughing again. Her face darkened even further, turning almost purple as she hawked. Finally she conjured something thick and slimy from her throat, spitting it onto the pavement in front of her.

"Leave me alone," she moaned, looking at the ground. "What's it got to do with you, anyway?" She rocked back and forth, eyes closed, arms wrapped around her bony body as if to keep it from breaking apart.

12

Genie

Crying dream last night. Third one this trip. Always about Michael. Fear of losing him, loneliness, wanting it both ways. In this one I'm kissing and hugging and touching him, even as we're breaking up. When he realizes what's going on, he turns icy. "I don't love you anymore," he says. "How can you say that?" I plead. "We promised we'd love each other always. That no matter what happened, we'd be best friends." I reach for his hand, but he yanks it away and begins to turn, spinning into a smoky blur. I get stuck in a loop and this reaching and pulling and spinning and blurring repeat themselves again and again until I awaken in bed with a pounding heart, tears and sweat in the morning cool.

A few days after Katie's departure, I was back on the road. The journey felt lonely without her. I missed her sarcastic commentary and dry English wit. At the same time, I felt a touch of exhilaration. It was wonderful to have someone with whom to share the humor and hardship of the journey, but I definitely connected more with others when I was alone. As traveling companions, two people form a closed unit. A solo traveler is open to the world.

The world, that is, and all its men. The biggest problem with being a solo woman traveler is that every horny Tom, Dick, and Kwesi gloms onto you like a blood-hungry tick and won't let go. *"Vous êtes SEULE?"* they ask, "You're alone?" and then, with growing excitement, *"Vous êtes AMÉRICAINE?"* There's an instantly recognizable look to the eyes of men who are about to give you a sleazy come-on—a hooded, dozy look intended to draw you in with the promise of candles, stringed instruments, expanding time, expansive beds.

But as annoying as the men's incessant overtures were, even more annoying was the inexplicable fact that I always felt guilty when I rejected them. Several years before, while traveling in Germany, I'd met an Italian guy at a youth hostel who wanted to go hiking with me. I said no, because he was already getting touchy-feely, and I knew I'd be fighting off his advances before we rounded the block. He reproached me with, "You must take risks when you are in a foreign country. Otherwise you miss it all."

Clearly this feeble attempt at persuasion was a garden variety example of the depths the male species could sink to in its tireless quest to self-perpetuate. We know this, right? And yet, in spite of this knowledge, I tormented myself for days, wondering whether I was cheating myself out of too much life. In another instance, a Swedish man whom I'd rebuffed asked me why I was creating artificial barriers between body and mind. We liked each other, why shouldn't we make love? And although I knew he was a New Age clone whose recycled arguments went all the way back to John Donne and "The Flea," I had to endure the nattering of my own mind for days, wondering whether there was something wrong with me, whether I was an ice empress, incapable of spontaneous passion.

These things and more make a shaved head and robes sound like a blessed relief.

After all my years of solo travel, I was convinced there was no tactic known to the Y chromosome that could surprise me. Then I met Jimmy Brahima.

"You are very interesting," he told me after less than five minutes' acquaintance. "*Très très intéressante.* Please, can I take you to bed?"

"No!" I shouted, furious and bored and disgusted. "No, no, no, no!" We were on a darkened street behind the stadium in Bobo-Dioulasso, Burkina Faso, a small city with tree-lined streets, lively markets, a couple of museums, and a famous mosque. I'd arrived that day from Ghana, after a long bumpy ride in a packed minivan. Burkina Faso was once a French colony, and the official language was still French. Fortunately, I was equipped for this, having studied for three years in high school and honed my skills during my month in Morocco.

Since Burkina Faso is known for its culture, I'd made my way to the stadium to see a youth choir concert I'd seen advertised, only to find that there was no concert. I'd gotten the time wrong, or the day, or the year, I couldn't figure out which. Tired, headachy, and near the breaking point, I'd been walking around in circles for almost an hour now, trying to find my way back to a hotel whose name I had forgotten. Along the way this irritating companion had attached himself to me, like something unseemly sticking to my shoe.

"Shhhh. . . ." He looked around, embarrassed, but there was

no one to hear. He leaned in for a kiss. I sidestepped him so quickly he almost fell.

"Don't touch me," I said between gritted teeth. I was about to follow it up with a command to get the hell out of here, when he startled me by suddenly backing up about ten yards. He did it so quickly, bouncing backward in tiny Charlie Chaplin steps, that I giggled with surprise. From that distance he shouted the following pronouncement:

"If a woman tells me not to touch her, I don't touch her, because I don't know what she is."

"What do you mean?" I asked, mildly intrigued.

"She could be a genie."

"Really?" I took a step toward him. He backed up. "A genie?"

"Oh yes. There are so many genies walking around. They appear to be human, but when they want to, they can grow huge."

"Are they all women?" I asked.

"No, there are males too, but the males don't show themselves to men." He looked at me speculatively, then continued. "If a genie is angry, it goes like this." He made a powerful sucking sound through his teeth, lips parting slightly to let the air sing through.

I tried to imitate him, but instead sputtered and drooled like a geriatric camel. I struggled to look forbidding, but laughter twitched the corners of my mouth uncontrollably, and soon I was cackling so hard I could barely breathe. After a moment Jimmy joined the escalating gigglefest until we were both bent over and gasping for air. Jimmy moved closer again now—I guess he figured I couldn't possibly be a genie with such a wimpy capacity for hissing. He demonstrated the sound a few more times, and with some practice I got it.

"Please," he said now, "let us go to the bar for some beers. Afterward I will help you to find your hotel."

Riding the wave of goodwill, I accepted.

"If you ever need to threaten a man, make that sound and he will run," Jimmy counseled me as I followed his lead through the labyrinth of darkened streets.

I promised to keep that in mind.

"I worry for you, *une petite fille,* traveling alone."

"Oh, don't worry about me," I said heartily. "I can take care of myself." We'd reached the bar, which had an outdoor courtyard with several wooden tables where African men in both Western and traditional clothes sat drinking, laughing, and shouting. I slid onto a wooden bench.

"But I do worry. Such a little girl. You need protection." Jimmy himself was dressed in spanking new blue jeans and a silky black shirt with the top two buttons undone. I half-expected to see a thick gold chain around his neck. His face, seen for the first time in the light, was striking in a sleek, chiseled way, long and narrow with high cheekbones and gorgeous thick-lashed eyes. The combination of his disco-age clothes and movie-star features produced an effect at once sleazy and seductive. I already regretted having agreed to a drink.

"Spare me the 'little girl' stuff," I said testily. "*Je suis très forte.* I'm very strong. Not to worry."

"I knew it." Jimmy leaned forward, his eyes wide and eager. "I could see it. Please, will you tell me your secret?"

I laughed, "There is no secret."

"You should tell your brother. Tell your friend. Teach me."

"No secret. I'm trained in self-defense," I said.

"Self-defense?" He lowered his voice to an excited whisper. "You mean you can . . . disappear?"

"Disappear? No. I wish. Self-defense—I can defend myself. Use my hands and feet to disable someone, knock him out."

He looked at me reproachfully. "I wish you'd tell me the secret. Don't be annoyed. You frighten me. I don't know what you are."

I shrugged helplessly. "I don't know what to tell you."

"Please. Let us agree. I will tell you a story of my friend, who met a genie, then you must tell me what you are."

I nodded and took a long swig of beer. I extended my hand. "Deal."

Gravely, he shook my hand. He looked at me for a long moment, then began:

"He saw her here, at this bar, sitting alone at a table. She was a beautiful round African woman. She was dressed in expensive European cloth. He himself is so skinny, with one leg shorter than the other, and not rich. Normally he would never speak to a woman like that, but her eyes stopped on him, and she smiled and nodded her head. He went to her and offered to purchase a drink, but she said no. She asked if she could go home with him instead.

"They walked to his house, but every time he reached for her hand, she said *'laisse moi'* and pushed him away, just the way you pushed me away before. Every several steps she asked him, 'Where is your house?' He asked her why she was in such a hurry to get there, but she only said, 'I need a place.'

"When they finally arrived she almost ran to the door. Inside, he tried again to pull her next to him, and she went *'fffffft!'*" Here Jimmy made the sucking sound, violently, his hands in the air and his eyes wild.

"Then she started undressing," he continued. "She took off one skirt, then another and another and another, then blouses, one, two, three, until there was a pile of a hundred, two hundred skirts and blouses lying on the floor. The room was filling

up and my friend could not breathe. He ran for the door, but the woman begged him not to leave. 'Stay!' she cried. 'Stay with me!'

"But my friend was too frightened. Even though she was the most beautiful woman he had ever seen, he opened the door and ran down the street to the house of his cousin. He remained in his cousin's house for two weeks. Finally he went back to his place. Everything was normal. No clothing on the floor, nothing. But from that moment on he was impotent.

"That is why if a woman says 'don't touch me,' I don't touch her. I don't know what she is."

I gazed at Jimmy, entranced by his fine cheekbones, expressive eyes, and wide, elastic mouth. I gulped at my second beer.

"Now," he said, "You must tell me what you are."

"Oh . . . I don't know," I teased. "I don't know if I can trust you with that information."

"Ma soeur!" he said eagerly, taking my hand. "Surely you can trust me. Have you ever in your life met a nicer person than me?"

I nodded.

"Where? In America? Ghana?"

"Lots of places."

"Lots of places? No. There is no nicer person than me. How can you say someone is nicer than me? When you told me not to touch you didn't I say, 'yes, *Madame*'?"

"Yes, but only because you were afraid of me. A really nice person doesn't ask a woman to sleep with him when they've only known each other for five minutes. Especially not when she's alone in a dark place."

"You must talk more quietly; you're talking very loudly." He eyed a portly man at the next table, who was staring at us with unmasked curiosity. "I was just making several options available to you," he whispered. "You never know what a person wants to do. I said, do you want to go to the concert tomorrow, to the museum, shall I go with you to the market? You said no. I said you are very interesting, can I take you to bed? You said no to that, too. I said all right. I was only giving you choices."

My head was spinning from the beer, and I started to laugh. The day's heat and exhaustion lifted off me, and I felt giddy and weightless. So what if I couldn't find my hotel that night? I'd surely find it in the morning, when it was light. *Perhaps I am a genie,* I thought, *full of hidden powers,* and the thought made me feel sexy, reckless. Something moved inside, not unlike the sensation before an impulse purchase, a rash, against-my-better-judgment stirring, a heart-knock of desire. I was lonely, too—why not indulge once in a while? Whose outdated ethic governed me? What was I defending, and why? Here was Jimmy, a physically stunning man, and vital, creative, alive. I could almost feel the heat of his hands against my body, the long smooth journey of my fingers down his back. Oh God, it had been so long . . .

I leaned forward and kissed his lips.

"You want to know what I am?" I asked softly. I was about to follow it up with something flirtatiously ironic, when Jimmy quickly scooted back his bench and stood up.

"Please," he said, "The bartender, he knows all the hotels. He will help you. Please be kind. Don't watch me. Don't follow me. Please."

And Jimmy was down the street and around the corner before I could tell him that of all my roadside suitors he was the lucky winner—that I was no genie at all, just a tipsy human female ready to step off her pedestal and seek a little comfort far from home.

13

She Kept Dancing

Sitting on buses and tro-tros, *I find myself repeatedly telling strangers the story of my life. Sometimes, hearing myself talk, I feel as if I'm doing it more for my own benefit than for the hapless individual sitting beside me, listening with such polite attention. Some need seems to drive my narration, as if through the telling I'm constructing a self-image that I can anchor myself to and believe in. I want the events to be linear and the lessons cumulative, building on each other like Legos: this led me here, and I learned this, and then I was here, and I was lost, and I found this.*

Life, of course, was never so orderly. It was more like my long hair used to be after a ride in the open back of a truck: an ungovernable tangle. Growth wasn't like that either. Growth happened when I wasn't looking. It happened later, after I'd given up hope. And love wasn't like that: so transparent and unequivocal, a balance sheet of pros and cons. Life was life and love was love. All the explanations came later.

◆

I hadn't noticed Brigitte until we pulled up to the curb in down-town Ouagadougou and she leaned over and tapped me on the shoulder. "If you don't have a place to stay during your visit," she said with breathless timidity, "you are welcome in my house."

I was used to sudden changes in plans and to West Africans' amazing, nearly overwhelming hospitality. I hadn't planned to stop off in Burkina Faso's sprawling capital, but I suddenly real-ized I needed to apply here for my Malian visa. It would be just my luck to arrive at the border and get turned away. Besides, after spending a largely sleepless night at the side of the road while our *tro-tro* driver went in search of a tire, I was in no mood to coninue traveling. My cream-colored T-shirt and olive skirt had turned road-dust gray, and my shorn hair—the only part of my body retaining any natural oils—was plastered to my scalp. Something new and odd was happening with my body, which for days had produced the sensation of sweating, though no actual moisture appeared. I felt like a kettle that rattles and shakes, but never quite manages to sing.

I stood guard over Brigitte's cloth-tied bundles while she used the phone box outside the upscale *Hôtel de l'Indépendance* to call her husband. Oceans of *motos* swerved around me. The air was thick with dust and exhaust, whipped about by the *harmat-tan*'s harsh gusts. The sunlight seemed to rob the landscape of depth, leaving it two-dimensional, like a painted set. Even with sunglasses on, the glare knit a hard ache behind my eyes.

Driving north from Ghana, the terrain had grown gradually drier. The color of the dirt had shifted, little by little, from red and brown to tan to almost white. The streets, buildings, and grass of Ouaga (as I soon came to call it) appeared washed out, as though they had been dipped in a bucket of bleach.

Brigitte was in her mid-twenties. She had a plump figure and a perky, impish face with round, shiny cheeks and eyebrows that leaped and danced when she spoke. She had managed to stay astoundingly clean on the journey from Bobo, where she'd gone to visit her cousin. Her bright orange and green print dress still looked freshly pressed. A matching cloth wrapped her head.

"I'm bringing a friend home," I heard her say. She paused for emphasis, then added, "a *white* friend," her voice simmering with excitement.

❖

An expensive taxi ride took us from wide, heavily trafficked downtown boulevards lined with stately buildings to a gravel-paved neighborhood on the outskirts of town, where solid cinderblock houses with clean-swept dirt yards alternated with vacant lots filled with rubble. Goats nosed around in the debris, munching on garbage. Not the pygmy goats of Ghana, but lanky Burkina Faso goats, with drooping ears and tails, and doleful, basset hound eyes.

Brigitte lived in one of the cinderblock rectangles with her husband—a midlevel customs official—their three children, and two servant girls. In the open-air bathroom, a mud wall separated the neatly swept section where a board covered a hole in the ground from the area where you carried your bucket of water to bathe. With a television, boom box, and telephone inside the house, it was a solid middle-class home.

It was love at first sight for me and little Rod. She stood shyly at the gate with her three middle fingers in her mouth, twisting her upper body back and forth as the taxi pulled up. As I swung my bulky pack out of the roof rack, she was already at my side, and I swerved off-balance to avoid hitting her. When I flopped onto the couch in the tiny living room, she came and sat silently on my lap.

Rod was five years old and had silky skin the color of fresh coffee grounds, kept creamy by her mother's daily application of shea butter. Her small face was a perfect oval with grave, wide-set eyes so dark you couldn't separate iris from pupil, and pouty, beautifully shaped lips which often hung slack in the unselfconscious gape of childhood. She seldom spoke, but always stayed within a few steps of me, often slipping a hand into mine as I sat writing or talking in the yard.

"This one's too quiet," Brigitte said, holding Rod at arm's length and brushing dust off her pink skirt with a brusque hand. "Here comes the smart one." Her face lit up with a smile as a chubby two-year-old careened through the doorway with a stocky teenager following a step behind.

"Lidia already speaks French, don't you?" Brigitte said to the little one. *"Tu parles français?"*

"Oui!" the baby shouted, and Brigitte laughed with delight. She barked a command at the teenager, who rushed out into the yard. "I've told her to get water for your bath," Brigitte told me. Brigitte and I spoke French with each other, while she usually spoke to the children and servants in her native Mossi. She turned back to the crowing Lidia.

"This one," she said, smiling, "this is my girl."

Her son Constantin came home a few hours later, dragging a book bag behind him, his school uniform covered with mud.

"Tintin!" Brigitte called sharply. "Did you greet our guest?"

He slid to a halt in front of me, a nine-year-old bundle of kinetic energy: hands, knees, and feet all trembling to go.

"Pleased to meet you," he murmured, sneaking a glance from lowered eyes.

"My pleasure," I said.

He flashed me a smile, dropped his bag in front of the couch, and took off running, out the door and through the gate.

"Change your clothes," Brigitte shouted as he tore around the corner. "Did you see him? That one is bad," she said, sighing and shaking her head. "Bad."

✦

Rod and Constantin shared a bedroom with two teenage servant girls, Nyanga and Yolan, while Lidia slept in a crib in her parents' bedroom. I shared the large bed with Brigitte. I never met her husband, who arrived home that night after we went to bed, slept on the couch, and left early the next morning on a business trip. When I asked Brigitte about him, she simply shrugged her shoulders.

"He's not mean," she said.

I was struck by the difference in appearance between Brigitte's children and the two servants. I knew that it was common in West Africa for middle-class people to have live-in servants, but this was the first time I'd witnessed it firsthand. While the two little girls had neatly braided hair, clean dresses in appropriate sizes, and sandals on their feet, Nyanga and Yolan walked around in faded sacklike prints, barefoot, their hair in fuzzy plaits that looked as though they hadn't been touched in weeks.

Yolan, the older girl, was seventeen years old, tall and robust, her affable face drawn in broad, clean lines. The other girl, Nyanga, was sixteen, according to Brigitte, but looked twelve. She stood about four foot ten, with slim hips and the barest hint of breasts. Her face was an impassive mask, eyes and lips locked in an expression of perpetual blankness. She looked as though she'd been through a war, and who knows? Maybe she had.

I never heard Brigitte speak a gentle word to these girls. If she spoke to them at all, it was to bark out commands, often adding the words "lazy" or "stupid" at the end. Yolan took this in stride, her sense of herself secure and unflappable, but the shouts seemed to hit Nyanga's small body like blows. At every insult she flinched, and her face grew more determinedly blank.

When I asked Brigitte if Nyanga and Yolan had ever been to school, she said no. They were simple village girls, she told me; their families could not afford it. When I asked her what these village girls were doing in the city, she shrugged.

"The big one's parents have died, and her family cannot keep her. Her uncle knew my husband in the army; he asked him to help. The other girl came with her. She is very 'shhhhh.'" She made a zipping motion with her lips. "No one learns a word from her." She shrugged. "They are lucky to have employment. Many such girls end up selling themselves to whichever man walks down the street."

I wanted to speak to Brigitte about her treatment of them, but I didn't know how, and I was wary of making things worse. I contented myself with indirect tactics, openly praising Nyanga and Yolan for their cooking, their washing, the care they took of the children. When I did this, Yolan giggled in embarrassment and Nyanga flashed a shy smile that completely transformed her appearance. Smiling, she revealed a classic African beauty, with her strong, narrow chin, high forehead, wide nose, and full lips.

Sometimes Brigitte regarded me strangely, as though suspicious of my intent.

"Don't you think it's a good idea to praise people when they do something well?" I asked cautiously.

"Oh yes," she said absently. "When someone does well you must tell him so."

Once Nyanga spilled water on the floor as she carried a bucket outside for my bath. After reprimanding her severely, Brigitte shook her head. "These girls," she said, "they are lazy because I do not beat them."

"They don't look lazy to me," I said. "They seem to work very hard."

She shook her head. "At another house they would be beaten, but I am too soft with them, so they take advantage of me."

It was hard to imagine the cowering Nyanga taking advantage of a mosquito, but I held my peace.

✧

On my first full day in Ouagadougou, Brigitte and I wandered together through *le Grand Marché*, an enormous market housed in a blocky cement building. "It used to be outside, the African way," Brigitte said with disdain.

Brigitte wouldn't let me pay for anything, insisting on playing the perfect hostess. She bargained fiercely to bring down the price of a woven bracelet I tried on from the equivalent of sixty-five cents to about forty. When she began buying vegetables for lunch, I stopped her.

"Why don't we go to a restaurant?" I said. "My treat."

"Restaurant?" She looked hesitant.

"Come on," I said. "We passed one yesterday when we got off the bus."

Still skeptical, she followed me to *La Grotte*, a restaurant in the international section of town, close to the chichi *Hôtel de l'Indépendance*. The restaurant was nestled behind another building, its white plastic tables shaded by umbrellas. Large white blossoms perfumed the air, and rotating fans provided a light breeze. Palm and banana trees surrounded the enclosure; the light that danced sideways onto our table was mottled and green. A brilliantly colored parrot perched nearby on a wooden post, keeping mum. The clientele was mostly white.

From the moment we entered, Brigitte grew quiet, looking

around her with widened eyes. She sat with her hands in her lap, not picking up the menu the waiter placed in front of her.

"Don't you want to order?" I asked her.

She shook her head. "I'm not hungry," she said, her eyes flicking back and forth.

"Are you sure?" She nodded. "Well, at least have a drink, okay?" She nodded again. "You can share my food," I added.

I ordered a chicken dish with *tô*, the staple of the region, a firm porridge made from pounded millet. When the waiter asked Brigitte for her order, she mouthed, "Coca Cola."

"Excuse me?"

She cleared her throat, "Coca Cola."

"Why do you order this dish?" she asked me, after the waiter had gone.

"What do you mean?"

"This isn't your food."

"I'm in Africa. I want to eat African food."

She shook her head with incredulity. "This food is too plain. I wouldn't serve you this food."

She continued to shake her head as I paid the bill, which came to roughly five dollars.

"A bit of a splurge," I said. She was silent all the way home.

❖

But sitting in the packed dirt yard the next morning, Brigitte was full of plans. It was a cool, fresh morning, the sky a guileless baby blue that bore no hint of the heat to come. We'd carried out the white plastic table and chairs and were eating our breakfast in the shade of a plane tree.

"You will find me a job in your country," she said. "I can do anything. I can cook, I can clean. All kinds of African dishes. I worked for a German family; they were very content with my work." She paused, then continued. "You will find me a family. They can send the plane ticket, then when I work, they don't pay me until it's paid for. They can get a visa for me."

"What about your children?" I asked.

"They will stay with my mother," she said. "It's only two, three years. I'll make a lot of money, then I'll come back. I'll open a restaurant, my own, like the one yesterday. Cook African food; white people will come."

"And your husband?"

"He doesn't mind." She flipped her hand. "He's not mean. You will find me a job?"

"I don't think—"

"I know it's not sure."

"It's really not—"

"You will try?"

I shrugged helplessly. "I'll try."

✣

That night, Yolan cooked a delicious dinner of savory chicken soup. When they weren't busy serving us, Yolan and Nyanga ate their meals out in the yard while we sat inside at the table. Rod pulled her chair as close to mine as possible, so that our knees touched while we ate. Lidia sat at a small table by herself, her face covered with food.

"Please can I go play, Mama? Please can I, please please please?" Constantin held out his empty bowl for inspection.

"And where is your schoolwork?" She turned to me. "Last week he missed half on his geography test."

"I did it, Mama. All finished, *tout c'est fini! Fini, fini, fini!*"

"All right, all right, go, my ears cannot bear to hear you," she swatted at him as he left.

"He is bad," she said. "He never wants to do his work." She

smiled indulgently at Lidia. "That one never gives me any problems."

"He's not bad," I said.

"No?"

"No. He's just a normal boy."

"Is he?" She seemed pleased.

"Uh huh," I nodded vigorously. "Just a boy."

Rod had finished her meal, and was tugging at my skirt. Her mouth was moving, and I brought my ear close. She was repeating the word boy, *"garçon, garçon, garçon . . ."* I lifted her onto my lap.

"How did she get the name Rod?" I asked.

"A white man," said Rod, in perfect French. *Un homme blanc.* I looked at her in surprise. Brigitte started to giggle.

"What white man?" I asked the little girl.

"Mama's boyfriend," she said, and went back to eating her soup.

"An American, named Rod," said Brigitte. "Peace Corps. He wanted to marry me, but my mother said no. I was only seventeen, and I was scared. If it were now, I would go with him. I would go like that." She made a whisking motion with her hand.

"So you gave her his name? Your husband doesn't mind?"

She shrugged again, a bored expression crossing her face. "I told you . . ."

My voice joined hers, "He's not mean."

✥

When I accepted Brigitte's invitation, I'd planned to stay two or three days. A week had gone by, and I was expecting my visa from the Malian embassy any day. As the time of my departure approached, Brigitte's conversations with me developed an urgency, as though there weren't time for her to say everything she wanted to say before I left. I too had begun confiding in her, talking about Michael and my dilemmas of the heart. Her response to my predicament was not unlike Santana's.

"You say you love him?" she inquired.

"Yes I do. Very much."

"Then what is the problem?"

I told myself to answer honestly, no matter how stupid it sounded. "It's like we're brother and sister," I began. "I thought my lover, my soul mate . . . I thought it would feel different."

"How should it feel?" she asked.

"Oh, I don't know . . . Exciting. Passionate," I paused for an instant. "Like travel. When I travel, I feel so *alive*. Every moment is charged. I guess I thought love would be more like that. You know, constant discovery. I know it's too much to expect, I *know* that, but—"

"You are like a man," said Brigitte. "Always wanting something fresh."

"It's not that," I said, a little too loudly. "It's just . . . I mean . . . Why should I force myself to stay in one place, with one person, if it doesn't make me happy? Just because some societal standard says I'm a bad person, a bad *woman,* if I don't? I never want to hurt anyone, believe me! But sometimes people get hurt, not by design, but just by the truth of how things are. I mean, I blame myself, of course I do, I blame myself *all the time.* But what can I do? All you can do is try to deal in truth, right, moment to moment? Try to do the best you can with the information that's available to you?" I stopped, shocked by my outburst, amazed to find myself crying. *God, girl,* I thought, *you're more lost than you even knew.*

Brigitte stared at me for a long moment, as though discovering something extraordinary.

"You can do any particular thing you want," she said slowly.

"Pretty much," I admitted. "Maybe that's the problem." I looked away in embarrassment.

"Does moving around make you happy?" she asked.

"Well, yeah, I guess," I paused, laughed awkwardly, swiped at my eyes with the back of my hand. "I don't know. Happi-*er.*"

Brigitte looked at me for a moment, then smiled and shook her head. "Just like a man," she said, squeezing my hand. "Except for this." She lifted her finger to my cheek and captured a fugitive tear.

❖

Rod became more affectionate than ever, clinging to my hand, sitting on my lap, hanging onto my legs. I sat with her some-times from afternoon till evening, stroking her hair and singing. Her presence brought up my latent mothering instincts. I loved children, always had, the touch and feel and smell of them. They opened my heart in a way that nothing else could. There was a part of me that wanted children of my own, yearned for them with a longing so fierce it stopped my breath. Michael, too, had wanted children passionately. He had even tried to persuade me, on occasion, to play a little Russian roulette between the sheets.

"I can't do it, Michael," I'd said.

"Why not? You're great with kids. Look at my nieces and nephews. They adore you."

"I adore them, too."

"Well then?"

"Because. I'm not ready. You know that. I want to do things. I'm not . . . stable enough yet. If I got pregnant now, I wouldn't forgive myself. Or the child."

Michael shuddered. "Don't say that," he said.

Now, with Rod on my lap, I was hard-pressed to remember what "things" I had to do that were so important. I wanted to squeeze her little body close to me, to bury my nose in her oiled and braided hair. Maybe I'd made a mistake. Maybe having children was exactly what I needed, the catalyst that would toss me headfirst into the clear cold pool of my own happiness. The ultimate wake-up call. Maybe. Maybe not. Unfortunately, I couldn't take a trial run.

❖

One evening, I sat next to Brigitte on her bed while she worked the sleeping Lidia's hair into tight little braids. Rod had already been put down for the night.

"Lidia never lets me do this when she's awake," Brigitte explained.

I watched her fingers fly, dipping into oil, then sectioning, braiding, sectioning again.

"I don't love my husband," she said to me. "I used to love him, but now I don't. He goes with other women."

"How do you know?" I asked.

"I've seen the woman. My friend has pointed her out to me." She made a disgusted face. "It makes me sick. And he doesn't give me money."

I looked around. "How do you buy things?"

"Oh, he pays for food, you know. School things. But anything for me, my clothes, my hair, I have to get it for myself. But he won't let me get a job! He wants me to have more children." She pulled another face.

I watched her fingers layer the braids into overlapping arches.

"As soon as I find someone else," she continued, "I'm going to divorce him. I just have to find someone first. I don't want to go around, going on dates. A woman isn't safe that way. But I must hurry, before another baby comes. Can you find an American husband for me?"

"I can't even find one for myself," I joked.

"I want an old man," she said. "Young men are too complicated. I want one who'll appreciate me. I'll give you a picture of me to give him and he can send his picture, and if we like each other, then he'll send me the plane ticket and I'll come."

I pointed out that the visa might still be a problem.

"He'll get it for me," she said. "If he's hot, he'll do it." She took her hands from Lidia's hair and ran her palms up and down the sides of her body, over her breasts, arms, thighs. She closed her eyes. "An old man, who'll treat me well."

I said nothing. After a moment, she opened her eyes and went back to her hair sculpture. Lidia started for a moment, opened her eyes, and whimpered. Then, seeing her mother, she closed them again and drifted back to sleep.

"What about Lidia and Rod?" I asked. "What will they do if you go to the U.S. and marry some old fart?"

She shrugged impatiently. "Their father will take them. I will send money. It will be better for them."

I looked down at the sleeping baby. "If I . . . If I had children like yours," I said, "I could never leave them."

Anger crossed Brigitte's face, and I was immediately ashamed. Who was I to lecture her? Single and childless, I was a veritable poster child for the transient lifestyle.

"They'll be okay," she said.

We sat in silence, Brigitte's hands resting on Lidia's braided head.

❖

"In your city, will you show me around?" she asked later that night, as we lay side by side on her white-sheeted bed under the gauzy canopy of the mosquito net.

"Of course," I said, eager to reestablish our intimacy. "We'll go dancing together, go shopping, to the movies."

"Oh yes," she said, "yes, that's it. I'll be in the movies. You're an actress, aren't you?"

I nodded, "But not in movies. On the stage."

"I'll do movies," she said. "That's the way to make money."

I laughed, and she turned her head sharply toward me.

"It's not that easy," I said.

"Oh, but I can do it!" she said, and in the dark, I could feel the motion of her hands stroking the sides of her body, her head thrown back. "I can do the movies like that, the love scenes . . . I know how to do it." She stopped abruptly. "Of course, if I had a husband, he wouldn't let me. On my own, I could make some money."

"Your husband probably wouldn't stop you. In the U.S., it's normal for women to work. Most women work."

"Oh yes?" she said. "Good."

❖

When I got back from the Malian embassy the next afternoon, passport and visa in hand, I found Brigitte in the smoke-filled kitchen, waving a large stick at Nyanga. The wispy girl cowered in the corner, wailing with fear.

"She's *bête!*" Brigitte shrieked, when she saw me, using the French word that means both "stupid" and "beast."

"What? What happened?"

"*Bête!* I had some mayonnaise—did you see the mayonnaise? I bought it—it was supposed to last until Easter—and yesterday she served it *all* to the people who were here. *All* of it. *Il faut économiser.* I don't earn the money here, it's my husband who earns the money. What's he going to say? He will blame me, he will blame *me,* and then . . . Stupid beast!" She held the stick above her head, her face livid. The girl sobbed loudly, pressing herself into the wall as though she hoped to push through it and disappear. My eyes teared in the heavy smoke.

Behind Brigitte, Constantin appeared in the doorway, sucking on his fingers, a guilty smile on his face. Afraid his presence would further escalate things, I gestured sharply with my head, and he scampered off. I approached Brigitte slowly, holding out my hand for the stick.

"Everyone makes mistakes," I said.

"The same stupid mistakes, again and again. I will beat her now. Never a word, this girl, never a sound, but she is trouble, she is bad!"

"She's not bad. We all make mistakes," I said again, evenly.

"I made the mistake, staying here with these stupid girls. I could be in America, with Rod, Peace Corps. There is a machine that washes, a machine that makes the food!"

"That's not her fault, Brigitte. She's just a child. Look at her, she's terrified. Please. I'll buy you more mayonnaise. A whole new jar."

Brigitte looked at me as though I were a stranger, an alien being she was seeing for the first time. I tried to smile, but my lips wouldn't do the trick. In the corner, the girl moaned. Out in the courtyard, I heard Constantin's cackling laughter.

How desperate we humans are, I thought. *How our hearts burn, feeding on their own desire as if it were tinder.*

Slowly, as though awakening from a dream, Brigitte lowered the stick.

✦

At eleven o'clock that night, Brigitte and I sat on the couch in the living room, drinking beer. It was my goodbye party. Brigitte got up, went to the tape recorder, and put in a tape—a funky, bluesy groove. She pulled me up, and we started to dance. After about twenty minutes, I collapsed back onto the couch, my head swimming. Brigitte kept dancing, her eyes closed. I stared at her, mesmerized by the extreme grace of her bulky frame. Her hips seemed to move independently of her upper body, which hovered above them, regal and still. Her behind taunted the beat, tantalized it, waiting till the last possible instant, till I thought she wouldn't make it, couldn't, then it snapped into place, twitching and popping like corn in hot oil.

Over the rhythmic thump of the music, I heard Rod's voice coming from the bedroom, soft and plaintive. "Mama. Mama. Mama. Mama."

I longed to go to her, but what good would it do? Tomorrow I'd be gone, and besides, she wasn't mine. I don't know whether Brigitte heard her or not. She just kept dancing.

14

Sand Angel

In Ghana, funerals are parties, with drumming and dancing all night long. The older the deceased, the bigger the bash. T-shirts commemorate the prominent ones, with inscriptions like "In ever-loving memory of Mercy Aidoo, alias Nanna," silk-screened on the front and "Rest in Peace" on the back. As one guy told me, "When a young man dies, it is a sad thing. But when an old man dies, it is just natural, so we figure we might as well entertain ourselves." Others put it more delicately: "We rejoice that the person has lived so very long and well."

Maybe this blunt attitude toward death is part of why the average West African seems so much happier than the average American. Perhaps the constant awareness that death could drop in makes people more fully inhabit their lives. My Ghanaian friends strenuously protest the comparison. "We are desperate here!" they say. Nevertheless, I dare anyone to walk down the streets of Accra and then San Francisco, observing the faces, and tell me the Ghanaians aren't happier. You might say that smiling is just a habit, a cultural mannerism, but I think it goes beyond that. These are not empty smiles. The approach to daily life is humorous and exuberant, even in difficulty, like popping a whole chili pepper into your mouth and relishing the burn.

For better or worse, Katie's absence had freed me to travel to whatever out-of-the-way place struck my fancy. One such place was the legendary city of Timbuktu. Its illustrious history as a trade center and seat of higher learning was enough to capture anyone's imagination, but even more intriguing to me was the boat trip up the Niger River. According to my guidebook, people along the river were living much as they had for thousands of years. The more sedentary groups inhabited fishing villages, while the nomadic tribes set up temporary camps, pulling up stakes and moving with the migration patterns of the fish. Even before her illness, Katie had been reluctant to make the journey. If anything happened, she'd said, we'd be too far from anywhere to get decent medical care. Now that she was gone, there was no obstacle to me hopping on a boat.

Before I left Ghana, I discussed the matter with a bikini-clad English expatriate I encountered by the pool at the Accra Novotel. The Novotel was the most expensive hotel in the city, practically the only place in Ghana where you could pay European-scale prices for everything from soap to sandwiches. On hot days, I occasionally splurged on the three-dollar fee to spend an afternoon by the blue waters of its heavily chlorinated pool.

"You don't want to go there!" the expatriate said in horror, reclining in a white plastic lawn chair while she rubbed cocoa butter onto her sleek, tan legs. "Timbuktu's a ghost town! There's nothing to see. It's not the great trading mecca it once was. No camel caravans laden with gold. Just a few beleaguered

beasts with feathers on their heads, and an army of guides waiting to mob you every time you step outside your hotel. Besides,
how good is your French? Mali is Francophone, you know."

Her equally sleek and sun-bronzed French boyfriend opened
his eyes and chimed in. "Sand," he said flatly. "A lot of sand.
Sand in the hair, sand in the eyes, sand in the bread you eat,
crunch crunch." He wrinkled his nose and mimed picking grains
of sand from his mouth.

"And the boat rides!" the woman continued, waving her
hand in front of her nose in horror. "You know how sometimes
a trip is really grueling, but when you finally arrive, you say,
'Well, it was hell, but I'm glad I did it?'" She paused for emphasis. "This is not one of those trips. It's just hell."

❖

The Niger is the third largest river in Africa, after the Nile and
the Congo. If you include its delta—the surrounding wetlands
created by the river's sediment—it's the largest in the world.
Starting in Guinea, the river enters Mali just below the capital
city of Bamako. It heads northeast across Mali until it reaches the
edge of the Sahara at Timbuktu, then turns due east. Shortly
thereafter it shifts toward the southeast in a great arc, passes
through Niger and Nigeria, and empties into the Atlantic Ocean.
In its entirety, the river basin overlaps nine countries.

I decided to catch the boat to Timbuktu in Mopti, a major
trading center about 200 miles southwest of the legendary port.
On my way to Mopti, I stopped for a few days in the city of
Ségou, where I saw the river for the first time.

It was after dark when I made my way through the dusty
streets to the banks of the Niger. I'd arrived from Ghana in the
late afternoon, found a guesthouse, eaten, and showered. The
day had been overcast, and the night was now very dark, with

neither stars nor moon showing through the thick cover of clouds. A few streetlights and glimmers from windows illuminated my way. When I reached the river I saw a vast stripe of darkness that was more like an absence than a presence. On the bank a group of men huddled around a fire. Coming closer, I saw the fire's light reflected in the water. Then I saw *pirogues*— the long, slender canoes of Mali—floating in darkness, their silhouettes supple bows against the reflected light.

It's hard to explain what I felt then, or why. The water's fathomless darkness seemed to beckon, as though it would draw me in. I'd never thought of myself as a spiritual person, and yet I'd spent my adult life seeking *something*. In that moment I felt that the river would change me, though I had no idea how.

The city of Ségou was a charming blend of old and new. Donkey carts, bicycles, mopeds, and taxis rattled side by side down the wide colonial avenues. Decaying mansions lined the boulevard, laundry hanging from their wrought-iron trellises, their yards full of banana trees. Alongside the great river, the earth had regained its color again, and red dirt like the kind I'd seen in Ghana replaced the pale desert dust.

Mali felt like another world. Here, the turbans of the desert began to appear. Old men walked the streets, their light-colored *bou-bous* reaching almost to the ground. The walled alleys made me feel as if I were in Morocco again. Hidden houses, hidden lives.

The Niger by day was a green expanse, striped with dark currents. The rocky beach was littered with bleached bits of paper and plastic. On my second day in Ségou I sat on a cement promontory overlooking the beach for much of the afternoon, observing the goings-on. Below me, women washed clothes, dishes, and their own bodies in the river. Some beat the clothes on the rocks, slapping, twisting, and wringing, while others scrubbed pots and pans with sponges made from the dry brown fiber of weeds. One woman sang a lyrical, slightly plaintive song in a high, nasal voice. The tone was pure and unadorned, beautiful in its openness—a bright free sound offering itself to the world.

Later, a group of teenage girls gathered on the beach, singing upbeat songs in brassy voices. They were playing a game. They stood in a three-quarter circle, holding hands, as one girl at a time separated from the chain, stepped back, then ran and hurled her body forward against the linked arms of the others. Red Rover, we used to call it, except these girls didn't form teams. For them it wasn't about competition, apparently, but about the exhilaration of hurtling your body into space and being caught and held.

Throughout the day, as I perched on my cement outpost, skinny children approached me, their faces smeared with dried snot and pale with dust. They wore oversized torn clothes and held tin cans or calabashes in their outstretched hands. They mumbled unintelligible strings of words in sugary voices, smiling vacant, ingratiating smiles.

From what I could see, these begging children were the poorest people I'd encountered on this trip. In Ghana I'd seen poverty, malnutrition even, but never such forlorn, naked hunger. The expressions on the children's faces chilled me, and I remembered that Mali, once a wealthy empire, was now one of the poorest countries in the world. I distributed what money I had on me, then shook my head apologetically and turned out my empty pockets until they wandered away.

❖

Halfway between the capital city of Bamako and the desert gateway of Timbuktu lies Mopti. The city of Mopti was originally built over several islands, which were later connected with dykes and landfill. In the fourteenth, fifteenth, and sixteenth centuries, when Timbuktu was a great commercial center and seat of higher learning, Mopti was little more than a village. Now Timbuktu has fallen into decay, and Mopti houses the Niger River's most vibrant port.

The port of Mopti is a sweeping expanse of pebble beach bustling with trade. In the packed riverside market, people hawk boat tickets, mats, cloth, blankets, and food for the journey. Others sell jewelry, leather goods, amber, and masks. Tablets of salt, also for sale, glow like enormous ice cubes in the afternoon sun. Women in bright cloth wraps with babies on their backs and men in *bou-bous* and turbans mill about, buying and bartering at top volume. Fabrics dyed in indigo, made in Guinea or by the Dogon people of southern Mali, are popular in Mopti. Standing at the top of a sandy slope, I looked down on a full range of blue and purple garments, from pale lavender to deepest navy, interspersed with splashes of other vivid fabrics, including decoratively painted rust-colored mudcloth.

I finally located Mohammed Hammed, an elderly gentleman in an electric blue turban who sold boat tickets to Timbuktu. He was standing on a wooden crate, next to a stand overflowing with oranges.

"You must go to the airport!" he shouted in French when he saw me.

"I don't want the plane; I want the boat!" I shouted back. I'd been warned by other vendors that Mohammed Hammed was hard of hearing.

"The steamboat, it is not in season!"

"I don't want the steamboat. I want the *pinasse*!"

In the wet season, tourists rode large steamboats to Timbuktu, but in the dry season you had only two options for river travel: the *pirogue* (canoe), or the *pinasse* (motorized canoe).

He stared. "You want to ride the *pinasse*? With all the African traders—black people—with their goods? No private cabin. No 'comfort-of-home.'"

"Yes, that's it. The ancient trade route," I nodded vigorously. "No comfort! Crowded, smelly, difficult. That's what I want."

He shook his head in disbelief. "Well . . . Let me see if I have a ticket . . ." He made a show of shuffling through a small stack of papers. "Hup! One left. *Six mille CFA*. Six thousand francs."

"Oh, come on! I saw you selling that guy a ticket for half that!" I indicated a portly African man who'd just walked away with a ticket and a bag of grain.

"You people take up space for two. You are not used to travel like we do. Will you be able to sleep like this?" He crouched, hugging his knees to his chest.

"Forty-five hundred?"

"Five thousand."

"Including food?"

"Oh all right," he said, with a *you-drive-a-hard-bargain* sigh.

I did the conversion in my head—a comforting trick when you know you've haggled terribly. *After all, it's only twenty bucks.*

"The trip will take two days," said Mohammed as he handed me my ticket. "Maximum three."

"I heard it could take a week."

He looked offended. "A week, never!" he scoffed. "Four days if you have very bad luck. But no. Not even four. Three days. Not more than three."

❖

I was just getting settled on the boat, arranging my backpacks, oranges, and burlap-covered jerricans of water around me, when a burly African man appeared above me, blocking the sun.

"All these people are savages!" he boomed. With a grand sweep of his arm he took in all the other passengers on the boat.

"They have never been to school. They live like animals. Me, I don't like savages."

"Hello?"

"*Bonjour*, I am Touré. *Comment ça va?* What is your name?"

"Tanya."

"Excellent! I'd like to sit here with you, Tanya, to profit from your company." He plunked his canvas satchel onto my grass mat. His French was rapid and murky—I strained to understand him.

"You are not sleeping here," I said, alarmed.

"I don't sleep," he said impatiently, making himself comfortable beside his satchel. "I go days without sleeping. Where are you from?" He glanced at my bag. "America?"

I nodded, and his eyes lit up with a familiar gleam.

"I want to go there with you, Tanya, to your country. Can you help me to get a visa?"

"I don't work for immigration."

"You can sponsor me. Vouch for my character."

"I—"

"I would like to go there and open a store for women's shoes. They say that women in America will pay $200 for a pair of shoes. One can easily get rich with shoes."

I sighed. "It's actually not—"

"Very rich."

"There are a lot of poor—"

"Ha!" He stretched out his legs, propped his head against his bag and said firmly, his tone brooking no argument, "The poor in your country would be rich here."

❖

The floor of the boat was piled high with sacks of grain, creating a treacherous, uneven surface. We spread our grass mats across it to stake out territory.

The *pinasse* was an oversized, pregnant canoe, with a roof over the middle and a motor in the back. Sitting in its covered center, I felt like Jonah in the belly of the whale, looking up at a sturdy rib cage of bamboo poles with woven raffia stretched across the top. Sheets of raffia rolled down over the sides at night to keep out the cold.

The boat was about thirty feet long and nine feet wide. The roof—which covered about two-thirds of the surface area of the boat, leaving the front and back open—was so low that a five-foot-five-inch person such as myself had to bend over to walk in the covered area. In the center of the boat, there was a sharp drop in the floor where the sacks were cleared to create a kitchen. Down there, a stocky adolescent girl was busily arranging pots, coal ports, charcoal, and a collection of stubby logs. There, too, was where the water-bailer stood, already performing his endless task.

All around me, men, women, and children ran on and off the boat, carrying tied-up bundles and wedging them in between the sacks. They'd see me, do a kind of startled double take, then launch into what I call "the *ça va* dance," a murmured stream of dialogue accompanied by hand gestures: "*Ça va? Ça va bien? Ça va la santé? Ça va la famille? Ça va le déjeuner? Ça va le Mali? Ça va le voyage?*" This continued on and on, with slight variations: "How are you? How's your health? How's your family? How was your lunch?" And you responded: "*Ça va. Ça va. Ça va . . .*" It took me several days in the country before I learned that you end the exchange by saying, "*Ça va tout.*" Everything's fine.

At first people left a wide margin around my mat, but eventually the boat got too full, and they had to move in closer. In the end, about thirty adults and fourteen children fit tightly atop the sacks, with about a foot of space between us.

"You people are educated," Touré said to me. He was spreading out his things now, making himself ever more comfortable on my mat. "You know how to make things: telephones, computers, cars . . . And you all read. Not like these animals here. Me, I like to read." He produced a dog-eared French novel from his bag.

"You know, not all whites read—"

"Well, I never met one who couldn't. You and me, we are alike, Tanya. *Toi et moi.*"

I couldn't shake Touré. Whenever I attempted to converse with another person on the boat, he placed himself in the middle, translating. When I misplaced things, which happened at least every half hour, Touré asked, "What are you looking for?" When I grudgingly named the item of the moment (water bottle, socks, sunscreen, etc.), he performed a vacuumlike search of the surrounding sacks, never hesitating to push other passengers out of the way or reach beneath the men's legs. Within minutes he would hold the missing item aloft, proclaiming proudly, "It is here!"

He was a muscular man, with a sly, wise face that seemed to smirk in repose. He had a strong jaw and cheekbones, and his golden-brown eyes had an Asian slant. His movements were abrupt and impatient; he seemed combustible. He ranted incessantly about the ignorance and stupidity of the other passengers, but at the end of these tirades he always burst out laughing. His laugh was infectious. For all his abrasiveness, he could win a crowd.

"Your French is not so good, Tanya!" he crowed, as I strained to interpret his marble-mouthed dialect. He had a huge vocabulary, and seemed to enjoy employing a range of words I'd never heard.

"You don't know the meaning of *that?*" he shouted with glee. "This is a word every schoolchild knows! It is too bad I don't speak English. The rest of these animals speak no language at all," he waved his hand in disdain at the other passengers, "no French, no English—only African dialects: Bambara, Songhaï . . . How is your Bambara, Tanya?" He barked with laughter.

The morning wore into afternoon. The announced departure time of the boat was 9 A.M., but by 3 P.M. it showed no sign of going anywhere. Some people got off the boat and browsed the market. Children ran up and down the shore. Ice water, peanut, and banana vendors came onto the boat, hawking their wares to those who'd stayed on board to guard their spaces. A dry breeze moved through the boat. Touré lay back against my backpack, gazing ahead in a zombielike trance.

"These people are all thieves," he announced abruptly.

"Stop that," I said, trying to shush him.

"I know them," he insisted. "I have been in prison."

"Really?" I paused to digest this new piece of information. "What for?"

"Commerce."

"Commerce?"

"You know, commerce," he shrugged impatiently, then made a series of illustrative gestures, pointing to his nose and sniffing, putting his thumb and forefinger to his lips and sucking in air, then tapping out a vein in his arm.

"I get the picture," I said dryly.

"So you see," he continued, "I know what it is like. There are thieves who ride these *pinasses* waiting for their chance. Sometimes the owners and their families are in on it." He looked suspiciously at the chunky adolescent girl de-stoning a pot of rice in the sunken kitchen. "I will help you to keep an eye on your things."

The irony that I should trust an ex-convict to guard my belongings seemed lost on him.

"Thanks," I said. Shifting impatiently, I asked him when he thought the boat would leave.

"The boat will leave when it is completely full," he said.

Buses operated under the same principle, but somehow I had never gotten used to it. I glanced around at the packed boat. "So you think about fifteen minutes?"

He laughed appreciatively. "You people," he said, shaking his head and wiping his eyes. "You live by the clock."

Where had I heard that before?

At four o'clock that afternoon, we left Mopti for Timbuktu.

✦

Going to the bathroom was a problem. I watched the other passengers for clues. A little boy was given a plastic bowl, which his mother then emptied over the side of the boat. Later, under cover of darkness, I noticed a woman sitting on the side wall, placing her body outside the rolled-down raffia shade, her hands clinging to one of the bamboo poles for support. For once I was grateful for dehydration.

When I finally had to go, I was in the uncovered front of the boat, huddled under a scratchy handwoven blanket. I'd come out to watch the stars. Men were stretched out all around me, but it was dark and half of them were asleep. I made my way to the side of the boat and then discovered the problem. Out here, there were no poles to hang on to. I giggled nervously.

"What's the matter?"

I was surprised by a nearby voice speaking precise, European-accented French. I couldn't make out the man's face—just the pale outline of a slim body topped off by a turban, like a dandelion with an enormous, puffed head.

I giggled, put a hand to my bladder, indicated the edge of the boat.

"I see," he said. "Here, hold my hand."

His hand was slender, delicate almost, and unusually smooth. His voice, too, was gentle and soothing. There was something very comforting about him.

I started to climb onto the low wall, then balked. "Ooooh . . . I don't know."

"Everyone does it," he said easily. "I will turn my head the other way."

So it has come to this, I thought as I leaned back, holding this stranger's hand. I'd done holes in the ground, seething pits, rooms full of sand, buckets, even the group toilet in Apam, but here was something new. For the longest time nothing would come out. *Come on.* I wanted to kick my body like a horse. The stranger would wait silently, it seemed, for as long as it took. Eventually it came, and with the sound of the water all around me, I could barely tell when my own flow began and ended. When I pulled myself up, the end of my skirt was soaked from dangling in the river.

"Thank you."

"Everyone does it," he repeated cheerfully, and returned to his contemplation of the stars.

I headed back into the covered section, ready for sleep. In the warm glow of the kerosene lanterns, I found it transformed into a cozy house. I picked my way through a carpet of bodies sleeping sardine-style, head to toe. I was glad, now, that I'd paid for extra space. But where was my mat? I scanned the boat, disoriented, trying to locate a vacant spot.

Oh, no.

Touré was sprawled diagonally across my mat, snoring. Only a tiny triangle of space remained between his body and a bamboo pole. I looked around for another spot, but every inch of space was taken. Sighing, I tried to squeeze myself into the available space, pulling my knees to my chest and resting my head against the pole. I tried to sleep.

I couldn't sleep.

"Touré!" I whispered, shaking him lightly, then harder. "Touré!"

I pushed him; I tickled him; I pulled him. No response. An old man just past Touré's head sat up and glared at me like an angry ghost.

"Je m'excuse," I mouthed.

The water-bailer temporarily abandoned his task and came over to help, shaking Touré's foot and calling to him in Bambara. I tried to move one of Touré's arms, and that's when I discovered something peculiar. At first the arm moved floppily, the way a sleeping arm should. Then it tensed and became steel. With all my strength I couldn't budge it. Either he was faking, or his guard never came down, even in sleep.

In desperation, I placed my feet against his chest and tried to roll him over. I was making no headway at all, until my foot slipped loose and kicked him in the face. He sat up sharply.

"Eh!" he shouted.

"Touré! You've got to give me just a little space to lie down."

"A little space," he repeated groggily.

"A little space," I pleaded.

He lay back down, grumbling, shifting his body a teensy bit to the side. I nudged him again, afraid he'd drift back to sleep. He moved a little more, but still not enough. The water-bailer spoke to him sharply in Bambara. He sat up.

"Aahh," I groaned, spreading out.

He stayed sitting the rest of the night. I didn't care.

❖

"You beat me up last night. You tried to kill me!" Touré shouted at me the next morning.

"You said you didn't sleep," I countered defensively. "You said you wouldn't sleep *here*."

"And so you attack me?"

"I didn't attack you," I grumbled. "I was just trying to *move* you."

"Is this how you treat your boyfriend in your bed?"

I paused for a moment. "I don't have a boyfriend."

"No wonder!"

It was 6 A.M. The day had dawned clear and breezy, with a pale yellow sky moving gradually toward blue. All around me people were chatting good-naturedly, leaning over the side of the boat to wash their hands and faces in the river. The sound of their laughter and the splashing of the water mingled with the chirping and warbling of countless birds.

Everyone on the boat chipped in a handful of rice, and the captain's daughter prepared a rice-water breakfast. Dinner the night before had worked the same way, with everyone chipping in rice and the girl cooking it up with a mixture of shea oil, onion, tomato, and a bit of okra, which gave it a slimy texture that made me gag. It had a slight fish flavor as well, though no actual pieces of fish. Touré explained to me that they cooked the rice with the fish, then took the fish out, removed the bones, and crushed the rest to a pulp to flavor the whole dish.

I hadn't been prepared to contribute rice, and the boat's owner seemed unaware that I'd purchased a ticket with meals included, so I gave him some extra money for food. Instead of using the coal port, the girl lit a log fire in a large iron bowl in the sunken kitchen area, right in the middle of the *pinasse*. The smoke stung my eyes. To make matters worse, she'd positioned herself right next to me while chopping the onions.

Mornings are not my best time of day. I've never been sure whether my work in the theatre is a cause of this or vice versa. On this particular morning, my body ached from the cold night on the lumpy sacks, and Touré's incessant energy was grating on my nerves. Was I stuck with him for the entire trip because of language? Then I remembered the man I'd met the night before, the one with the smooth voice and delicate hands.

"Hey, Touré," I said. "Did you know there's another guy on this boat who's fluent in French?"

"Yes," Touré said huffily. "I have seen him. He does not do the prayer. You should stay away from him, a man who betrays his own religion." He leaned in closer. "I've heard he is meeting Christian missionaries in Timbuktu."

❖

Over the course of the morning, we saw an astounding array of birds. They dove and waded, hovered and floated. I recognized a few of them: heron, sandpiper, pelican, starling. Others were completely unfamiliar. Some had colorful plumage and large curving bills; others' heads were adorned with feathery sprays. Some balanced near the shore on long, spindly legs, while others darted along the bank so quickly their short legs blurred to invisibility. Still others circled overhead, brightly garbed in yellow or red or black, each trilling its particular song.

Midday found us pulled up on the bank of the river. One of the steering cords had broken and was being repaired. The population of the boat made a mass exodus to the shore, teetering down a shaky plank, bare feet clamped to the slippery wood. Despite my best efforts at balance, I ended up ankle-deep in squishy mud. It was worth it, though, to relieve myself in the relative comfort of the great outdoors. We were passing through a series of lakes, and the shores of the river were marshy, filled with high grasses and reeds in brilliant shades of green.

Two hours later, we were back on the water.

"Why are you going to Timbuktu?" I asked Touré, after we'd finally gotten underway.

"Timbuktu? I am not going all the way to that place. Too much sand. I'm getting off in my hometown of Diré. I am going to see the marabout. Someone has cursed me."

The marabout was a Moslem holy man believed to have supernatural powers, the Malian equivalent of the fetish priest.

"Look." He pushed up his sleeve and showed me the inside of his arm. One patch was noticeably paler than the rest. The skin appeared to be peeling off in fine, uneven layers, like shale.

"Everything else in my body is fine," he said. "I went to the hospital and did all kinds of tests, but they could not find anything." He paused. "Shall I tell you how I know it's a curse?" He leaned in confidentially, glancing around. "My flip-flops disappeared. Twice in a row. I left them outside my door at night, and the next morning they were gone. Then in the evening, they were back."

I looked at him curiously.

"That's how they do it!" he insisted. "They take a part of you to give to the spirits so they know how to find you."

"Why would they give them back?" I asked.

"They got what they wanted! They aren't thieves."

❖

Five times a day the call to prayer sounded, and the majority of passengers rose like a wave and faced Mecca. The sight of them in their blue, white, and lavender robes and turbans, rising and falling in near unison against the backdrop of the river, was graceful and unexpectedly moving. They knelt on their prayer mats, prostrating themselves, their mumbling forming a hypnotic chorus. I envied them this ritual, at once private and shared. My Moroccan friend Abdelati once said to me, "I look forward to the hour of prayer with eager anticipation." *It must be a great comfort,* I thought, *to know that wherever you are, whatever you're doing, five times a day you—and everyone around you—will drop everything and speak deeply with God . . . or even just with yourself.*

One man kept drawing my eye. He was tiny—maybe five foot two—with small bones and delicate features. He wore the usual pale cotton *bou-bou,* but instead of a turban he wore a little wool cap, even in the heat of day. When he performed the prayer, bliss seemed to radiate outward from his entire body. His eyes turned upward in an expression of devotion more complete than any I had ever seen. He positively glowed with joy, from the tips of his fingers to the soles of his bare feet. I was transfixed.

On the second afternoon, after finishing the prayer, he turned suddenly and came toward me, pointing emphatically. His face was animated, eyes lit by an urgent question. He pointed at me and then pointed up. He tilted his head back, peering skyward. Then he looked at me, hands spread wide, eyebrows raised.

Confused, I looked around for help.

"He wants to know why you don't do the prayer," said Touré. He tapped the man on the shoulder, pointed at me, then made the sign of the cross. "I told him you are a Christian," he said.

"But I'm not a Christian," I protested. "I'm an agnostic-leaning-toward-atheist Jew."

"What?"

"Just tell him I'm not a believer."

Touré looked at the man. He pointed at me, crossed himself again, then shook his head sadly and moved his hands across each other in a negating gesture, like an umpire calling "out." He then prostrated himself on the ground in the manner of the Moslem prayer, got up, and repeated the negating gesture. Then, in a final dramatic action, he pointed toward the sky, sweeping his arm as if to include anything that could possibly be up there. He shook his head again, vigorously, and once again moved his hands in the "out" symbol, as if to say, "Nothing there."

The man looked at me in disbelief. He made a gesture as though gathering up a fistful of grain and throwing it over his head, then looked up again to heaven. His face wore the purest delight.

Touré shrugged at me. "He says you must believe. God is there."

The man nodded at me, beaming. It was the same conversation I'd had a hundred times since arriving in Africa, but this man's passion made it fresh.

I shook my head at him. "I'm sorry," I said gently. "I wish I could believe, but I don't." I shrugged helplessly. "I can't."

The man simply nodded at me, beaming.

"He says you will," said Touré.

❖

The landscape settled into a kind of monotony, as we floated past broad stretches of grassy savanna dotted with low bushes and spiny trees. Here and there a baobab stood, squat and defiant, its prickly branches thrusting combatively into the air. Occasionally we passed villages—clusters of rectangular, flat-roofed huts the same color as the earth. Some of these grew crops, their brilliant green, carefully tended plots like flashes of neon amid the surrounding drabness. From time to time we'd see sheep or goats grazing on the sparse savanna grass. Near the villages, men fished on the river in *pirogues* or *pinasses*, some with billowy sails, and women stood along the bank, smoking fish, bathing, or washing clothes.

At the center of each village was a mosque. These mosques were exquisite, wildly fanciful creations, like something out of Dr. Seuss. They, too, were built of mud, with turrets and towers of varying heights, and short pieces of wood sticking out all over at odd angles. Mud can be a shifty substance: I later learned that the wood was there at least in part to allow people to climb up and apply a fresh layer if a spot cracked or wore thin.

On the third morning of the trip, we were passing a village when the little man approached me again. Excited, he pointed to me, then to himself, then to the village. He repeated the sequence a couple of times.

"He wants you to visit him in his village," said Touré.

"Is that it?" I asked, confused, pointing to the passing hamlet.

"No, no. In the desert. He will bring you there from Timbuktu."

"Really? That would be fantastic."

The man put his fingers to either side of his head like little horns, then made a lusty biting gesture at his arm, as though tearing away the flesh with his teeth.

"He says he will kill a goat for you," said Touré.

"But I'm a vegetarian," I said. A fish-etarian who sometimes eats chicken, actually, but I didn't want to confuse things. Touré made the biting gesture, with less gusto, and shook his head sadly.

The man repeated the fierce gesture, and nodded.

"He says meat is good," said Touré.

The man pointed then to a little boy standing on the shore. He nodded, smiling, and rubbed his belly.

"He says that boy would be very good to eat. He says you could get a lot of money for the head."

I gaped in disbelief.

Touré burst out laughing. "He is joking with you! He has heard what the white people think of Africa." He shook his head. "He is an interesting person, isn't he?"

I laughed, and so did the little man, silently, beaming and rubbing his flat belly. He then launched rapid-fire into a new sequence of gestures.

"He says there is plenty of rice in his village for you to eat," Touré translated. "This village is only a small camp, some distance into the desert. A car goes there twice a week from Timbuktu. Or you can take a camel."

"What does he do there?"

The man moved his hands vigorously from side to side. I looked at Touré in bewilderment.

"Isn't it obvious? He makes charcoal!"

"Obviously." Charcoal, I'd been told, was made by burning wood in a deep underground pit, then applying pressure to compact it. How the gesture illustrated this wasn't entirely clear to me, but I didn't ask.

"He wants to know what you are doing on this boat."

"Me? I'm just . . . traveling." I walked the fingers of one hand across the back of the other. Now it was the little man's turn to look bewildered. He spread out his hands and cocked his head inquisitively.

"Why?" I looked at Touré, who nodded. "Why," I repeated aloud. I looked at the man. As usual, his wool cap covered his skull. It was impossible to gauge his age, though I guessed somewhere in his mid to late forties. The skin was stretched tight

across the bones of his face. Deep smile lines had carved themselves beside his mouth. His eyes were so kind, his expression at
once so innocent and penetrating, that I felt tears rise in my own
eyes. I tried to imagine his life: sweltering days spent digging
holes in the desert and pressing the charcoal into them, walking
for miles in search of water, eating meals of rice and sauce with
his family, sleeping curled up between siblings and cousins in a
tent, then dragging his heavy sack on a bumpy camel ride to
Timbuktu, where he would catch a *pinasse* and travel along the
river, hawking the hard black lumps that were his livelihood to
the people in the villages he passed—people who had known
him all his life—always delivering a smile with his goods. How
could I explain my strange life to him? How could I tell yet
another person here that with everything that had been given to
me, I was still restless and unsatisfied? That I felt driven to wan-
der the earth in search of some elusive key that would unlock
the chamber of my own happiness? How could I explain that I
chose physical hardship: dysentery, heat rash, dizzying rides in
crowded vehicles down bumpy, potholed roads—hardship he
had no choice but to endure—that I *chose* all of this, because it
was the only thing that made me feel truly alive?

"To see things . . . I guess," I offered lamely.

The man pointed to my red spiral notebook, which was
perched on the sack of grain beside me. He put his head down
and hunched his shoulders, making a scribbling gesture on his
hand. He looked up at me with an inquiring expression.

"How can I see when I'm always writing?" I shrugged.
"Good question. Sometimes I feel that when I'm writing is the
only time I can see."

He looked at me in perplexity, and again I was at a loss.
Maybe it's because my parents are academics, I wanted to say, *but I feel*

that no matter how big a mess I make of my life, if I write it all down carefully, it'll come out all right.

"Why don't you write at home, in your own country?" asked Touré.

I shrugged, turning to him. "I guess I was just born restless. Wherever I am, I always want to be somewhere else."

Touré gestured, translating my response. The little man shook his head sadly, looking at me with downturned mouth and mournful eyes.

"He says you are a very bad girl," said Touré. "Your mother and father are so worried about you—they want you home. His mother too, she will be glad to see you, for his sister has gone far away, to work in Bamako."

"Did he really say all that?"

"Of course!" said Touré, mock offended.

I laughed. "Well, I can't wait to meet his mother. When do we go?"

"Aren't you afraid, to go so far into the desert?" Touré looked at me curiously.

"With him? How can I be afraid with him?" I looked at the generously lined face, the warm, twinkling eyes. "What's his name?" I asked.

The man gestured helplessly, spreading his hands wide, palms up. Straining his neck, he let out a high chirping sound.

"He cannot tell you," said Touré. "He does not have letters."

The man was deaf! All this time I'd thought he was gesturing because of the language barrier. I'd imagined he spoke a regional dialect so different from Touré's that even they had to talk to each other in a kind of universal sign.

Suddenly the man pointed at my feet. He began stroking his own pale soles with a doleful expression.

"He wants you to give him your shoes," said Touré.

What? Here I am thinking this guy is some kind of guru, and it turns out he's just after my shoes? My enthusiasm evaporated like a teardrop in the Sahara.

"I need them," I said, my lips tight.

He wagged a finger at me. Smiling craftily, he pointed to my backpack. With infinite care, he built a boot in the air around his foot.

He knew the sandals were not my only shoes. He'd spotted a pair of boots in my backpack, practically new. He touched his heart, then repeated a gesture I'd seen him make before, flinging an invisible handful of grain into the air.

"He says when you give, you are in the heart of God," said Touré.

"Is he still trying to convert me, or does he just want the shoes?" I snapped.

Touré considered this. "I will ask him," he said.

"No . . . Don't."

What the hell was wrong with me? The man's feet were dry and cracked, covered with yellowing calluses. When had I become so hard?

But what good would it do anyway, one pair of shoes to one person, in a year they'd wear out and—

Stop it. Look at this man.

I looked. The woolen skullcap, the slight body swathed in its cotton robe, the crinkled face and glowing eyes, the hopeful smile, the bare feet. I stood there for a long moment, suspended in indecision.

Just take the sandals off and give them to him.

I didn't.

❖

Afternoon found me on the roof of the *pinasse*, basking in the sunshine, the wind tousling my hair. It was a perfect day, the sun warm but not oppressive, the breeze delicious on my skin. The Niger spread brown and languid before me. The sky was a pure, deep blue, the marsh grass to the left a vibrant green. To the right, spectacular red rock formations rose above the equally red earth.

Whenever we passed a village, children materialized out of nowhere and tore down the shore, pointing and shouting, waving wildly at the strange white creature perched on the boat. I waved back at them, feeling like the homecoming queen on her float.

The air was filled with birdsong, harsh and lyrical, legato and staccato—a polyphonic symphony. A hawk circled overhead. Earlier in the day we'd seen three hippos, bathing serenely in the middle of the river, their backs rising from the water like the mountains of a sunken land. Another couple sunned themselves on shore. Touré warned me to steer clear of them, both in and out of the water. They were very fast, he said, and they'd been known to chase people down and trample them to death.

Great, I thought wryly, *one more thing to worry about.*

But nothing was worrying me now. My broad-brimmed straw sunhat cast a half-circle of shade on my face. I kept taking my sunglasses off and putting them on again: off to experience the colors; on to cut the glare. I was singing: *"I'm on the top of the world, looking down on creation and the only explanation I can find—"*

Suddenly the captain of the ship, who'd been standing a few feet in front of me, nose to the wind like a mascot, jumped off the roof to the deck below. The boat was heading straight for the swampy shore. He grabbed a pole and threw his weight against it, trying to deflect the nose from collision, but we were moving too fast—the pole jumped back at him. He sprang out of the boat as though someone had pushed an ejector button, and crashed into the water below.

I stared at the water, paralyzed. Where had he gone? Was he hurt? Just as I was about to scream for help, he hopped out of the water onto the bank, shouting and waving his arms.

At that moment, the nose hit the shore with a resounding crack. Wood splintered. Water began pouring in. A few scattered shouts from the deck below built quickly to a cacophony.

Wow, I thought, with a kind of dull incredulity. *This is really an accident.*

People started running off the boat. I suddenly realized my notebooks were still in the back of the boat, under the roof. One of them was loose, on my mat; two others were in my small daypack. There was over a month of writing there, precious detail I didn't want to lose. *I knew I should've mailed them home!* I decided to wait until everyone was out of the way before jumping down. No fire-in-the-movie-house crush for this girl.

When the flow of traffic stopped, I leaped lightly to the deck. The water was coming in slowly—only ankle-deep so far. Plenty of time to get my notebooks.

To get to my things, I had to make the precarious climb over the sunken kitchen. When I got there, I found Touré, dragging my two packs and his own satchel toward the shore end of the boat.

"Here, put these on your back," he said, dropping them. I knelt to detach the daypack from the larger one. Touré had connected them the night before by interlinking the straps. He'd said they were less likely to be stolen that way.

"What are you doing?" he yelled.

"I'm detaching the small pack."

"There's no time for that! Put the packs on your back!" He headed off, toting his bag.

I tried to follow his instructions, but in my haste I got tangled in the straps. I couldn't imagine negotiating the climb from the boat to the shore with that load on my back. I had the irrational notion that if I put on the heavy pack, my part of the boat would sink faster. Out of the corner of my eye I saw my current notebook—the red spiral one—sitting on my grass mat. I reached for it.

Until that moment, I'd never really understood the way a boat sinks. I figured that with the water coming in so slowly, it would be a good half hour before the boat was really under. What I didn't realize is that when the weight of the water hits critical mass, the boat just goes down.

Suddenly water—at my chest and rising. I tossed the bags and dove. But did I dive? Or was I just suddenly in the water? *My hat!* The leather braid yanked my head back, choking me. Ripped it off, paddling wild, roof coming down, dark. *Dark.* Underwater—how long?—turning, flailing in slow-motion darkness. *Which way is up?* Thrashing, heartbeat, loud—*Did I clear the roof?* Then light, murky and green, and I popped up into it, gasping.

The water was eerily calm. I looked around, confused.

Any children in the water? Fuck it—get to shore. What a selfish asshole you are.

I swam for the muddy bank, where children and adults were running down the shore, chasing after floating luggage.

"La blanche! La blanche!" A man extended a scratchy hand. I almost pulled him in, trying to gain my balance in the slippery mud.

Touré came running up the bank toward me.

"Look what happened to me trying to find *your* luggage," he shouted, showing me a gash on his arm. "And this one tried to kill me; she tried to strangle me!" He indicated a slim young woman standing nearby with a baby on her back. She held a naked, shivering little boy by the hand. "She grabbed me here," indicating his turban. *"Sauve moi! Sauve moi!"* he yelped, affecting a shrill soprano.

"She was probably afraid," I said.

"Is that a reason to strangle me?"

Just then I heard a high-pitched sound, somewhere between a chirp and a scream. It came again and again, sharp and staccato, repeating at regular intervals like an alarm. I looked around, agitated, trying to locate where it was coming from. The brown surface of the water was smooth, undisturbed except for the end of the boat sticking up like a shark's fin and the baggage drifting lazily downstream.

"What's that sound?" I asked Touré, but he was gone, chasing the bags. I began to scan the floating debris for my things. I was thinking, again, of my notebooks, wondering if they could possibly be saved.

"Madame, your bag?" The captain's adolescent daughter was beside me, panting with exertion, pulling me inland. Her chubby hand gripped my forearm too tightly. She parted the high grass and pointed to a soggy duffel bag.

"No, that's not mine," I said distractedly, watching the river. "Have you seen a small gray daypack? Or a red notebook?"

She shook her head, dragging me along the shore to where more retrieved items lay drying.

"This?" she asked, pointing. "This?"

"No, not mine," I said. People were darting among the luggage in a panic. A fight seemed to have broken out over a cloth-tied bundle. Two women were pulling at it. Clothes went flying.

"What is that sound?" I asked again. The shrill cries were coming at shorter intervals now, one after another.

The girl shrugged. "A bird, maybe." She pointed to a leather satchel. "Yours?"

"No, no . . . There are two, a gray daypack and—"

Just then I saw my red spiral notebook floating downstream.

"Oh!" I ran down the bank, stripped off my skirt, and dove for it. When I got back to shore, holding my sopping notebook, the air seemed unnaturally still. The high-pitched sound, I realized, had stopped.

Catching my breath, I turned inland to survey the landscape in which we were stranded. Shielding my eyes, I saw that the muddy bank and high grasses soon gave way to drier land. Sandy dunes capped the horizon, bare with spiky grass at the tip. Low shrubs were scattered around the base of the dunes. The scenery I'd found so beautiful a half-hour before now appeared bleak: shadeless and unforgiving.

When the flow of luggage abated, the captain's daughter returned, still in a tizzy. She showed me several more unclaimed bags, none of them mine.

"I am so sorry we have not found it," she said, shaking her head. Her hands flew despairingly to her face.

"It's okay." I clutched my notebook, laid my other hand on her shoulder. My passport and travelers' checks were in a money belt around my waist, soggy but intact. "At least no one was hurt," I said soothingly.

"Yes," she nodded, eyes wide. "They say there was a man who died."

"Really?" A knot of anxiety formed in my chest. "Who was it?"

"I don't know," she said. "Only, an old woman, she saw him, trying to swim."

I searched for Touré, the fear hardening, moving upward into my throat. I found him arguing with the husband of the young woman he'd "rescued." Apparently this had caused some jealousy. I grabbed his arm and pulled him aside.

"They say someone drowned."

"Yes, yes," he said distractedly. "Your friend. He is dead."

"What?"

He turned to face me. "The deaf mute. He was caught in the boat. He did not know how to swim."

"The . . . That man?" I imitated the hand gestures, and Touré nodded.

"Are you sure?" My mind doubled back frantically. Hadn't I seen him?

He shrugged. "I did not see it, but that's what they are saying."

"But—" I stopped suddenly. *Oh God. That sound.*

But how? I thought. *Those were not the cries of a person in the water. A person in the water couldn't have kept up such a steady stream of sound! He'd have been splashing around, gulping, gasping, wouldn't he? How could the sound go on so long?*

Unless he was in the boat. The back of the boat was sticking up; his head could've been just above—But I was staring right at the boat, how could I not—if he'd been in there I would have seen—But I wasn't looking, was I? I was thinking of my notebooks. My notebooks—

Oh no. No.

"Why didn't someone save him?" I whispered.

"They did not see him in time."

◆

Most people's things were recovered. The men cracked open the bamboo ribs of the roof, and things trapped within floated up, including my two packs. As they dove to dislodge stuck items, I held my breath, afraid I'd see a waterlogged body emerge, pale and softening. It never came. The current, swifter than it appeared, had long since carried him away.

We scrambled to set up camp, scrounging among the shrubs for firewood, searching the recovered sacks for edible grain. Throughout this process, a toddler's cries permeated the air.

These were not a normal child's cries, but raw, hair-raising sounds, as though she were suffering some excruciating physical pain. Her eyes were bleary with tears; mucus ran from her nose.

This went on for hours. The young mother, edgy and embarrassed, alternated comfort and threats. Occasionally the crying stopped for a few moments. Each time it started up again, people groaned. It was as though the child were expressing, vocally, the private anguish of the entire boat. It was all I could do not to plug my ears.

[...]ce, as the mother lifted the child to her breast, the little dr[...], and I saw that it was not a girl, but a boy. I felt a com-[...]g, for the grief he would have to stow.

[...]at boy is traumatized by the accident," I said to Touré.

[...]e's spoiled," he said. "He needs to be slapped."

✧

[...]ght fell. The darkness was alive with humming and whirring [in]sects, punctuated by the occasional birdcall. Soggy and pathetic, we huddled around small fires at the foot of the dunes, holding clothing and blankets toward the flames to dry. I turned my bulky sleeping bag over and over, trying to dry it inside and out without burning a hole.

The woman Touré had nearly come to blows over sat near me with her baby on her lap. Her little boy, still naked, shivered beside her on the log. Searching for a dry garment to give him, I came across my emergency blanket, a paper-thin sheet of something metallic—gold on one side, silver on the other. This blanket, I'd been told, could reflect back enough of your body's heat, in a pinch, to save your life. I unrolled it, shielding my eyes from the reflected firelight, and wrapped it around the shaking child. He shrieked with delight and began to run from campfire to campfire with his arms outstretched, a superhero in a shining cape.

As I returned to the task of drying my sleeping bag, I gradually became aware of a thin man standing beside me, watching my manipulations with amusement.

"Are you feeling better?" he asked. His light, soothing voice and flawless French sounded oddly familiar.

I shrugged, turning my face toward the flames.

"You know," he said, "when you cry, it brings everyone else down."

I looked at him in disbelief. "Well, they should be down. A man died."

"Men die every day."

"But it shouldn't have happened. The river's not wide; it's not even very deep. We could have done something, if we hadn't all been chasing our luggage. Including me with my notebook, God help me."

"That's right!" he said, with sudden energy. "God helped you! It was our brother's time."

"I don't believe that," I said, wishing for once that he could convince me, that anyone could.

"If you'd seen him," he said, "would you have done something?"

"Yes! I think so. I mean, God, I hope so. I mean—"

"*Did* you see him?"

"No, but I heard—"

"But did you *see* him?"

I shook my head.

"Neither did I. And I promise you, if I had seen him, I would have gone in after him, even if I had died myself. But why do you think, with all these people, the only one who saw him was an old woman who could not swim?"

I started to say that I'd like to believe him, but that I'd never seen any evidence that the universe was not completely, absurdly random—but my throat closed up. He looked in my eyes for a long time, searchingly, as though he might transfer some faith this way. I felt a sudden urge to grab his narrow shoulders and kiss him, so hard that our teeth knocked, to bite, to squeeze until we both lost breath. My throat ached as though a stone were lodged there, and my face went hot.

"So you should not cry," he said.

"But we should remember," I croaked, "so we learn from it." My eyes welled up. I turned my head from the fire, and cool air bathed my face.

He sighed. "People have lost shoes, identity papers, everything. Cakes and cloth they were going to sell are ruined. They have nothing to bring home to their families, not even money to get back to their villages. They must keep cheerful. No one has forgotten. Each person, alone, will think of it. And around these fires tonight, people will talk of it. They are talking of it already."

It was then that I recognized his voice. The night he'd held my hand while I balanced on the boat's edge seemed light-years ago now, an entirely other life.

His name was Yaya, and he was studying to be a minister, a Christian convert from a prosperous Moslem trading family. He'd been a student activist and lived in exile in France for two years when the political climate got too hot, hence his impeccable French.

"Do you know how you can tell that it is not yet your time to die?" he asked.

"How?"

"Because you are sitting here alive."

We pulled up a couple of sacks of damp grain and sat close

to the low fire, occasionally feeding it twigs from a nearby pile. Above us a perfect half-moon had risen, dazzling and cold. My sleeping bag was almost dry.

"Once I was in a car accident outside Bamako," he continued. "Seventeen people in my van. Every person died, except me. I walked forty kilometers to my brother's house in Bamako, covered all over in the blood of strangers. I did not know why I was alive. But now I know. God was saving me, to do his work."

"Why you?"

He pondered this for a moment.

"Because I am so handsome," he said at last.

I looked at him in astonishment. He kept a straight face for a few seconds, then burst into laughter: a high-pitched, goofy giggle.

Touré strode over from a neighboring fire. For the last half-hour I'd heard him in the background, entertaining a group of elderly men with some dramatic yarn.

"Tanya!" he shouted. "I have put together two sacks of grain over there for you to sleep on, so you do not have to lie on the earth, where it is wet."

"Oh thank you, Touré," I said amiably, "but my friend Yaya here already found me some sacks." I indicated the ones we were sitting on. "They're pretty dry," I added, smiling.

Touré started, then thrust his face close to Yaya's as though checking his skin for blemishes.

"I *see*," he said and strode haughtily away.

❖

Several times throughout that long, achy night, as I lay curled in my sleeping bag on the lumpy sacks, I heard Touré imitating me to his cadre of rapt geezers.

"We could have saaaaved him! Oooooh, we could have done

something!" Touré yowled in a weepy falsetto, while his audience howled with laughter.

Finally, as the sky began to gray, I'd had enough.

"What's funny, Touré?" I shouted across the expanse of sleeping bodies. "What's the joke? A man died. A human life."

"You are right," he said somberly. "Sorry."

As I lay back down I heard him cooing, very softly, "a huuuuman liiiiiife."

⁎

When I finally slept, I dreamed of the deaf man. I was wandering through an American supermarket when I heard his cry. Over and over it came. I tore through the aisles, frantically searching. The sound seemed to be coming from behind some cereal boxes. I ran to the shelf and began to pull the boxes off, trying to get to him. Uncooked grain spilled from the fallen boxes, littering the floor. But behind each brightly colored row there was another line of boxes in sleek primary colors, each a different brand. Santana was beside me, piling a cart high.

"You are wasting so much food," she said, as I flung the boxes to the ground. Then I saw that they weren't cereal boxes but brightly colored spiral notebooks.

The cry began to recede, and I ran down another aisle, trying to find its source. As I ran, the aisles of the supermarket became a maze of narrow dusty streets. With each passing moment, the cry grew fainter and more desperate. I knew that I had to find him, that time was running out. I kept tripping over piles of wet notebooks, catching myself, barreling on. Just when I thought I'd found him, I came smack up against a blank mud wall.

I woke to activity. All around me people were untying bundles and unpacking bags, draping clothing and papers across the tall grass to dry in the early morning sun. The air was still cool, but in direct sunlight the heat of the impending day was beginning to show its teeth. I went in search of my backpacks, which I'd dropped behind a low bush. When I finally found them, Touré was right there, standing guard. His own belongings were there, too, spread across the bush to dry. They included a shirt, a pair of pants, and his current "commerce": three pairs of women's shoes and twenty or thirty sample-size bottles of perfume.

"You've got to be more careful of your things," he berated me. "You should have kept them next to you when you slept. Your *friend* should have advised you."

"Oh come on, Touré. Who wants my soggy backpacks? No one's gonna steal after this kind of tragedy."

"Oh, *please!*"

Ignoring him, I opened my pack. I spread my belongings across the grass, shaking out clothes and fanning pages, opening pill bottles to see what had crumbled and what was intact. A picture of Michael was stuck face-to-face with one of my father. When I separated them, some color from my father's clothes had stained Michael's face. Freud would have had a field day.

A few dunes away, a hubbub arose. The sound of shouting and slaps broke the morning calm. Touré and I hurried over to see what was happening. We navigated the low dunes awkwardly, our sandals catching in the tangled shrubbery and sinking into the sand.

When we arrived on the scene, the whole population of the boat was there. Yaya stood at the edge of the group, shouting for order.

"What happened?" I asked him.

"They say that man stole clothing from people's luggage. They want to beat him."

At the center of the group stood a skinny old man in a threadbare *bou-bou*. Several women were holding his arms, shoving him roughly back and forth. They were wiry women in their thirties and forties with weathered, careworn faces. They shouted in piercing tones, shaking his shoulders with their stringy, muscular arms.

"I told them they must let me speak to the man first," Yaya continued, "to find out why he did it."

He tried again to speak to the women, but his voice got lost in the din.

"What makes them think he did it?" I shouted.

"The women noticed things were missing. They started opening bags to search. They found the missing items in his bag."

"Then they are right!" yelled Touré. "He is a thief. We must beat him and throw him in the water." He shoved his way toward the center of the group, shouting and waving his arms.

"No!" Yaya pushed through the crowd. Standing at the center, he gained the group's attention with a piercing whistle, then dropped his voice and began to speak.

Touré interjected angrily. Some people cheered their support for Touré, but others shouted them down. When the noise subsided, Yaya continued. His dignified demeanor seemed to command respect.

The old man stood a bit to one side, his blue-gray turban half-unraveled and hanging down his back. As the argument continued, he stared at the ground. His face showed neither hope nor dread, but a kind of dull resignation, as though he were waiting in a soundproof chamber while a jury decided his fate.

Eventually Yaya prevailed. Holding the crowd at bay with sharp words and an outstretched hand, he led the old man over the crest of the dune and out of sight.

The two men were gone over an hour. At first people waited angrily, shouting and gesticulating with barely contained violence. One man grabbed another by the shoulders and shook him. I was convinced a fight would erupt, until they burst out laughing and fell into an embrace. After a while, people began to drift away. The women went first, returning to check on the children and prepare rice for the afternoon meal. Soon the men followed, wandering away in twos and threes, deep in conversation. By the time Yaya and the old man reappeared at the tufty crown of the dune, Touré and I were all that remained.

"Well?" said Touré, leaping to his feet.

"It will not happen again," said Yaya. Touré was about to object, but Yaya continued rapidly, raising his hand as though fending off a blow. "The women have their clothing back," he hissed. "Isn't that enough? Or will you beat him now, by yourself?"

They stared at each other for a moment, locked in a standoff.

Then Touré turned abruptly toward the old man, who took a quick step backward in fear. Touré turned back to Yaya with disgust.

"I will be watching him closely," he said. "And you too." He poked a finger at Yaya's face. "I think I have seen you somewhere before." He stomped off across the dunes, giving the other passengers a wide berth. The old man slunk away, too, throwing Yaya a small, grateful smile.

"Would they really have beaten him?" I asked Yaya, as we watched Touré's retreating back.

"People get very carried away when someone has been stealing," he said slowly. "Often if a thief is caught in the market, he will be beaten to death before the police can even arrive. People work so hard for these things, for nothing. And they will give them to you. But for you to come and take them . . . No."

I remembered a scene I'd witnessed at the market in Ségou, in which a group of about thirty women had surrounded a woman accused of stealing. They'd pulled off the outer layer of her garments, her body spinning helplessly as the cloth unwound. Then they'd taken off their rubber flip-flops and slapped her with them, the shoes blurring the air like a swarm of flapping wings until the police came and dragged the woman away. I shuddered.

"So why did he do it?" I asked.

"He said he could not help it. God made him do it. I told him God would never do such a thing; it must have been the devil. But he said no—it was God. God whispered in his ear and told him so."

❖

The day was hot and dry, the pale sun so relentless that even the marsh grass seemed to wilt beneath its gaze. Since there was no bush high enough to offer any real shade, Yaya and I made a tent of a blanket and four sticks and sat under it for several hours, talking. I drank thirstily from my water bottle, which I'd filled the night before with boiled river water. At this point it scarcely seemed worth the effort of purifying it, since I'd downed several glasses of lukewarm coffee which had probably never reached a boil. Still, I persisted. Yaya filled his cup directly from the river like the other passengers.

"I have drunk this water my whole life," he said, chuckling. "If the creatures in my stomach have not killed me yet, it is unlikely they will do so now."

Yaya told me that the devil had appeared to him as a teenager on the very day that a white man in Timbuktu had handed him a Bible. As he carried the Bible home through the desert, a man jumped out from behind an acacia bush and blocked his path. The man had red eyes, as if from drinking, and an enormous penis, far bigger than any human's could possibly be. At first Yaya thought the man had attached something to it, to scare people. Yaya pulled out his curved Tuareg knife, to show the man he wasn't afraid, but the man just laughed, and the penis darted toward Yaya, like a snake. Then, by some intuition that seemed to come from outside himself, Yaya held up the Bible and said, "Jesus Christ, bless and save me." Hearing this, the man flew straight up and disappeared, leaving a trail of fire. From that day forward, Yaya was a Christian.

❖

My digestive system was quick to protest the river water. I was squatting in the bush for the third time that day when a small child approached me.

"*Ça va? Ça va?*" she murmured.

"*Ça va*," I sighed, putting my head in my hands. I could never get used to African children's complete nonchalance about bodily functions.

I thought the child would leave now, having cheerfully humiliated me, but instead she tugged at my sleeve, pointing toward the shore. She drew a shape in the air with her hands.

"What?" I said with some irritation. "Another boat?"

Our hopes had been raised and dashed several times that day, as overcrowded *pinasses* passed us, heading back toward Mopti. I'd briefly considered boarding one of them, heading straight back to Mopti and the comfort of a phone line to the U.S., but I couldn't bring myself to do it. I felt allied with the community of the boat. The thought of carrying this experience back to Mopti alone felt unbearably lonely. Besides, I still wanted to see the fabled city, no matter what shape it was in, and to feel the Sahara's hot sand between my toes.

The girl continued to tug at my sleeve. Sighing, I yanked up my underwear, let down my skirt, and accompanied her back to the shore.

Three *pirogues* had arrived from a nearby fisher camp, offering to transport us to their camp for the night, then onward tomorrow to the village of Aka, where we could catch a new *pinasse*. Word had been sent back to Mopti to send us a replacement boat, but no one knew how long it would take to arrive. The men argued strenuously over what to do. As usual, Yaya and Touré were on opposing sides.

"These men would divide the group," Yaya explained when he saw me approach. "They say that those who can afford passage on a new *pinasse* should go forward in the *pirogues*, while the rest stay behind and wait for the replacement. I tell them it is not right that some of us should go forward leaving others here alone to suffer. We must remain united. A small group, alone in this place, will be vulnerable to bandits."

"And I tell him," blustered Touré, "that it is not right that you, Tanya, must get sick from the river water and burn your skin waiting many long days in the sun!"

"Oh no, please don't make this about me," I said quickly.

"You be quiet!" snapped Touré.

Touré's group won out. As the sun set, I sheepishly loaded my bags into one of two long, narrow *pirogues*, along with sixteen of the boat's more prosperous passengers. The river glowed rosy orange in the failing light. Several young men from the Bozo fisher camp waited on the shore, jousting amiably with the long poles they used to propel the *pirogues*.

Touré pointed at a couple of stout, middle-aged men. "Those two are afraid to go in these *pirogues*," he chortled. "They've never ridden in such small boats, without motors. It is because of them we must take two boats. We could have paid less and all gone in one."

I was surprised to see the old man who'd been accused of stealing among those who could afford to leave. No one commented on his presence, but I noticed that he made sure not to ride in the same boat as Touré.

Touré climbed into the front of one of the canoes, and I squeezed in behind him. I saw no possible way that all the passengers could have fit into a single *pirogue*.

Yaya and I had shared an emotional goodbye, with prolonged hugs and promises to write. I was therefore startled to see him dragging his duffel over the dunes toward the water, just as we were about to push off. As he approached the boat he slipped and fell, covering his hands and knees with mud.

"What's this?" shouted Touré when he saw him. "You will leave the very poor to suffer alone?"

"I will go forward to Aka and send word to their villages, so that their families will not worry," said Yaya primly, attempting to brush off his pants with his muddy hands.

"Oh, *please,*" groaned Touré.

Yaya pushed his way onto the seat behind me. The two stout men, who were sitting in the back, grumbled uneasily at the rocking of the boat.

We poled along in silence as the sky slid smoothly toward darkness. My feet sat in freezing water. I slapped them against each other, wiggling my toes to keep them from going numb.

The other *pirogue* glided a few feet ahead of us, its silhouette graceful as a newborn moon. The actual moon hovered pale and plump on the horizon, coating the black water with a silver sheen. Each time I looked up, there were more stars. Touré sat in front of me. Tentatively, I touched his arm.

"Beautiful," I said.

"What?"

"The stars."

"Don't you see them over there, in your place?"

"Not so much in the city," I told him, "with all the lights."

He nodded thoughtfully. "I heard there aren't many trees there, either."

Hours later, I saw eight makeshift shelters glowing pale in the moonlight.

"Tanya," said Yaya, tapping me from behind. "This is the Bozo fisher camp."

The shelters were lean-tos, with wooden poles spaced unevenly along the sides, grass mats spread between them, and straw thatch across the top. In the moonlight they looked terribly fragile, as though they'd topple like dominoes if you leaned on one of the poles. In front of each shelter was a circular mud structure with a grate on the top.

"For smoking fish," said Yaya.

The Bozos had built a bonfire in anticipation of our arrival. After we dragged our *pirogues* from the freezing water, the chief came down to the shore to greet us. He was a middle-aged man, tall and thin, with a deeply lined face and gentle eyes. There was something regal in his presence, an effortless stillness that commanded respect. We stood before him in a ragged, shivering clump, while he spoke a few words of the Bozo language in a formal tone and presented us with an armload of blackened fish. One of the portly men stepped forward, thanked him on behalf of our group, and accepted the fish in the folds of his *bou-bou*. The chief smiled then, looking in my direction.

"Bonjour," he said. He asked me, in careful, precise French, where I came from and what I was doing there. Then he turned to Touré and spoke a few quick words of Bambara.

"He says you must eat plenty of fish, because you are a stranger here," said Touré, "and you do not look well."

We huddled around the fire, eating delicious fish: crackling outside, succulent within. Touré took enormous bites, shoving almost an entire fish into his mouth at a time. Yaya and I raised our eyebrows at each other.

"Savage," whispered Yaya, and we giggled conspiratorially.

As we ate, an animated conversation took place between the men. The women and children had bedded down early, a slight distance away. I thought briefly, regretfully, of how disconnected I was from these women. Language limitations and mutual shyness locked me into the company of men. Turning toward the fire, I asked Yaya what the men were talking about.

"He says it is because of God that we are suffering like this," Yaya translated for me, indicating the plump man who'd accepted the fish for us. "And *he* says no," he indicated an older gentleman in a deep purple turban. "God gave us the world and free will; we bring about our own suffering."

◆

In the pale yellow dawn, a very fat, very black woman stood over me, hands on her hips, shouting repeated greetings in the Bozo language.

"*Ils sont les vrais Bozos,*" Touré said, "the real Bozos."

"*Les vrais Bozos,*" the woman repeated proudly, a broad smile on her face.

I sat up. In the watery morning light, I looked more closely at the small cluster of huts. Most of them had only three walls. Looking through the open fourth wall, I saw that they contained nothing at all, just grass mats and a few pots piled in the corner. I was used to the essential nature of African homes, but it seemed to me there was usually *something*—a table, a stool, a few clothes on a peg.

"They are nomads, like the Tuaregs," said Yaya. "Wherever the fish go, that is where they live."

In spite of myself, a small thrill went through me. This was exactly the sort of thing I'd hoped to see.

The men and older children had taken out the *pirogues* and nets for the day. Women were smoking fish on the round grates. They arranged the fish, then placed reed mats over them until the skin was black and crisp. An adolescent girl was repairing one of the ovens, slapping a layer of wet mud over a layer of dried mud mixed with sawdust, then smoothing it down with her hands. Younger children stood near the shore, fishing. Their homemade poles consisted of sticks with strings and hooks attached.

"I know fishing!" Touré boasted. He approached a toddler and grabbed her stick. "Just watch!" he said to me.

The little girl looked at Touré and then at me. She started giggling, hiding her face in her hands. Touré danced the hook along the surface of the water, repeating, "I know fishing!"

Within moments he had a bite.

"See!" he cried. "I told you I knew fishing!" He yanked the fish from the water.

Touré threw the fish to the little girl. She pulled the hook from its mouth mechanically, never taking her eyes off Touré as the bloody gills popped out. She tossed the fish into a basket where it flopped slowly to its death.

◆

Before we set off again, Touré and Yaya each pulled me aside.

"You know that man you've been talking to?" said Touré, dragging me behind one of the shelters. "That *Ya-ya?* I knew his face looked familiar, but I could not place it. Then when he said he lived in Bamako, I realized. My cousin works for the Bamako police. He showed me a picture of a man who lures tourists to his home by acting friendly, then steals their luggage and disappears. It was him! I *know* it was him."

"Oh, come on, Touré."

"Come on, what?"

"That is just too paranoid."

"Was I paranoid about the thieves on the boat? Was I paranoid?"

"You know, Tanya, many Moslems pray to the devil," Yaya whispered to me as we carried our belongings down the narrow rocky beach to the *pirogues.* "They know God is stronger, but the devil can help them out with small things. Your friend over there, Touré, you see those beads he always carries? He uses those beads to pray to the devil. He told me that when he was in prison, it was the devil who saved him. He said it is because of those beads that he got out."

"You cannot trust that man. He will steal from you!" said Touré.

"You must be careful of a man who will make a friend of darkness," said Yaya.

It was the fifth day of our three-day trip.

◈

Late that afternoon we arrived in the village of Aka. White sand beaches gleamed; sun-bleached mud walls hid a maze of narrow streets and houses that seemed to grow seamlessly out of the earth. The town was bookended by two fantastic mosques. Silhouetted against the bright sky, they looked like elaborate sand castles, with their fantastic jumble of coneheaded towers and their wooden pegs sticking out in every direction like the sculpted hairstyles of the women in Accra.

Within a half-hour of our arrival, Touré was in a shouting match with an elderly woman selling firewood from a shack above the beach. The woman, who couldn't have been more than five feet tall, stood surrounded by piles of thick, gnarled branches. Hands on her hips, she answered Touré's bullying shouts with some shrill scolding of her own. Finally Touré threw up his hands in a gesture of defeat, shaking his head.

"She's mean," he said to me. "She doesn't want to sell the wood at a decent price because she says she can get more from the bigger ships."

"Well, if that's her livelihood . . ."

The woman spoke to me in Songhaï, shaking her head.

"She says your husband is mean, but you are nice," said Touré. "She thinks I'm your husband."

I smiled at her, pointing to Touré and making a mean face. Her nose appeared to have been ripped open in some sort of accident. It had healed with heavy scarring, leaving the nostril enlarged and oddly shaped. She was striking all the same, with wide cheekbones that made a "V" to a narrow chin, and vivid, sparkling eyes. She reached out and grasped my hand, pulling me to her side.

"She says you are just like her daughter, the same age."

The woman took me in her arms in a tight hug, stroking my hair. Touré barked a few words at her.

"I told her if she wants you to be warm," he said, "she'd better sell us some firewood."

❖

That night I strolled along the beach enjoying the cool air. Touré and Yaya walked on either side of me. They weren't speaking to each other.

"Tell that man not to push me into the ocean," said Touré testily.

"Come on."

"Tell him!"

Four young girls blocked our path. Saucy and flirtatious, they extended plastic plates and buckets filled with small golden cakes, giggling as they pushed each other's hands out of the way. They wore Western skirts and T-shirts that looked like the donations of American missionaries. One of the T-shirts was hot pink, with the words "No Devil" written in sparkly silver letters. Another advertised a Christian summer camp. The clothes fit tightly, hugging the girls' budding figures and exposing their taut midriffs.

"Buy this cake, it is so sweet," one of them crooned.

"No! Buy from me. Mine is sweeter!"

Touré stepped toward the girl in the "No Devil" shirt. He pushed aside her plate, putting his face about two inches from hers. He said something, and she gave a swift, cheeky response. They seemed to be bartering a price.

"What's he doing?" I asked Yaya.

"He wants her to meet him later tonight," he said.

"But she's so young!" I cried. "She can't be more than fifteen."

"Those girls want it," said Yaya. "Look at her." The girl was smiling, wrapping a corner of Touré's turban around her finger.

"Oh, come on! Some adult probably put them up to it. Either that or they're desperate for money."

Yaya was about to retort, when Touré turned toward me.

"*She* is cuter than *you*," he said.

I looked at the girl. To my surprise, I felt a twinge of jealousy. It occurred to me that Touré had made no moves on me, not out of respect or restraint, but because he didn't find me attractive.

"To each his own," I said airily, turning away.

❖

On our third night in Aka, a member of the local police force invited us to a party to celebrate his recent wedding. He was young—barely out of adolescence—slight and earnest. In his stiff uniform he gave the impression of a boy seriously at play.

That night Yaya and I walked the winding streets of Aka, clutching a piece of paper on which the young man had drawn a map of the town, marking his house with an "X." Touré was otherwise engaged. Finding our way around tiny Aka was surprisingly confusing. The dirt paths and one-story mud brick dwellings all looked the same. We were on the brink of giving up, when a middle-aged man noticed our perplexity and offered to accompany us.

Rows of candles burned in the courtyard, and kerosene lamps hung from wires strung between the trees. Beneath the wide, starry sky, the effect was pure magic. The yard was packed with people, laughing, eating, and drinking. Heads turned as we moved through the party, and I heard a few gasps. Among the shining dark faces, I must have looked like a pale ghost. A toddler standing near the doorway saw me and began to wail in terror, shoving his head into his mother's crotch. People crowed greetings in Bambara, Songhaï, and French, while Yaya and I moved down a receiving line of elderly men, shaking hands.

"*Ça va, ça va, ça va . . .*" I murmured, ducking my head, smiling until my cheeks ached. I made my way through platters of smoked fish, *tô*, rice, thick doughy pancakes wrapped in leaves, and bowls brimming with savory stew. The villagers were dressed in their best clothes, the men in *bou-bous* of waxy, embroidered fabric, with matching pajama pants peeking out beneath; the women in voluminous, richly colored cloths and head wraps, their ears and throats glinting with gold. I felt woefully underdressed in my blue batik sundress, its pattern already faded from too much scrubbing.

Laughter and scattered applause came from the other side of the courtyard. There was some kind of game going on, and people were gathered around, watching. Though every chair was filled, people rose at our approach, offering us their seats.

"No, please sit," I gestured, but they shook their heads vigorously, and Yaya pushed me to accept.

"You are a stranger here," he said. "They will be ashamed if you stand."

The young groom came forward to shake my hand. He looked even younger without his uniform, his slender body swimming in layers of heavy brown and gold cloth. He stood before me beaming, offering multiple *ça va*s.

"He wants you to be the guest of honor," said Yaya. "To start the dancing with him."

"Really?" I giggled. "How will I know what to do?"

"Just follow," said Yaya. The groom gestured with his hand for me to wait, then disappeared into the crowd.

"Where's the bride?" I asked Yaya.

He looked around. "It may be that she is doing some ceremony with her women friends. They must bathe her in the river."

"Why?"

He shrugged and offered the familiar response, "That is what is done."

Music rattled through a battery-powered boom box. A woman singer's high, wailing voice slid up and down the scale, slipping in and around the notes with agile fluidity. It reminded me of Arabic music, its multilayered rhythm cyclical and infectious. The crowd formed a circle, clapping and shouting. The groom appeared at the center and gestured for me to join him. Several pairs of hands pushed me forward.

I love to dance. I gave myself to the hypnotic music, tossing my head, swiveling my hips, and stomping my feet with utter abandon. The groom laughed in surprise; the crowd hooted and cheered. I closed my eyes, and for a few moments I forgot everything.

When the song ended, the crowd applauded wildly. The groom took my hand and gave a courtly nod. Another song came on, and within minutes the courtyard was alive with shimmying, arm-waving bodies.

"They didn't think you could dance like that," said Yaya. "I didn't think so either," he added.

"There's a lot you don't know about me," I said, flashing him a playful grin.

Buoyed up by the adrenaline of my performance, I stayed on for several hours. Everyone wanted to dance with the white lady. By the end of the night I was giddy with exhaustion, the back of my cotton sundress soaked with sweat.

The groom presented me with a small plastic bag of pungent peppermint tea, and another tied-up bit of plastic holding sugar.

"Because you have blessed his wedding with your presence," Yaya said. "He will remember this always."

"As will I," I said, and bowed my thanks to the young man.

❖

Although the villagers offered shelter, Yaya and I decided to spread our grass mats on the beach. The night was mild, and I couldn't bear to trade its breezy freshness for the close warmth of a hut.

We walked through Aka's deserted alleys toward the river. The moon was waning now, just the other side of full. The houses of the sleeping town looked beatific, bathed in a cool white light. As we walked, Yaya told me about Stacy, the American missionary waiting to meet him in Timbuktu.

"We pray every day that we will marry," he said.

"Why pray to marry? It's not like it's out of your control."

"We pray that conditions will be right for it to take place."

"Do you *want* it to take place?"

"Yes . . . I think so." He paused. "I am not sure," he blurted. "I love her, but . . . the attraction. I am not sure. That is why we pray."

I looked at him in surprise. His attitude was a far cry from Brigitte or Santana's practical approach to matrimony. Most West Africans I'd encountered considered a match good if the potential spouse came from a decent family and was neither abusive, dishonest, nor excessively ugly. Marriage to an American, with its implicit visa to the land of plenty, would be the answer to their prayers. Perhaps living in Europe had changed Yaya's perspective.

"I have similar issues with my boyfriend," I admitted.

"Yes?" He looked at me eagerly.

I told him about Michael: my profound love and equally profound confusion. The evening's entertainment had loosened me up, and the words flowed easily.

"I feel the same confusion about Stacy," said Yaya, when I had finished. "But I will marry her anyway," he added, after a moment's pause. "The satisfaction I seek can never be found in human love. I get my deepest fulfillment from the love of God."

❖

Yaya and I lay side by side on our grass mats. The sky arced above us like a speckled ceramic bowl, so thick with stars that every inch of space seemed crammed with pinpricks of light. The more you stared at a given spot, the more stars you saw, layer upon layer. Since Yaya had only a light blanket, I opened up my sleeping bag and put it over both of us. I rolled onto my side, facing away from him. He turned toward me and began massaging the tight tendons of my neck with brutal precision, working his way downward. I groaned in delicious agony.

Something familiar was happening. I recognized it immediately and marveled at its universality, even as my heart began to cavort like a crazyball against my ribs. While his hands worked on me, I lay absolutely still, scarcely daring to breathe. Suddenly he was pressed hard against my back, and his hands were around the front, squeezing my breasts with a muscular intensity that caught me by surprise. At once I was wildly, acutely awake, my head pounding, my body pulsing subtly against his. But I couldn't bring myself to make a definitive move, to turn around and kiss him, to commit.

My mind raced dizzily, trying to arrange the thoughts. What was wrong? He had a girlfriend, no, he was engaged! And we'd confided in each other, trustingly, as friends. This, on the heels of that, felt sleazy. On the other hand, I wanted him. A *lot*. My body was responding to his touch with a yearning I suddenly realized had been growing since our first conversation, on the night of the accident. I remembered the deaf man, then, and sorrow shot through me. Suddenly everything about this evening felt false: the attention heaped on me at the wedding, Yaya's confession about Stacy, my own facile, oft-repeated words. I pushed Yaya away with a throaty sound, and rolled to the other side of the mat.

"I want to sleep," I said.

Silence.

"I'm sorry," he said stiffly.

I lay there, motionless, for a long time, listening to the sound of Yaya's breath. Eventually it slowed, grew regular, and quieted. Then I stuffed my face into the fetid T-shirt I'd balled up for a pillow, and cried.

That night, in my dream, I was wandering through the desert when I spotted the deaf man. He was just a tiny speck in the distance, but I knew it was him. Delighted, I ran toward him. Soon I saw that he was waving his arms. As I drew closer, I saw, too, that he was sinking. The sand was almost to his waist. What I had taken as a gesture of greeting was a gesture of panic. I called out to him to hold on, that I was coming. I tried to run faster, but the sand was too deep. My calves burned with the effort. A wind whipped up; sheets of sand stung my legs and arms. Off to the side I heard music and turned toward the sound. Beneath a giant tent, a dance party was taking place. MC Brown was there, but he had Yaya's face. He grabbed my arm and pulled me toward him in a kind of swing-dance twirl.

"Won't Nadhiri mind?" I asked.

He lifted me in the air, dunked me between his legs, then set me back on my feet again.

"She thinks you only want me because I'm white," I told him.

Yaya/Brown laughed at that, a harsh, cruel sound.

"Stop it," I said, and tears came to my eyes. Suddenly I realized I'd forgotten the deaf man. I tugged at Brown's arm, trying to get him to come with me. I couldn't seem to convey the urgency. And then it wasn't Yaya or Brown I was dancing with, but Michael.

"How can he drown when there's no water?" he said with utter contempt, as though I was the stupidest person he'd ever met.

"He's drowning in sand," I said.

"There is no sand."

"There's sand everywhere!" I cried, and woke myself up with the shouting.

❖

At noon, a new *pinasse* arrived. As I dragged my packs toward the water, the mother with the disfigured nose ran down to the beach and pressed a plastic bag full of fried rice cakes into my hands. We hugged each other hard, while she gave me what I'm sure was good counsel in Songhaï.

The owner of the new *pinasse*, a short, irritable, fast-talking man, was unhappy about taking on more passengers. His boat, he said, was full.

"Get in the boat," Touré barked at me. "Get in the boat now, and we'll deal with him later."

I paid a boy in a *pirogue* to ferry Touré, Yaya, and me out to the waiting boat. We heaved our luggage over the side and climbed in.

"Pardon, pardon."

We tiptoed through a dense garden of bodies. As with the other *pinasse*, the floor was piled high with sacks of grain, and we had to bend low as we moved beneath the bamboo-framed raffia roof. We finally found a small clearing in front of some soldiers and wedged ourselves in, sliding down into the crevices between the sacks of grain. One of the soldiers' long guns, laid carelessly across his knapsack, was pointing straight at me. I gingerly pushed its muzzle aside.

"Maybe the owner was right," I said to Yaya and Touré. "This boat is too full. It's not safe."

"It's safe, it's safe," said Touré. "He's just trying to get more money out of us."

"How can you say it's safe?" my voice rose in pitch. "Look around you! There's no way out. If there was an accident we'd all drown."

Yaya spoke soothingly. "They will all be full like this," he said. "The other boat was the exception."

"Well then . . . then . . ." My voice wobbled and tears rose swiftly to my eyes.

"Oh, not again!" exclaimed Touré. He got up with a loud sigh and started shouting at the other passengers.

Within five minutes we had a spot by the side of the boat. I felt both sheepish and relieved. It became a running gag between Touré, Yaya, and me that every time the boat slowed down, or brushed against a sandbar or a piece of floating wood, I faced the water, put my arms over my head in a diving pose, and said "I'm ready to swim." Touré and Yaya were even joking with each other. Touré said they were cousins, Kulubaly and Tangara, but Tangara was the slave of Kulubaly, so Yaya ought to treat him with respect. Yaya said he couldn't respect a Kulubaly: they ate too many beans. We were all growing giddy from so much laughter.

Touré was looking through his bag for a photograph he wanted to show me, when suddenly he let out a shout.

"Hey! Where are the shoes?"

"What?" I asked stupidly.

"The ladies' shoes! I was bringing them to Diré to sell. I had three pairs; now there are only two."

"I think you sold a pair," Yaya said. Then, to me, "I thought he sold a pair."

Suddenly Touré was on his feet. He swung himself over the kitchen with surprising agility, picking his way through the mass of bodies at an extraordinary speed. When he got to his destination, he reached down and grabbed someone's *bou-bou* at the throat. It took me a moment to recognize the old man who'd gotten himself into trouble on the first boat.

"This man is a thief!" shouted Touré. "He stole on the last boat and because of this . . . posing imbecile . . ." indicating Yaya, "we let him go free to steal again. And now he has stolen my shoes!" He yanked the old man to his feet. "I should have beaten you last time. This time you're going to pay. This time I'm going to open your bag, and if I find those shoes, I'm going to throw you off the boat."

"No!" shouted Yaya. He stumbled through the crowd, drawing shouts and curses as he stepped on people's limbs. "You cannot do this!" he insisted.

Touré spun around. "You stay out of this! I am tired of you telling me what to do," he snarled. "You who have left the faith and taken another."

"You see?" Yaya shouted, looking around frantically for support. "He oppresses me because of my faith! He oppresses me because I work for justice, like Jesus Christ himself was oppressed."

"You stand up for criminals because you do not know them," yelled Touré. Yaya had reached him now, and Touré let go of the old man and grabbed the top of Yaya's *bou-bou* instead. "You are a weak, soft man. You have never had to pay your own way. Stand back, weak man! Life is for the strong." Touré shoved Yaya, who stumbled and fell backward onto the legs of a child. The child began to scream.

"And you," cried Yaya, lurching to his feet, "you feel you are fit to judge. You who are a criminal yourself, who have not been to school past the second form. Who can scarcely read!"

"I can read! I can read!" roared Touré.

"Then read for us. Read for us if you are so smart." Yaya reached into his robe and extracted a small black-bound volume. "Here is a book of Mali law. Read for us where it says that you may throw an old man in the river." He tossed the book at Touré's feet.

Touré looked down at the book, then slowly back up at Yaya.

"I do not have to read for you," he said. His voice was low and ferocious, simmering with fury. "I do not have to prove anything to you. You traitor! I will throw you off the boat!"

Touré advanced on Yaya. Yaya raised his arms to defend himself, and their hands locked in the air like the antlers of two stags. Touré had easily fifty pounds on Yaya, and in no time he was propelling him backward toward the edge of the boat, while the other passengers shuffled desperately out of the way.

"Stop it!" I screamed, moving toward them.

"You stay out of this, *tubabu!*" Touré flung the words in my direction. "This is not your place." It was the first time Touré had called me a white lady.

From the center of the boat, an enormous woman dressed in bright red cloth rose slowly to her feet.

"Stooooooop iiiiiiiiiiit!" she bellowed, her voice deep and penetrating as a foghorn. "*Stop it! Stop it! Stop it!* You are behaving like two small boys in the village who run around with no pants on." Scattered laughter and cheers came from the crowd. "You, sir," she shouted, pointing a thick, authoritative finger at Touré. "You leave that old man alone. You are talking that way to him because you do not respect your father!" A rumble of assent from the population of the boat.

"You go right ahead," she continued. "You go right ahead and open his bag, but if you do not find your shoes, it is you we will beat and throw in the water."

For an astonishing moment, there was complete silence. Then Touré smacked the bamboo pole beside him, hard, with the flat of his hand.

"Savages, all of you!" He turned his back on the boat and faced the water. "Me, I don't like savages."

◆

Touré moved his satchel to the roof and stayed there all day. I peeked my head up and called to him a couple of times, but he ignored me. Yaya and I sat in silence as well, each of us brooding on our own thoughts. The countryside around us was flat and sandy, with patchy grass, thorny shrubs, and flat-topped, spiky acacia trees. Once in a while a runty palm. We were well into the Sahel now, the area where savanna and desert come together. Just a short hop to the Sahara itself.

In the late afternoon, the boat pulled up to the shore of a fishing village with a lively riverside market.

"This is Diré," Yaya told me. "Touré will descend here."

I accosted Touré on the rocky shore, pushing my way through a crush of young girls who plied me with bags of cakes and sticks of charred meat. I was determined to have a proper goodbye.

"Savages, all of them, idiots!" he spat, when I asked him how he was feeling.

"Oh Touré," I sighed, suppressing a smile. I put a hand on his arm. "Thank you for taking such good care of me. I'm sorry things had to end so—"

"You and me," he interrupted, leaning forward conspiratorially, "we are alike, Tanya. *Toi et moi.*" He grinned, then, and it was as though a spell had broken and he was once again his blustery self. He continued, "Someday I will come to America and find you."

"And then?" I said cautiously.

"And then? And then, Tanya, you will come to my house, and we will laugh, and say, 'Oh, you remember that boat ride, in Mali? It was so crazy, my friend, but it was *sweet.*'"

❖

We arrived at Kabara, the port of Timbuktu, as dusk was falling. We were still about an hour's truck ride from the city itself. The port was unremarkable, with a long wooden dock and a familiar assortment of colorful, dilapidated boats.

As we made our way off the *pinasse*, I found myself directly behind the old man. He seemed weak on his feet, so I took his arm. Stepping off the ramp, he stumbled and fell to his knees in the shallow water, spilling some of his belongings.

"Oh no!" I cried, "Are you all right?"

He nodded, fumbling around in the water for his things. I tossed my bags onto the shore and crouched down to help.

Some ceramic beads had come unstrung; they floated on the greenish brown surface of the water like tiny inner tubes. I fished them out and then spotted a dark lumpy object, partially submerged. It was a woman's leather shoe.

Timbuktu was founded in the eleventh century by the nomadic Tuareg tribe, who used it as a seasonal camp. A hundred years later, the king of the vast Mali empire laid claim to it. By the fourteenth century, it had become the Port of Africa—the center of trade between northern and sub-Saharan Africa. It was also a center of Islamic education, with more than a hundred Koranic schools and a major university.

Most of the trade at that time was done by camel caravan. From the trading post of Timbuktu, gold and humans were transported north, while salt, cloth, and horses went south. The human slaves, I suspect, were unmoved by the city's glory.

Ten days after my journey up the Niger began, I walked the streets of that mythical town. Having come with no real expectations, I wasn't disappointed to find that the once-glittering trade mecca was now a sleepy desert village which was gradually being buried in sand. After all, I'd been forewarned about the extra crunch in the bread baked in the city's dome-shaped mud ovens. I was even prepared for the guides, who swarmed all over me the moment I stepped outside my hotel room, as promised.

But those who told me there was nothing left of Timbuktu were wrong. Guides aside, the city's more than 30,000 inhabitants moved noiselessly through the streets in their pale or colorful full-length garments, their faces shielded from the sand and sun by layers of cloth. Their lives took place in those streets, and in the flat-roofed mud houses with their intricately carved, iron-studded wooden doors. These individuals didn't seem to know that they were living in a ghost town. Contrary to modern mythology, they were definitely not ghosts.

There is a mosque—one of three in Timbuktu—which the locals told me was the oldest in West Africa. It was the third place I'd visited that claimed to be the oldest mosque in West Africa, but the others shriveled in comparison. Originally built in the late thirteenth century and rebuilt many times since, it is located on the western outskirts of Timbuktu, its hulking cone-shaped tower looming above the city's otherwise flat skyline. Since the mosque is no longer operational, I was permitted to enter. Walking among the pillars of its high-ceilinged chambers, I felt a growing sense of wonder. The silence itself felt old. Like everything else in Timbuktu, the mosque was made of mud, a product of the sand that surrounds it, the same sand which, in the not so distant future, will swallow it whole.

◆

Stacy turned out to be a Bible-thumping blonde from Louisiana. The most endearing thing about her was the way she made the French language sound like a Tennessee Williams play. The least endearing was the condescending tone she took with Yaya. Her pet name for him was "Donkeyhead."

The last time I saw Yaya was on my third day in Timbuktu. He and Stacy came by my hotel room, and the three of us went together for a camel ride out into the Sahara to visit a Tuareg camp. I'd often dreamed of crossing the Sahara on camel, but that ambition died about halfway into the galumphing forty-minute ride. Major saddle sores.

The desert landscape was less uniform than I'd imagined it. Instead of an unbroken expanse of sand, the rolling white dunes outside Timbuktu were dotted with thistles, patches of grass, and occasional scraggly trees. When we arrived at the camp, I sat on a small dune, writing in my journal, while hard-shelled scarab beetles tottered over and around me. Below me, dome-shaped tents with raffia walls hunkered low to the earth. Golden-skinned Tuareg children with crew cuts and mohawks sat below me in the sand, watching me with avid curiosity. Their knees and elbows were knobby, their bony scalps covered with scabs.

I looked up. Yaya and Stacy were playing in the sand, unrolling his long turban and holding it like a sail in the wind.

"Try not to move," he said, but they couldn't do it. Again and again they fell, laughing, to the ground.

I thought of him then, the deaf man. The light in his eyes, the questions he asked. He wanted to know why I traveled.

To see things, I'd said at the time, but that wasn't right. I should have said, *To see what else is possible.*

I put down my notebook and began to sing, to the tune of "Clementine":

Rode a camel, rode a camel, rode a camel on the dunes
On the dunes I rode a camel, rode a camel on the dunes.
Kissed a Tuareg, kissed a Tuareg, kissed a Tuareg on the
dunes . . .
Got a heatstroke, got a heatstroke . . .

Still singing, I lay down and flapped my arms and legs against the earth. Grains got in my eyes and mouth. My teeth crunched. My eyes teared. A few minutes later, Yaya came and sat down beside me.

"What are you doing?" he asked.

"Making a sand angel. Where's Stacy?"

"She's in the Tuareg tent, shopping for jewelry."

"I could tell her a thing or two about you," I said slyly.

He smiled. "But you won't."

We looked at each other. I smiled back.

"I miss Touré," I said, hugging my knees.

"You know," he said with some surprise, "I miss him too."

✣

On my last day in Timbuktu, I climbed onto the rooftop of West Africa's oldest mosque to watch a pale sun set over the Sahara. The rippling sand gleamed beneath it like an ocean of bones. The night air already held a chill.

Two weeks had passed since the day a devout man with cracked feet and glowing eyes had asked me for my shoes. I remembered the disappointment I'd felt when he asked. I'd taken him for an angel, and there he was behaving like a human being. I realized, suddenly, that I'd spent much of my time in Africa befuddled by the notion that if a friend asked me for something, it rendered our entire relationship suspect. But what friendship isn't a balancing act, an ever-shifting dance of altruism and self-interest? How naïve I'd been, to imagine that *any* human exchange could take place in a vacuum, let alone one between a person with shoes and a person without.

It struck me, then, that the only changes we humans are capable of are small ones. You can beat yourself up for years, wishing you could be kinder, happier, more decisive and secure. And then one day you realize you've made a slight shift, moved your inner lens a fraction of an inch to this side or that. Not a whole new self, a remade identity, just a little change in perspective. A loosening, really, an out-breath, a drop of acceptance in the salty ocean of the soul. You haven't solved everything, maybe you haven't solved anything, but if you're lucky, that small shift will be the difference between holding your life in grace and simply holding on.

I knelt and put my forehead to the dusty rooftop in honor of the passenger on our *pinasse* who never reached his earthly destination. I wanted him to know that he'd made a difference on this earth, that he'd touched someone, even if it was only a wandering white girl of questionable faith. He hadn't gotten a proper send-off on his new journey, so I did my best to give him one now.

"Goodbye, my friend," I whispered. "Go in peace."

Malaria

If traveling has given me anything, it's given me this: the ability to float gently down the river of events—to relinquish control. In Africa, the boat leaves when it's full. You might wait an hour; you might wait two weeks. If you spend that time tipping forward into the future, you sink. The best thing to do is just to sit on the boat and look around at the other humans who are sitting there with you. You might discover that you like the view.

I've said it before: Mosquitoes don't like me. Conversely, I don't particularly mind them. The same goes for flies, gnats, and other small circling creatures. This simple fact always exasperated Michael.

"Relax into the bugs," I'd counsel him as we hiked along in

some damp, tropical place, a cloud of insects swarming around his head like a dark halo.

"Easy for you to say," he'd snarl from deep within his swirling aura, his hands flailing angrily at the air.

In spite of Michael's occasional flings, I never really doubted that he'd wait for me. In my brief romantic history, male partners, once hooked, had been exceedingly devoted, and none more so than Michael. The only question was whether I'd go back to him. In my mind, the equation was simple: Mosquitoes didn't want me. Boyfriends did.

✦

While working in Ghana, I watched with infinite compassion as one by one my fellow volunteers were laid low by malaria. Behind my compassion was only the smallest hint of triumph. To get malaria, you had to be bitten, and my blood was bitter horseradish to your average mosquito.

At first, I followed the precautions anyway, just to be on the safe side. I dutifully popped my chloroquine and Paludrine and covered up in the evenings, wearing long-sleeved T-shirts and lightweight pants, applying repellent, carefully checking my mosquito net for holes. But as time wore on I became increasingly careless. The repellent was the first thing to go. I hated the hot, sticky feeling of it, like an airtight layer of latex on my skin. Not to mention the smell. The long sleeves went next. Three weeks after my arrival in West Africa, I'd sat on the stone steps of the one-room schoolhouse that was our living quarters in the village of Afranguah, enjoying the delicious whisper of the night air on my bare arms, while my European co-workers sweltered in their long sleeves and jeans, reeking of toxic substances. And still they came down with it, sweating and shivering on their air mattresses in the stifling cement room while the rest of our brigade was out digging and carrying. I never gloated, at least not on the surface, but I considered myself supremely blessed.

❖

After returning to Ghana from Mali, I flew across the continent to Nairobi, Kenya, still malaria-free. I'd gone to Kenya to join Debbie, my best friend since childhood, who'd flown out from the States to meet me for a month. She brought with her a letter from Michael, telling me that he was seeing someone. He still loved me, he said, but he was sick of waiting with no promises, and she was gentle and attentive and, well, *there.* What was he to me, anyway, he asked, a booby prize to come home to when the travels were done? He was tired of feeling like the lunkhead in the corner, staring at the wall while the free-spirited object of his affections danced her way across the globe.

A jolt went through me as I read his letter, but I squelched it. He adored me: hadn't he said a thousand times that I was the love of his life? The world's greatest miracle? When I first found out he was sleeping around in my absence, I was wild with jealousy, but I'd since learned not to take it too seriously. I had it from reliable sources that none of his dalliances had lasted more than a couple of weeks. By the time I got home, in a month or two, this one would surely be over, too.

"Enjoy yourself," I wrote to Michael, struggling to maintain a playful tone, "but don't commit yet. Your girl will return anon."

❖

Debbie and I had decided to meet in Kenya long before I left the U.S., at a time when I was hazy on the geography of the African continent. I'd told her that if she'd get herself to Africa, I'd meet her wherever she wanted. Being a visual artist and a nature lover, she chose East Africa: Kenya and Tanzania. A couple of months into my trip, when I'd come to understand that this would not mean a few days on a bus but rather another ultraexpensive plane ticket, I tried to persuade her to come to West Africa instead. No go; her heart was set. She might go to Africa only once in her life, she said. She wanted to see some animals.

Nairobi, with its sleek high-rises and traffic-ridden streets, felt more like New York City than Accra. The people were different too. Still friendly, but much more reserved. Tourism, I supposed, had had its effect. There were no roadside fires in the downtown area, no food stands even, except a lone woman selling pineapple chunks in plastic bags. Very few people wore traditional clothes on the streets, and no one carried anything on her head. Besides all that, there were a lot more white people around.

Nairobi was the first place in Africa where I felt unsafe. Everyone I met there, without exception, had been robbed. When Debbie and I went out for a walk on our first afternoon, the receptionist at our lodge told us to leave our watches and jewelry behind. People could grab them off our bodies as we walked down the street. No long dangling purses or money pouches in clear view, either—that was asking for trouble. Even with all these precautions, I was pickpocketed a few days later, when Debbie and I went to an outdoor market to purchase camping supplies for our safari. I bought a sweater, pocketed the change, walked to the next stand for a hat. When I reached into my pocket to make the purchase, my change was gone.

I couldn't stop talking about West Africa, even after we got out of Nairobi and crossed the border into Tanzania. I missed my friends in Ghana and Mali, missed their exuberance, their openheartedness, their brash, unapologetic zest for life. While

Debbie exulted in the colors of the earth, the brilliant greens and reds unlike any she'd seen before, I found fault with the food (bland), the people (cold), and the places we visited (touristy). In addition, I was worried about Michael. I tried to maintain my cavalier attitude, sending him cheerful postcards with no mention of his new friend, but I couldn't help obsessing a bit. I asked Debbie if she thought I should go home right away. When she said it depended on what I wanted, I told her thanks a lot for the help. When she said maybe I should go back to work things out with him, I grew belligerent. Would it really make any difference? I demanded. If he liked this new woman, the die was already cast.

After two weeks, Debbie informed me that her time in Africa was half over. Could I do her a favor and let her enjoy it without constantly having to hear about how much better it was on the other side? And another thing. She was willing to listen to me talk about Michael—that's what friends are for, after all—but she felt like no matter how she responded, she couldn't win. Every word out of her mouth seemed to piss me off.

I got the message. I was spoiling both her time in East Africa and my own, doing the very thing I thought I'd learned not to do: looking at everything through the lens of expectation. Holding tight. I resolved, from that moment onward, to savor my moments there.

One thing in East Africa I could find no fault with was the landscape. As a native of Kansas, I've always been a sucker for wide open spaces. The vast planes of Tanzania, spotted with herds of elephants, zebra, and antelope, gave me a feeling of expansiveness that made me short of breath. Nothing glowed like those skies. The sunsets were spectacular, feasts of orange and gold, lilac and rose, amethyst and violet and deep, deep blue. The clouds piled upon each other in sharply defined layers like an otherworldly mountain range, the spaces between them glimmering lakes.

For a person who grew up seeing wild animals primarily on television or in zoos, the sight of large groups of them running free was a revelation. I had to keep reminding myself they were real. In the Ngorongoro Crater, we rode in our jeep in the center of a wildebeest migration. I stood with my upper body poking through the vehicle's sunroof, while all around me a roiling sea of animals galloped, their thick bodies and enormous heads supported by thin legs, their glossy manes rippling in the sun as their pounding hooves flattened the grass. The furious drumming of their hooves exhilarated me.

"I'm a wildebeest! I'm a wildebeest!" I shouted, and my voice was lost in the madness, subsumed into the unrelenting symphony of hooves.

After our safari, we returned to Arusha, our jumping-off point, to plan the next leg of our trip. That night Debbie came down with malaria. We remained stranded for more than a week in that strange little town filled with desperate safari hawkers, while she lay on her bunk, throwing the covers on and off, going through the feverish dance I'd witnessed so many times. I cared for her as best I could, administering the appropriate doses of medication, bringing food and water, applying damp towels to her forehead, chasing the aggressive safari salesman from our door. Throughout all this, I marveled at my own continued health. By the time Debbie was safely on the plane and I'd set out alone for places unknown, I was convinced that my body was invincible, a fortress of immunity.

◆

A week later I lay on a lumpy mattress in a barren hotel room in the town of Tanga, Tanzania, lazily watching a fan turn above my head. The air was stupefyingly hot and still. As I stared at the fan's hypnotic spiral, an extraordinary languor seeped into my limbs. My arms and legs felt weighted down, as though an army of Lilliputians had anchored them to the bed with tiny ropes. As my mind began to drift toward sleep, a small voice in the back of my head made the following delicate suggestion: *Before you conk out, why don't you put up your mosquito net?*

My eyes scanned the room vaguely.

I don't see any mosquitoes, I told the voice. *Probably the fan's keeping them away. And besides*—at this point my face undoubtedly wore a faint smirk—*mosquitoes don't like me.*

❖

Three days later, in the coastal village of Pangani, I awoke in the morning with the sensation of a thousand tiny needles pricking my flesh. I'd spent the past two nights camping on the roof of the Pangadeco Hotel with Clemens, an East German medical student with bright green eyes and astonishing black lashes, whom I'd met in Tanga. The Pangadeco was a "find"—a completely empty hotel less than a hundred yards from the beach—and the previous days had passed in a blissful haze of sun and sand. At night Clemens and I had walked for miles into the lukewarm shallows of the ocean, moonlight floating lightly on the water like lace on black velvet. Back on the beach, we'd watched tiny crabs skitter sideways across the sand and drop into their holes, so light on their ballerina claws they left no tracks. The only blot on this idyllic time (besides my nagging anxiety about Michael), was the fact that it was the sacred month of Ramadan, the Moslem holiday in which no one eats between sunrise and sundown. This meant there was no food to be found during the day except coconuts and underripe miniature bananas about three inches long.

But on this third morning, when I sat up, my head seemed to soar above my body at a great height, as though resting atop an impossibly tall, spindly neck. I stumbled down the stairs to the toilet, awkwardly balancing my unwieldy head, and noticed, with the morbid fascination that accompanies such observations while traveling in the developing world, that my feces had turned a bright, almost neon yellow. The beast had entered me at last.

I carted myself to the local hospital for a malaria test, only to find that Ramadan was coming to an end, and the hospital was closed for the festivities. Back at the Pangadeco, the owner telephoned a German doctor who lived in a nearby village. Over a crackly connection, the doctor told me I should assume it was malaria and begin treating it right away, rather than waiting to get a test. If it were *malaria tropica*, the most virulent strain, and I didn't treat it, I could conceivably die from it, she explained, whereas taking unnecessary medication might screw with my system a bit, but it wouldn't kill me. Armed with this advice, I broke out my supply of mefloquine.

Mefloquine was the strongest antimalarial drug available. Peace Corps members took it weekly as a prophylaxis, but the doctor in southern France, where I'd bought my medications, advised me to bring along only a small amount, to use as a cure if necessary. He'd given me a combination of more moderate drugs to take as prevention.

"This mefloquine is too toxic for your body. You should not take it weekly if you will be in Africa for more than two months. This is not just the personal opinion of Dr. Marc Sillard," he'd told me sternly, pointing at his chest, "But the strong recommendation of the World Medical Association. I give it to you as a cure only in case of emergency. If you are near a hospital and can be tested, they may give you something else."

Peace Corps volunteers I met in West Africa reported all sorts of effects from their weekly mefloquine dosage, from depression and mood swings to startlingly vivid dreams and hallucinations. Their weekly dosage was one tablet. The curative dose was three tablets in a single day.

By the time I took my mefloquine, the fevers were in full swing. My body behaved like a furnace gone haywire, my temperature modulating up and up like the ending of a Barry Manilow song until it broke in a dramatic display of sweat and shivers, only to begin the process all over again. I kept a bucket of brown water next to my sleeping bag, wetting a grungy washcloth and placing it masochistically against the hottest spot I could find—stomach, underarm, inner thigh—as every hair on my body stood bolt upright on its follicle in protest. Although I was ravenously hungry, when I finally got access to food, I was unable to keep it down. Even with something as innocuous as rice, I would eat one spoonful and my throat would close on the second bite. Still, my mind remained detached, even slightly intrigued.

"Malaria's not so bad," I said to myself.

My first mefloquine-altered night was spent in a surreal state, somewhere between acute wakefulness and grotesquely etched, brilliantly colored dreams. I watched helplessly as everyone I'd ever met paraded through my head, their edges blurred and the colors slightly off, as though captured on home video with a handheld camera. All my loves and betrayals, from early childhood onward, came forward in random order to take their shaky bows: my seventh-grade best friend who deserted me when I was kicked out of the in-crowd for gaining weight and "dressing like a Martian"; the mentally disabled boy at my elementary school whom I championed and then betrayed by throwing a single pea in his direction during a cafeteria food fight; the man who whispered "dirty Jew" in my ear on a cross-country bus; the acting coach whom I worshiped with fervent, unparalleled lust; my adoring father and chronically nervous mother; Michael, Michael, Michael, Michael . . . all of them praising and accusing me, grabbing hold of my hands and legs and hair, breaking my heart again as if for the first time. I shouted their names, sat up again and again, cried and begged forgiveness.

And then, suddenly, I opened my eyes. I had to write a letter to Michael. I shot out of my sleeping bag, slipped under my mosquito net, and skidded across the cold cement to my backpack, where I fumbled madly for my notebook and pen. Suddenly there was no time at all—no time to form the words, no time to get the stamp, no time for the letter to cross the ocean and sit in his mailbox. In this moment I understood everything, and he had to understand right now, too. I loved him; I needed him; I cherished him. He was my life.

✦

By the time morning came I had no patience left for either letter-mailing or malaria. I had to get back to Dar es Salaam, where I could find a reliable phone. I would call Michael and tell him how I felt. Then I'd put myself on the first plane home. My journey was over; the endless searching, doubting, questing for self. I knew what mattered. Thank God I'd figured it out in time.

I started to get up to pack my backpack and was stunned to discover that I could not stand and cross the paved roof to reach it. I stood up and sat down again three times in rapid succession, my legs folding beneath me like a marionette. The dizziness in my head was so severe that palm trees, ocean, clothesline zoomed by me as if on a high-speed carousel.

"What are you doing?" Clemens called from across the rooftop. "You've been screaming all night long," he added with visible irritation.

"I've got to get to Dar es Salaam," I said.

"Are you crazy? You've got malaria. You're not going anywhere."

"But I have to," I told him, my voice rising. "I need a reliable phone line. I have to call."

"Call in a few days," he said. "Look at you. Who do you think you are? Stay in bed for Christ's sake."

"I have to call," I said. "What's the big deal? How much work is it to sit on a bus?"

I started to stand up again, and again I found myself sitting. My head ached like the worst kind of hangover. The colors of the world were too bright. Still I kept trying, over and over, with the perseverance of an athlete training for a race. Never in my life had there been a challenge I'd set my mind to and been unable to achieve, from winning the county spelling bee to writing and touring original plays to traveling alone through Africa. I wasn't going to be defeated by six feet of cement rooftop.

But I couldn't do it. I rose and fell and rose and fell like a crazy jack-in-the-box before I dove headfirst into the hot morass of my sleeping bag and began to cry like a child throwing a tantrum; heaving, moaning, wailing, shaken by violent sobs which gradually gave way to a bottomless river of fluid grief. The sudden knowledge of my arrogance pressed down on me like a boulder. I could not stand and walk across the cement. Michael was gone and might never come back to me. Things were fragile. Things could be broken. Things could be lost.

I spent two days prostrate on that rooftop, hobbling down the stairs in the evening to ingest a few grains of rice. Clemens waited in a state of growing agitation for me to recover.

"Go back to Dar es Salaam," I told him on the third morning. "Continue your trip."

"And if you die here?" he said angrily. "I would be responsible."

"If I died here," I said wearily, "you'd never know about it."

The next afternoon, I stumbled to the bus station. Clemens carried both my pack and his own. My fevers were gone, but I was still dizzy and weak.

The seven-hour bus ride along the tropical coast of Tanzania to Dar es Salaam was among the longest of my life. Every bump in the road traveled up my spine like dynamite and arrived with a jolt at the base of my skull, creating the sensation that my head was splitting apart. A couple of young men in the seat behind me found my groans amusing, and at each bump they would chime in with me, the three of us moaning in raucous harmony.

When we arrived in Dar es Salaam I dumped my luggage at a cheap hotel I'd stayed in before. Clemens helped me flag a taxi and told the driver to convey me to the hospital.

"Have a test," he said. "Find out what is wrong."

I nodded. "Thank you."

"You'll be okay now," he said. He strode away without a goodbye.

❖

Dar es Salaam was a modern city, but friendlier and slower paced than Nairobi. Boats of all sizes, from dinghies to passenger ships, crowded the noisy port. As we drove by the sprawling Kariakoo Market, I saw streetside fires and food vendors that reminded me of Accra. Seeing them tugged at my heart as though someone had wrapped a thread around it—a bittersweet ache.

At the crowded hospital, a nurse drew my blood and sent it upstairs to a lab. She told me to wait—the doctor would call me when he had the results. I sat for three and a half hours in a dingy waiting room while patients filed in and out of the doctor's office. The close air smelled of vomit and ammonia. A yellow plastic basin sat on the floor, with patches of wet on either side of it. Sandals and shoes picked up the moisture, leaving hieroglyphics of circles, stars, and dashes on the cement floor.

When the results of my test arrived, they showed malaria in my bloodstream.

"I took mefloquine!" I cried.

The doctor shrugged. He was a middle-aged man with thick glasses, stern and focused.

"Different strains respond to different things. Try this." He handed me a prescription for a new round of drugs.

"But mefloquine's supposed to knock out everything!"

He shrugged again and glanced toward the door where dozens of other patients huddled on wooden benches, waiting.

Back at the hotel, I took one of the new pills. My room was bare and functional, like every other room I'd stayed in in Africa.

A bed in the middle of the floor, a mosquito net hanging above it from a wooden ring, a bare bulb dangling from the ceiling, an overhead fan. The shared toilet and showers were down the hall. I turned on the fan and it creaked slowly to life, clattering loudly as it gathered speed, stirring the stagnant air. I lay on my bed, allowing the breeze to cool my limbs. Now that the telephone office was just a few short blocks away, I was suddenly reluctant to call Michael. I told myself that I'd wait until tomorrow, when I felt better. I wanted to have all my wits about me when I called.

An hour later I was shivering again, my body tingling with fever. What was this? A relapse? A side effect of the new drug? As I piled on blankets, I grabbed the pill bottle. Scanning the instruction sheet that was tucked inside, I found the words "can cause severe side effects and in rare cases death, when taken in conjunction with . . ." A long list of medications followed. One of them was mefloquine. I sprang out of bed, a strange buzzing in my head. I looked at the paper again. There it was in tiny, barely legible print. Mefloquine.

I stepped into my flip-flops and ran down the steps of the hotel with my rubber soles flapping.

"There is a doctor just next door," the woman at the desk told me, after I'd blurted out my story. "You can go and speak with him."

In the building next door, I scanned a list of offices until I found the words "Mr. Paul Chiteji, Private Medical Doctor, room 305." I ran up a slippery, poorly lit staircase to the third floor. The building was eerily empty—most of the offices seemed to be closed.

"Please be in," I muttered under my breath.

Next to number 304 I found a small, empty reception room with no one behind the desk.

"Hello!" I called desperately.

A slender, smooth-faced young man emerged from an inner room. He wore a green sports shirt and dark blue pants.

"Is the doctor in?" I asked breathlessly.

"I am Doctor Chiteji," he said.

"You?" I was startled. He looked about seventeen.

"Certainly," he said, smiling. "How can I help you?"

I poured out my story.

"Let me look at this." He reached for the bottle of pills. He examined it for some time. "You should discontinue to take these," he said at last.

"What about the malaria?" I said. "And what about the dose I already took?"

"Your mefloquine has surely vanquished the malaria," he said. "Most likely the test has misdiagnosed. You must return to the hospital for another test. This drug has not harmed you. Look! You are alive. Only, if you are concerned about the effects, it is best that you discontinue the drug." He laughed, then, and took my hand with surprising tenderness. "Sistah," he said, "don't worry. Be happy."

❖

Dar es Salaam was hot. Really hot. Walking even a short distance in the sun, I felt like a cookie left overlong in the oven. All internal suppleness was baked out of me, leaving my insides a dry, charred husk. My mouth was parched and cottony. No amount of water helped, because all moisture migrated instantly to the surface of my body. Places I didn't know could sweat leaked liquid—elbows, eyebrows, feet. For an hour that afternoon the power was out, paralyzing the ceiling fan in my room. I took a shower to cool down, got out, toweled off, and a moment later I was wet again, just as though I hadn't dried myself at all.

When the day cooled to evening, the power came back on,

and I could move again. I took myself to dinner at a fancy hotel, where I sat at a table, still trembling a little.

"What is the trouble, please?" asked my waiter, looking at me with concern. He was neatly dressed in dark pants and a yellow button-down, a bright white towel over one arm.

"Oh, it's nothing."

"Pardon?"

Looking into his kind face, I again poured out my story.

"Please, you will speak with the manager. She will surely help you."

Docile as a goat, I followed him. The manager was a plump Danish woman with red cheeks and blonde hair cut in an efficient bob.

"Oh yes," she said sympathetically, upon hearing my story. To my embarrassment, I had started to cry again while I was telling it. She patted my arm awkwardly. "All right."

She called the American Embassy doctor at his home number. His voice had the particular music of South India. He spoke to me at some length, asking lots of questions.

"The young doctor was quite right," he said at last. "It is most probable that the malaria was already gone. It showed up on the test simply because some of the dead cells remained in your bloodstream. The symptoms you are experiencing now are side effects of mefloquine. It produces different responses in different individuals. For some the effects—dizziness, vivid dreams, et cetera—can last up to two weeks. You must rest now. Tomorrow, come to my office and we will perform another test."

❖

Just as he had suspected, the test showed no malaria. Crisis averted, I had no more excuse for avoiding the telephone office.

A bored-looking woman slapped a scrap of paper onto the

wooden counter in front of her and instructed me to write down the number. She then showed me into a wooden booth with a paneless window and a phone with no dials. Beside the phone a low wooden seat came out of the wall. Through the window, I watched her attempting the connection. When she got through, she would signal me to pick up the phone.

Sweating in my wooden cubicle, my heart knocked ferociously against my chest. What would I say to him? What *could* I say?

The operator nodded at me. "You may pick up now," she said.

I lifted the receiver. "Hello?" I shouted. "Hello?"

"Hello," said Michael groggily. "What time is it?"

"Sweetheart, listen," I said. I spoke in a rush, fearing the connection might break. "I want to come back to you. I know I said I wasn't sure, I wanted to leave things open, but I'm sure now. I got sick, and I realized a lot of things. About what's important. I want us to be together. Will you wait for me, sweetheart?"

A long silence followed my proclamation.

"Hello?" I said after thirty seconds or more had passed.

"When?" he said in a flat voice.

"What?"

"When will you be home?"

"A month. Two at the absolute most. I'm almost out of money, anyway." I giggled nervously. "I would head straight home, but my brother's coming to see me next week, and he'll be here for two weeks. We'll probably do Zanzibar, maybe another safari in the Serengeti. Then I just want to visit the island of Lamu; everyone says it's amazing. And I heard about an orphanage near the border of Ethiopia where I could volunteer maybe for just a week or two. And then home. That's it. But most importantly, I'm ready to make a commitment now. No more leave it open, wait and see. Two months, tops, I'll be in your arms."

Again there was a long silence.

"Hello?" I said.

"It's too late."

"Please don't say that, sweetheart." Tears sprang to my eyes. "I know I've put you through hell, but . . . I didn't realize. Everything's new now. Didn't you say I was the finest creation of the universe?" I babbled. "That you'd never love anyone the way you love me?"

"If you're serious," he said suddenly, "come home tomorrow. Not next week. Not next month. Tomorrow. And we'll talk about it. I'll see how I feel."

"Yes, I mean, that makes total sense. But, you know, my brother's coming next week. Why don't we compromise. One month. I'll skip the orphanage. Just two weeks with him, then a super-brief look at Lamu—"

"Tanya! You don't get it, do you? There's no room for haggling here. This isn't a marketplace. I'm compromised out. Let someone else compromise this time. Let your brother travel alone! Yes, I love you, Jesus Christ, of course I do, but there's someone fifteen minutes away who loves me, who wants me, who thinks I'm just as exciting as the island of Lama—"

"Lamu."

"What?" Silence. "And anyway. If I take you back now, who's to say you won't leave again next month—"

"I won't."

"Or next year? You're a traveler, and I can live with that—I love who you are—if I knew that you'd come back to me, if I knew that you'd at least be faithful to me."

"I will! I told you, I had an epiphany. I'm sure now."

"You're sure now, but how sure will you be once you have

me safely back in your camp? Once you've proven to yourself that you can get me back anytime you want?"

"That's not fair."

"Isn't it?"

We sat in silence this time for more than a minute while the line crackled with static. My eyes and nose were streaming. I tried to breathe quietly. Through the window of my wooden booth I saw the operator looking at me with curiosity.

"Tanya," he said at last. "I love you. Get on a plane tomorrow or the next day, and we'll talk. Okay?"

Yes, I thought, *yes.* Why couldn't I say yes?

"Okay?" he said again, his voice cracking.

❖

Back in my empty room, I lay on the bed staring up at the still spokes of the ceiling fan. The power was out again. My body created a damp impression of itself on the sheet. I was playing a little game where I'd turn my head sideways, then turn it quickly back toward the ceiling. Each time I did this, the spokes of the fan appeared to turn for a moment and then grind to a halt.

I've got to go back, I thought. But he hadn't promised anything. He'd said we'd talk. What if I flew home, disappointing my brother, who was traveling all this way to see me, only to find that Michael had chosen this other woman? And Lamu— everyone said it was idyllic: a peaceful, sunny dream. No cars, only donkey carts. People who returned from there looked rested, happy. Perhaps there was something to be discovered there, some important bit of wisdom that couldn't be gleaned anywhere else. *Stop it,* I berated myself. *There's always another place.* My brother's visit, though—why was Michael so stubborn? He'd waited this long; what was three more weeks?

I flashed on Michael's presence then, the warm curve of his

back, his morning scent: a loamy blend of soap and sweat. The way he sang made-up songs in my ear as I woke up: *It's going to be a beautiful day . . . Tanya's going to make the ocean spray . . . She's going to laugh and shout and play. . . .*

My heart expanded painfully in my chest. I loved him. That's what this feeling was, wasn't it? Love?

I closed my eyes, Michael's song still unraveling in my head. *On the tree there cries a bluejay; people eat Grapenuts and horses eat hay. . . .*

As I floated away on my mattress, I saw donkeys, one after another, plodding down a dusty trail toward the sea.

Author's Note

In the early 1990s, I was fortunate enough to spend a year in Africa, mostly in the western part of the continent. This book is based on memories of that year. I offer it to you, not as a journalist or a scholar, but as a storyteller. Names and identifying details have been changed to protect the identities of those involved. Characters, conversations, and events have occasionally been combined or streamlined to evoke the essence of the experience more clearly.

During my time in Africa, the AIDS virus had not yet taken its toll in an obvious way on the places I visited. This isn't to say that no one had contracted the virus, but that the scope of the problem had not yet become apparent, especially in West Africa. In that sense, this book offers a glimpse of a bygone era. Not an idyllic time, by any means, but one in which the preoccupations of the communities and individuals that I met were different than they are today, when this disease has claimed so many millions of lives.

Acknowledgments

My deep gratitude goes out to the following people: Ali Caddick (née Bacon), travel partner extraordinaire, who listened to my scattered scribblings with unflagging enthusiasm; Jonathan Lethem, under whose wise guidance this material began to find form; Carol Lloyd, without whose intervention these stories might still be sitting under my desk in a dust-gathering heap; Don George, who shared his excitement and published many of these stories on *Salon.com*; Jeff Greenwald, who generously and skillfully helped steer this book through crucial stages of development; Elena Felder and Laurel Carangelo, beloved housemates and insightful readers; Tanya Pearlman, Larry Habegger, and James O'Reilly of Travelers' Tales Books, also Kristin Herbert and Brad Newsham, all of whom contributed valuable suggestions and support along the way; Amy Mueller, for expert dramaturgy; David Dower and the Z Space Studio, for time, space, and encouragement; my agent Richard Parks, who ushered the manuscript through the world with kind and diligent attention; Maura Santangelo, in whose Umbrian farmhouse I completed a substantial chunk of the rewrites; my editor Edward Kastenmeier, for guiding me gracefully and adroitly toward the finish line; Russell Perreault and Sloane Crosley, for making me feel so supported by Vintage; Stuart Friebert, Diane Vreuls, and the late Del Fambrough, great teachers who instilled in me a love of language and respect for words; Debbie deNoyelles: dear friend, great reader, great travel companion on the road of life; Richard Talavera, who held onto the original documents and taught me a lot about unconditional love; the individual Moroccans, Ghanaians, Burkinabes, Ivorians, Togolese, Malians, Tanzanians, and Kenyans, too many to list, who blessed and astonished me with their openness and generosity; and finally my family: Harry and Betty Shaffer; Juliet Shaffer and Erich Lehmann; Len Shaffer; Ron, Mary Frances, and Gabriel Shaffer; Sophia Lehmann, Jonas Duke, and Jacob Lehmann Duke; David Green, the Green family, and Niblet; all of whom supported me throughout this process in innumerable ways.